OUR LADY OF GUADALUPE

Our Lady of Guadalupe

Faith and Empowerment among Mexican-American Women

Jeanette Rodriguez

Foreword by Fr. Virgilio Elizondo

UNIVERSITY OF TEXAS PRESS   AUSTIN

44 28665719

Requests for permission to reproduce material from this work should be sent
to Permissions, University of Texas Press, Box 7819, Austin, TX 78713-7819.

∞ The paper used in this publication meets the minimum requirements of
American National Standard for Information Sciences—Permanence of Paper
for Printed Library Materials,
ANSI Z39.48-1984.

Library of Congress Cataloging-in Publication Data

Rodriguez, Jeanette, date.
    Our Lady of Guadalupe : faith and empowerment among Mexican-
American women / by Jeanette Rodriguez ; foreword by Virgilio
Elizondo.—1st ed.
    p.   cm.
    Includes bibliographical references and index.
    ISBN 0-292-77061-8 (cloth : alk. paper).—ISBN 0-292-77062-6 (pbk.)
    1. Guadalupe, Our Lady of. 2. Mexican American women—
California—Religious life. 3. Feminist theology. I. Title.
BT660.G8R58   1994
277.3'082'082—dc20   93-31267

The author and publisher are grateful for permission to use excerpts
from the following:

"Broken Spears," "The Fall of Tenochtitlán," and "Flowers and Songs of
Sorrow" from *Native American Spirituality*,
edited by Miguel León-Portilla; copyright 1980 by Paulist Press.

La Chicana: The Mexican-American Female,
by Alfred Mirandé and Evangelina Enríquez; copyright 1979 by the
University of Chicago Press.

The Image of Guadalupe: Myth or Miracle?,
by Jody Brant Smith; copyright 1983 by Jody Brant Smith; published by
Doubleday, a division of Bantam, Doubleday,
Dell Publishing Group, Inc.

Guadalupe—From the Aztec Language,
by Fr. Martinus Cawley; published by Guadalupe Translations, Guadalupe
Abbey, 1983.

La Morenita: Evangelizer of the Americas,
by Fr. Virgilio P. Elizondo; published by the Mexican-American Cultural
Center, San Antonio, TX, 1980.

To Lola, my mother, and Gonzalo, my father,
who brought me into the presence of God
and who manifested God's unconditional love for me,
and to my husband, Tomás Holguin, and my children, Gabriella and Joshua,
who challenge me to love with all my heart, mind, soul, and strength.
This work is also dedicated to the Mexican-American community,
which brought me into the healing and liberating presence of
Our Lady of Guadalupe.

Contents

Foreword

The best way to introduce this first publication by Jeanette Rodri- guez is by introducing Jeanette. One of the exciting things about this book is that it is as much about Jeanette as a believing Hispanic woman as it is about Mexican-American/Chicana women. It is not rigid and detached theology but passionate and involved, yet truly system- atic and critical. I have enjoyed Jeanette's friendship over the years and have admired her struggles along the arduous path leading to her doctorate. She provided a beautiful model of what she writes about in this work: the silent and persistent strength of Mexican-American women.

I first met Jeanette several years ago when she came for a doctoral fellowship interview at the Mexican American Cultural Center in San Antonio with the Fund for Theological Education. All the members of the reviewing board were men. She was young, charming, articulate, feisty, and brilliant—a vibrant person who brought excitement to her desire to do theology. Were we hearing her correctly, did she really say theology—a woman doing theology?

At this point, I have an obvious confession to make. We men were not accustomed to women doing theology. Sure, women were in reli- gious studies and religious education, but theology? Wasn't that as much the job of men as the priesthood and preaching? But immediately the thought came through—why not? And as I thought just a bit more, it became evident that the only theologians we as Mexican Americans had ever had were women! The recognized theologians were all for- eigners who spoke another language in many more ways than one.

What was so odd was that we had never recognized the best theologians right in our midst.

I am sure that you have not seen their names in print, on books, or on articles. They have not written or taught in the universities or seminaries, but they have been very active and articulate in our centers of religious reflection and learning: our homes, with their *altarcitos*, religious decorations, and God-based *dichos*. They have not been university professors, but they have certainly been professors of the school of life in the midst of death-bearing social circumstances.

As theologians are supposed to be the interpreters of our faith experience, so the Mexican-American women have been the main interpreters and transmitters of our dynamic faith experience. Our *abuelitas*, *viejitas*, and *madrecitas* have been the functional priestesses and theologians of our *iglesia del pueblo*. This is not a separate or parallel church but the very basis of faith which has financed the institutional superstructures, which have remained quite distant and foreign from the ordinary lives of the people.

Theologizing is nothing new or artificial to Mexican-American women—it is only that academia and the institutional church have been so involved in their own myopic and incestuous affairs that they have neither seen nor heard the *sensus fidelium* of the people at large. It is done quite naturally in the ordinary language of the home and of the barrio. It comes out of our unquestioned experience of God's protective and guiding presence in our lives. We certainly have a special feeling of God in the churches and in great religious celebrations, but it is definitely not limited to that. God is everywhere and I never escape the divine presence. Thus there are images of the sacred in buses, bars, homes, bodies, jets, brothels—everywhere! The church, as *el templo*, is the center but it is not the exclusive place of God's presence.

The theological discourse of the church which comes through the *padrecitos* is usually so elevated and complex that it says little of value to the ordinary people. The priest is not ignored, but his complicated and confusing language must be reimaged and reinterpreted by the theologians of the people. The ordinary agents of this personalizing interpretation have been the women. As I have heard from many working women: the church is so complex, but La Virgencita is like us, very simple . . . the church does not understand us, but she does, we know it! They communicate through womanly intuition, which bypasses the rational process, but is definitely not irrational—just suprarational. This drives intellectuals crazy.

When I question my students about some of their most significant memories of their early faith journey, neither Anglos nor Hispanics mention a priest or a nun, but they usually refer to something grandma or mom and dad used to say or do. And among Hispanics it is almost always something we remember about our *abuelita, tía, madrina,* or one of the *viejitas* of the barrio. They have been "the ancients"—the custodians and transmitters of the wisdom of the Mexican-American people of God in the southwestern United States.

The church tells them so many things, but the church seldom asks them. Unfortunately, this has impoverished the academic and institutional theological discourse of the church. In many ways, the incredible wisdom and power of our past generations of giants of the faith—our virgins, martyrs, and confessors—is being buried each day as our *viejitos* die off. But is has not altogether disappeared, and in many ways it is making a strong and conscious comeback in the lives of our people. *Vox populi, vox Dei!* The work of Jeanette is a major contribution and, I hope, the beginning of a new methodology for systematic theology: begin by listening to the voices of the faithful. The ancient books, tradition, and works of other scholars are fine and Jeanette has demonstrated how to put all this into the service of the people. But the best works of others—past or contemporary—cannot substitute for the essential starting point of a living and life-giving theologizing enterprise: the ordinary faith expressions of the people.

Jeanette clearly brings out how the simple and spontaneous statements of the people are neither simplistic nor superficial. They express the roots, core, and aspiration of a well-ordered world vision. She does not force them into the constructs of someone else's worldview and then judge them falsely, but easily uses instruments developed by others to help enlighten and clarify the components of our own Mexican-American worldview.

Her cross-cultural dialogue at the level of religious symbolism and meaning is fascinating and ends up bringing out new aspects of both: the people being studied and the instrument used for studying them. This is not easily done and could only have been accomplished by someone who is truly bilingual, bicultural, bicognitive, and biliterate. Jeanette is such a person and her work is a marvelous essay in this new type of dialogue across the invisible but very real boundaries of religious-cultural absolutes which encase our worldview and prevent us from seeing, hearing, and appreciating the uniqueness of the other precisely as other. We often judge the other from within the categories of our own worldview but seldom make the effort to allow the two worldviews to conduct a true dialogue with one another. Jeanette does this. It is exciting and revelatory.

Her work deals not just with the religious-cultural but with the intercultural and interreligious. Thus it opens the way for further work along this all-important line. What I have found fascinating is that Jeanette puts herself at the service of the women she wants to write about. She does not dare to speak for them, but enables them to speak for themselves and through their voices come forth powerful and refreshing theological notions not only about Our Lady of Guadalupe, but about God and women. Our Lady of Guadalupe is about God and us—she redefines us in terms of God and God in terms of our own most sacred imagery.

Because devotion to Our Lady of Guadalupe has been delegated to the realm of popular religiosity, the tendency of theologians has been either to ignore it or to look upon it in a simplistic way as the piety of the simple folks. Theologians need to reincorporate themselves into the ordinary body of the faithful if they are to exercise their ministry of theologizing for the people of God. The people are hungry and want to be part of the theologizing enterprise, but all too often they are either ignored or "taught" but not actively involved. The wealth of Jeanette's work is that she sets out from the very beginning to involve the faithful—it is living faith which she sets out to explore.

We as Christians must never forget: "It has pleased God to hide from the wise and the intelligent what God has revealed to mere children." The most authentic manifestations of God's presence are the expressions of the faith of the poor and simple of society. They are the first-rank theologians—interpreters of God's presence. Scholars seek to interpret what they think they know; the people speak freely about what they experience. While the discourse of academic theology is often quite removed from the struggles and anxieties of daily life, the religious language of the marginalized and oppressed draws from the cries and dreams of the people.

"¡Se quedó!" So answered a simple Indian woman when asked what was so uniquely special about Our Lady of Guadalupe: she stayed. Powerful! She came, she loved, she entered into our hearts, she is ever present to us. She is not difficult to get to: we can touch her, see her, and listen to her story.

Malinche, Guadalupe, Chicana! What do these three great women have in common? They have brought new life out of a situation of devastating chaos. For too long we have seen Doña Marina as the traitor who is responsible for the conquest. What nonsense. The victim is made into the villain. She was sold out by her own people—it was not she who betrayed her people, but her people who betrayed her. Yet she interceded with Cortés, she who helped him to understand the people he would have conquered with or without her. She survived and mothered one of the first mestizos—one of the first of the new race. She was sold as a slave, given over as a mistress, and abused in many ways, yet she never lost her self-composure or dignity; thus she is remembered as "Doña Marina." They could use her body, but they could never destroy her inner self; she would go along externally, but internally she always knew who she was and never allowed herself to be destroyed. She was a woman of silent strength who endured without despair what she could not change or control. She survived and her children prospered—they have become a numerous people. She is the prototype of Mexican-American women: even when abused or insulted, their inner selves cannot be touched or soiled. We have made the mother of *mestizaje* the villain of the conquest so that we could easily ignore and even despise the face of our Indian mothers, who even when raped, abused, and abandoned gave their lives of hard work and suffering for us, their mestizo children.

But God is more powerful than we are. God will not allow us to be ashamed of the *rostro y corazón* (face and heart) of our Indian mothers. God will intervene in our history through Our Lady of Guadalupe, who converts our shame into pride, our curse into blessing, our violation into virginity, our obscurity into radiance, our dying into life.

When the Spanish church was trying to crush and dominate the natives in the name of the Gospel, it was Our Lady of Guadalupe who intervened and introduced something new. She is now the mestizo mother who makes present the compassionate *rostro y corazón* of God. The overall art appears to be European, the face mestizo, and all the color coding and symbolism Indian: three in one but not three distinct images. God will be present not by way of opposition but by a new harmony which will recognize and dignify all without exception.

When the dominant Anglo culture has tried to destroy our ancient Mexican customs and traditions, to whiten our skin and turn our black hair blond, to ridicule our foods and family life, it is our Chicana women who have resisted quietly but strongly with their ongoing devotion to and celebration of the mother of defiance, Our Lady of Guadalupe—La morenita!

These great prototypes are alive today in Mexican-American women of faith. Jeanette begins her theologizing by carefully listening to the voice of the faithful. She is truly ministering as an organic theologian who, being a very personal and intimate part of the believing community, seeks to understand the meaning of our common faith. In so doing, she is effectively engaged in the ministry of theologizing. Her very objectivity comes from her subjective involvement in the process being studied, and I am convinced that there is no other legitimate way of theologizing than from within the community of faith. Each one of her interviews adds a precious piece to the puzzle of the meaning of Our Lady of Guadalupe among Mexican-American women. This is not theory, but life giving life to life! The responses are as simple and profound as the Gospel statements of Jesus. In speaking about what Our Lady means, they are in effect redefining their own concept of womanhood. In recreating the tradition, they are being recreated themselves.

This is not a question of proving one thesis or another, but of listening to the voices of the women who in Guadalupe see and recognize their own inner selves for what they truly have been all along, but have been neither seen nor appreciated as such by society at large, including Mexican-American society. They are strong in a quiet way without having to tell the world about it. This is certainly true of my mother and many of the women I have been privileged to know and work with.

They have been strong in a quiet way throughout our history, but they have definitely not been passive or inactive! Their devotion to the home and their families allowed us to survive and prosper against all odds. Their love for us gave us a profound sense of inner security in spite of the fact that society gave us no chance. Their ingenuity and hard work kept the beans and tortillas on the table and clothes on our bodies even when there appeared to be no money around the house. They rocked us to sleep, were there to cry with us, to encourage us, to sing the beautiful songs of our tradition. Their wrinkled faces, curved bodies, strong arms, and calloused hands are living sacramental signs of their sacrificing love for us, their children. They exhibit the radiant beauty of life-long dedication. They don't have to say much, for their countenance says it all.

There is nothing weak about Mexican-American women. They are not into boasting, but neither are they into silence. Their voices were heard and will be heard all the more in the days to come. Through these women, Jeanette takes us to new perspectives on God, women, and human beings. Precisely because her work is so spatially and historically situated—so particular—it will truly have universal implications for the people of God everywhere. It will truly be good news for all men and women of faith.

VIRGILIO ELIZONDO

Fiesta de Nuestra Señora de la Candelaria

February 2, 1993

Preface

I walk into a cave without knowing why. As I walk deeper into the cave I notice movement to my left. I turn and see a column of monks. There are twelve or fifteen of them, dressed in full robes of brown and white burlap, their faces covered by hoods. They are moving in unison, carrying a large mural. I come around the mural and look up to see the image of Our Lady of Guadalupe. I ask them what they are doing, where they are going with this image of her. They do not answer me but continue on wordlessly. I turn, and I see that they are moving the mural into a vault. They push it in, close the door of the vault, turn a knob, and then seal the vault with a brick wall. Then I understand. I scream, "No! No, you can't do this! Don't you know what you are doing? Stop! Why are you doing this? Please answer me."

No one answers. They begin sealing the wall with plaster. I scream: I cry, "No!" I wail, "Don't you understand? She is the life of the people. They need her—she is their truth, their wisdom, their hope, their power!" The monks start to move away from the plastered wall, deep into a tunnel. I run after them, wailing and screaming, "Please, someone, show me that you have a heart. I understand that the system is making you do this, but someone please show me, someone respond!" The monks continue to walk in unison, all but one. The lone exception turns around and I see one huge tear on his cheek. And for one moment I feel relief, perhaps even hope. He understands, but he seems incapable of acting on his own, of acting outside the group or the system. But he feels and he knows, and if he knows, then others must know also.

I wake up. I find that I have actually been crying. My pillow is soaking *wet. And I sit up with the last words echoing: "He knows and others must know, and I know."* [Author's recorded dream]

What I know is the result of having lived and worked with Mexicans and Mexican Americans in California. What I know is the result of six years of research in California and Mexico. What I know is the result of contemplating the image of Our Lady of Guadalupe. I wish to share with you now this journey of six years.

After working in the missions of Guam and Micronesia for over three years, I arrived in Berkeley in the early 1980s to pursue doctoral studies. In addition, I accepted a lay leadership position with the Roman Catholic Diocese of Oakland as a consultant for Hispanic lay leadership development. Previously I had worked in New York with Hispanics of many different backgrounds, but now for the first time I was exposed to Hispanics of Mexican and Mexican-American descent. In the six years that I enjoyed the privilege of working and growing with them, I came to learn about and be devoted to the Guadalupe event. It is my intent to share my vision and understanding of Guadalupe with you. Before I begin, however, I would like to identify several difficulties I have encountered with this subject matter.

First, most of the material on Our Lady of Guadalupe is polemical in nature: either the event is cast as a device of the early Franciscan friars, invented for the purpose of Christianizing the people of Mexico, or it is written from a Catholic perspective as an apparition which is accepted on faith. Second, Our Lady of Guadalupe is often experienced as a Marian image to support and encourage passivity in women, and thus is viewed as an instrument of patriarchal oppression and control. On the contrary, Guadalupe is active and liberating. I agree with Elizabeth Johnson (1985, 1989) that the feminine religious imagery in the Christian tradition must be freed from the projections of male theologians and the priestly hierarchy. Therefore, in my study I propose that Guadalupe continues to be a vital presence for those who believe in her and that she manifests the maternal face of God. My study is one of the few concerned with the usefulness of this symbol for Mexican Americans today, and it is the only study to address the symbol's importance for Mexican-American women.

Third, most of the literature on Guadalupe is concerned with the validity of the apparition. But my personal interest is more focused on the application of faith in this symbol and its potential for empowerment. Her story and image exist in the people's memory (whether or not in fact) and I treat Our Lady of Guadalupe as a presence which exists for those who believe. It is a reality that people believe in her.

Ideas of how to arrive at the truth differ from culture to culture. In Western thought, the "affective" (or "emotional" as opposed to "cognitive") has traditionally been connected with the "irrational." Truth is suspect in Western thought unless it has been arrived at intellectually, using the logic of the mind. I believe, however, that there is also a logic to the affective: we can arrive at the truth through affective and physical senses and that truth can be equally valid. For proof, we need only look at the poets and artists who are capable of accessing that which lies deep in a person's soul. Although a contribution to the truth may be reached by a different path, it is still a contribution to the truth.

The truth revealed to me by the Mexican-American women of my study is that Guadalupe tells them something about themselves as well as something about who God is. Despite being taught that God or the Divinity is beyond male or female, the habit of referring to God as "He" and "Him" often creates the belief that God is male. It feels uncomfortable to think that "Guadalupe manifests God": Until the recent feminist scholarship in Mariology and a return to feminine images of God in Scripture, there has been no "category" for the female or feminine face of God, although close examination of Scripture will yield female metaphors for God. Our Lady of Guadalupe is a metaphor for God in popular religious form. Though my intellect raises caution and questions, I affectively assert that Our Lady of Guadalupe is of God. My struggle is to articulate how I intuit that. You will see that the women of the study have this struggle: although she is of primary importance to them, and they prefer to petition her before petitioning God, they understand that she is not God.

What does this experience, this Guadalupe event, signify theologically and anthropologically? Belief in an image simultaneously reveals information about the believer and about the Divine. Although it is generally accepted that there is no value-free and totally objective discipline and/or knowledge, theology, like any science, is influenced by the subjective presuppositions and contentions of the researcher.

When we begin to look deeply within ourselves, asking ultimate questions, we are entering the field of theology. As researcher and theologian, I define theology as the systematic attempt to articulate an individual's or a group's experience of God or the Divine, and one question I address is the theological significance of Our Lady of Guadalupe for the Mexican-American women in my study.

Religion and culture are inseparable within Mexican-American culture. I draw from the insights of anthropologists on the questions of voice and authority. Who has the authority to go into a field and describe an entire culture? Who, also, has the authority to describe another person's or group's religious experience? A responsible researcher asks, "How can I best represent the other, while recognizing that I am present?" For me, this question became, "How can I best represent what these Mexican-American women have said to me?" I have sought to articulate the experience of Mexican-American women in light of one religious image. I am not going to dominate the discussion, but I am also not anonymous, nor am I without a voice, feelings, and thoughts.

In the science of anthropology, the term "multivocalic voice" recognizes that both the person or group being studied and the professional conducting the study influence the results. The researcher has a role and an obligation to reveal herself as much as she tries to reveal the informant, being as truthful as possible for the reader's sake. For example, I have admitted that I became a devotee of Our Lady of Guadalupe, sharing with you something of my emotive self.

I am of Ecuadorian descent, and during my childhood I lived in New York. I grew up with the image of Mary as La Madre Dolorosa, the Sorrowful Mother, and I saw how the women around me incarnated this image. But until 1981 I had never heard of Our Lady of Guadalupe. I did not know who she was; I did not know the story. I had experienced no contact with her.

Like the women interviewed for my study group, I have been acculturated to some degree. I am second-generation; I am a woman; I am a mother. I have the same kind of Hispanic spirituality and devotionality as they do. I too have been alienated—as a woman in the Catholic church, as a Latina in U.S. society, and as a working mother.

But I am privileged in that I am fair-skinned and have received a higher level of education. I have also had the opportunity to do theological reflection. I believe I was also born with a volatile character. When I used to ask my mother questions about why things were the way they were, she would answer "así es la vida"—because that is the way life is. I remember as a very young child refusing to accept that and saying back to my mother, "But it doesn't have to be that way. I don't believe that it has to be that way. I cannot accept it." This explains my attraction to a proactive and decisive Marian image. When I began working with Mexican-American women in 1981, I noticed their affective bond with Our Lady of Guadalupe and saw the influence she had in their lives. Like any good educator, I wanted to use the tool that worked best for them to help them along in their own liberation process. But when I began my research, I discovered a theological and psychosocial implication that I thought they themselves were unaware of—Our Lady of Guadalupe provides them with a spiritual form of resistance to the sociopolitical negation of Mexican-American women. The Mexican-American women drew me in on an affective level, and in return I am able to give them some insights into Our Lady of Guadalupe's message and her presence.

As both participant and observer, I have undertaken what James Clifford (1988: 7–8) calls "an experiment of cross-cultural translation of religiosity." Like all authentic human experiences, the experience of the Divine is a relational one in which the boundaries between self and others fall away. With this contribution to theology, I wish to give objective form to the subjective experience of having faith, of being a believer. I want to participate in the process of emergence which is helping us to comprehend the relational experience better.

Despite the polemic difficulties of Our Lady of Guadalupe, she maintains a position of prominence, power, and value. Although Our Lady of Guadalupe would not be considered a source of political activism, certainly she is a source of empowerment. What could be more empowering to a people who have been systematically and repeatedly negated than acceptance of their dignity and humanity? She offers that to her people, who are gifted, capable, and generous, yet who lack a sense of their own worth. Our Lady of Guadalupe looks into their hearts and souls and gives them value. Once they are accepted and embraced and loved, then they believe in themselves. It does not matter what they can or cannot do, who or what they are, where they come from, or even where they are going. They give glory to God just in being themselves. Like flowers bursting through the earth seeking sunlight, people turn to Guadalupe for nourishment, acceptance, and direction in a world that ignores them.

At first I thought her message was especially and possibly exclusively for Mexicans and Mexican Americans. My research and personal reflection now tell me that Our Lady of Guadalupe truly comes to show her love, compassion, help, and defense to all the inhabitants of the Americas.

Because she can empower her people—my people—I am committed to disseminating her message. I struggle to make her credible in the twentieth century by making known her effectiveness as a source of empowerment. The word "power" comes from the Latin *posse*, to be able. In our patriarchal society, we learn to think of power in terms of having *power over* someone or something. But the ultimate source of power and empowerment is having *power with*: having one's dignity and humanity accepted in the world, having the capacity to be in relationships, having the power of memory, sharing the power of expressed feelings. In Christian tradition, God embraces that which the world has rejected. Guadalupe again offers God's loving embrace for the rejected people of the Americas.

Acknowledgments

There are so many people to thank, so many who have journeyed with me, challenged me, received me, and believed in me. You know who you are, and my gift to you is my service.

Friends in Mexico and the United States have spent many hours listening to me and assisting me in articulating what Guadalupe means to me and to the Mexican-American people: Dr. Yvette Flores-Ortiz, Paul Morentz, M.D., Eva Lumas, Dr. Maura O'Neill, Fr. Rosendo Urrabazo, John Diercksmeier, Dr. Adelaida Del Castillo, Susan Flores-Dow, Dr. Deena Gonzales, Dr. Lea Ybarra, Dr. Dolores Jiménez, Donna Williams, Mary Cross, Kay Zappone, Fr. Michael McDermott. Their helpful insights, encouragement, and "presence" sustained me.

I would like to thank the Cervantes-García family for their hospitality during my research in Mexico City. I am also grateful to Fr. Alfonso Alcala, Fr. Mario Rojas, and Margarita Parente-Martínez, and to the Center of Guadalupan Studies in Mexico City for their time and assistance. Special thanks to Fr. Martínez, expert on early Guadalupan literature, who resides at Our Lady of Guadalupe Abbey in Oregon.

In 1990 I accepted a position at the Institute for Theological Studies (ITS) at Seattle University in Washington state. Here I found a place and community where I felt personally valued, and where my work took on a more healing and confident shape. I owe my gratitude to Drs. Loretta Jancoski, Sue Secker, Trish Wismer, Pat Howell, and the late Dr. Leo Stanford for their encouragement to put into writing that which I had experienced pastorally. I also wish to thank my colleagues who helped clarify my understanding of an integral model of education and ministerial formation: Jim Eblen, Mike Raschko, Katherine Dyckman, Marianne Labarre, Sharon Callahan, and Phil Boroughs. I would be remiss if I did not thank my graduate assistants Don Linnertz and Beverly Heeke for their time, patience, and typing skills. Also, this manuscript is much better for Kathy Lewis's thorough copy-editing and Allison McLean's thoughtful comments, editorial suggestions, proofreading, and typing.

I want to acknowledge and thank my colleagues at the Academy of Catholic Hispanic Theologians of the United States. Their commitment and vision of articulating an Hispanic American Theology has been inspirational. I wish to especially thank Drs. Orlando Espín, Arturo Bañuelas, Pilar Aquino, and Roberto Goizueta. This book matter would not have been written if not for *Madre de Sol* (Mother of the Sun), a trilingual play in English, Spanish, and Nahuatl performed at the Mexican American Cultural Center (MACC) in San Antonio in 1982. This is where I met Fr. Virgilio Elizondo, founder and president of MACC and first Chicano theologian in the United States. My work draws from and builds upon his original and creative contribution. Other invaluable works I used were authored by Fr. Clodomiro Siller, Jody Brant Smith, Janet Barber, and Fr. Martinus Cawley.

Lastly, but pervasively, I give thanks to my husband, Tomás Holguin, for his love, support, and patience during this long process.

Introduction

There are 12.6 million people of Mexican descent in the United States (U.S. Department of Commerce 1988) and everywhere Our Lady of Guadalupe is known to them: a brown-skinned woman surrounded by the sun, cloaked in a blue mantle covered with stars, standing on a crescent moon held by an angel. She looks down, and the expression on her face is one of kindness, compassion, and strength.

The image of Our Lady of Guadalupe is found throughout Mexican-American neighborhoods: as a statue or painting adorning a sacred corner of the home, as a medallion worn around the necks of young and old believers, as an image on T-shirts, on the sides of buildings, and even on business logos. The name "Guadalupe" is given to both girls and boys and is bestowed not only on parishes and churches but also on streets, towns, cities, rivers, and mountains.

To be of Mexican descent is to recognize the image of Our Lady of Guadalupe. In the barrios and businesses of Mexican Americans, Our Lady of Guadalupe has a home. She shares the technological, fast-paced, elitist, and secular milieu of the United States with her many compatriots, who also share her dark skin and her language. In fact, it would appear that this religious image of a solitary woman is never far removed from the Mexican-American "phenomenon" in the United States.

This book emerges from a study investigating the perceptions that Mexican-American women have of Our Lady of Guadalupe, what—if any—relationship exists between them, and the context of that relationship. Who is Our Lady of Guadalupe today? More importantly, who is she for these women? Has the legacy of this feminine religious image had any effect on the lives and identities of Mexican-American women? Is Our Lady of Guadalupe a curious relic from the past or does she serve an important purpose in the lives of Mexican-American women today? As an educator, theologian, and pastoral clinician, these questions were of increasing importance to me as I struggled to assist Mexican-American women in their quest for meaning and identity in their homes, their church, and their society. Out of this commitment and concern for their religious and psychosocial health, I began to focus on questions involving the influence of Our Lady of Guadalupe on their lives. Out of that same concern, this book is offered as a resource for women to be affirmed through the message of Our Lady of Guadalupe.

Similarly, who is the Mexican-American woman of today? Do the Spanish Conquest and the U.S. takeover of northern Mexico in 1848 have an impact on the contemporary Mexican-American woman? What is the result of living one life in American schools and another one at home and in her community? She is seen by some as emotionally dependent while putting the needs of others before her own, archetypally a patient wife and mother. What is the impact of living with "those macho Latino men" on the women, often labeled neurotic and masochistic? Do Mexican-American women follow the "model" Mexican personality type characterized by pervasive feelings of inferiority? Within Mexican culture, women have been viewed as untrustworthy, violated, submissive, and passive all at the same time. How can these women be expected then to be warm, responsive, and devoted to their family? The Chicana is portrayed as a wife of a domineering man and a mother of a large family, passive yet untrustworthy. Often treated in an exclusively maternal role, she is designated a lowly status and expected to give completely of herself to her family.

As Mexican-American women take part in the day-to-day affairs— both familial and social—of their lives, they cannot help but question and redefine themselves as women in U.S. society. Faced with clashing cultural and social values, struggling as "women of color" within a predominantly white society, Mexican-American women daily meet the image of Our Lady of Guadalupe. For these women, Our Lady of Guadalupe is a model that arises out of their own cultural living, a model of feminine strength that appears in both the secular and religious worlds.

The Study and Its Framework

Struck by the prominence of the feminine image of Our Lady of Guadalupe in Mexican-American culture and concerned with the ways in which Mexican-American women might relate to and identify with this image, I set out to study its effect on their lives and identities. I chose to do an exploratory study that would identify these women's perceptions of Our Lady of Guadalupe and describe the nature of the relationship between them—the first step in understanding how Our Lady of Guadalupe influences the daily existence of Mexican-American women.

By no means is this understanding complete. A total picture would be interdisciplinary and include many factors that have not been addressed in this study, such as anthropology, education, economics, political science, and immigration policy. To focus the study and to avoid broad generalities, I examined Mexican-American women with a single lens which includes psychosocial, religious, and developmental factors. Each dimension of this perspective helps to elucidate the other dimensions, offering a more comprehensive picture of the relationship of these women to Our Lady of Guadalupe. This perspective offers professionals (specifically educators, clinicians, and pastoral workers) a tool with which to assist in Mexican-American women's empowerment.

My working assumption was that an individual's experience is grounded in history—in a specific historical, social, and cultural context, interacting with other people. An individual's experience is shaped by culture, history, and economics; similarly, a culture's experience is shaped by its history.

Intrapsychic life (emotions, fears, motivations, aspirations, religious yearnings) is also influenced by experience and the interpretive framework we assign to that experience and is an integral part of being human. How we respond to intrapsychic and interpersonal life experiences depends on our stage of development, whether exploring psychosocial or theological categories.

Because there had been no development of a systematic psychology of Mexican-American women at the time of this study, I found it necessary to take an interdisciplinary approach. I developed a psychosocial religious framework, which emerges out of my own discipline of Religion and Personality Sciences, which in turn draws from psychology, religious studies, anthropology, and sociology. Such an approach first began in the 1960s under the name Chicano Studies, incorporating sociology, anthropology, psychology, and the humanities. The theorists I draw from include Jerome Frank (1961) for the psychosocial dimension, William James (1958) for the religious dimension, and James Fowler (1981) for the faith developmental dimension. In addition, I utilized the contributions of Carol Gilligan (1982) for her insights into ways women relate, and Gloria Anzaldúa (1987), who captures the soul of the mestiza or Mexican-American woman through her poetry.

The image of Our Lady of Guadalupe as a source of empowerment is even more noteworthy in light of the growing feminist movement in the United States, which seeks to eradicate the exploitation and domination of women as well as to give precedence to the self-development of people over imperialism, economic expansion, and material desires (hooks 1984:324). There are four basic tasks of feminist scholarship and specifically of feminist theology: (1) to rediscover women's position in whatever area we are discussing, (2) to critique patriarchy, (3) to create a new understanding that is based on or emerges from women's experience, and (4) to transform the world and the church. In my study I articulate Mexican-American women's position in the world; I acknowledge that because we live in a patriarchal society the voices of these Mexican-American women have not been heard; I attempt to create a new understanding about who God is, using the relationship between Our Lady of Guadalupe and the Mexican-American women of my study; and I hope to transform the church with this new perception of Our Lady of Guadalupe.

Overview

Chapter 1 describes the historical and cultural setting of the apparition of Our Lady of Guadalupe. As noted earlier, experience is rooted in and arises out of a historical context. The apparition of Our Lady of Guadalupe has its roots within a particular historical setting (the sixteenth-century clash of Spain with the "New World"), and this setting played an important role in how it was experienced from a psychosocial and religious perspective.

This chapter utilizes well-known historians of the period, such as Miguel León-Portilla (1963) and Jacques Lafaye (1976), as well as Michael Meyer and William Sherman (1987) and Alfred Mirandé and Evangelina Enríquez (1979), because of their unique perspectives on history: the former write out of the experience of the Aztecs, and the latter from the experience of the Mexican Americans. Virgilio Elizondo (1978, 1980a,b,c) is included because of his specifically Christian reading of this history. Women historians, such as Martha Cotera (1976a,b), Anna Britta Hellbom (1967), and Ana Nieto-Gómez (1975), offer an interpretation of the same period from the perspective of women and include effects of the Spanish Conquest on the female population.

Chapter 2 describes the story of the apparition of Our Lady of Guadalupe to Juan Diego in 1531, with both Christian and Nahuatl interpretations. The original story as told in the 1531 *Nican Mopohua* (Here It Is Told) is recounted, as well as an indigenous interpretation by anthropologist/priest Clodomiro Siller-Acuña (1981c), who offers a liberationist interpretation of the Guadalupe event. In discussing the text and its interpretation, the works of Ernest Burrus (1981, 1983, 1984) stand out as some of the most thorough historical-critical studies.

The imprinted image of Our Lady of Guadalupe contains codices. A codex is a book or manuscript with ancient symbols and words; thus Our Lady of Guadalupe is a story in pictures. The technical study of this codex has been done primarily by Jody Bryant Smith (1984) and Philip Serna Callahan (1981). Apart from one study on the stars of Guadalupe's mantle (Rojas Sánchez and Hernández Illescas n.d.), there has been no technical work on the image by Mexican scholars. One explanation for this dearth of scholarship may be that the apparition is considered such an essential part of the Mexican identity that any analysis and/or proof of its validity is rendered a "nonissue" for Mexicans. The fact of the apparition matters less than the fact of their faith.

Given that Mexicans and Mexican Americans believe in her, how can we best understand her meaning to them?

In Chapter 3, the focus moves from the image itself to the first perceiver of the image: Juan Diego. This perception was a powerful faith experience for the poor and marginalized 52-year-old Christianized Indian. The perceptions of Juan Diego may offer us an understanding of others' faith experience in perceiving this image. He is part of the event and is the interpreter of that event to his culture. Our Lady of Guadalupe is not merely a popular story but is actually a recorded religious experience of Juan Diego. His religious experience underwent certain changes which follow a pattern. Although Juan Diego lived in a different time and culture, I have found James Fowler's 1981 *Stages of Faith* schema useful for my own understanding of his experience.

The psychosocial perspective concerns itself with the assumptive worldview of the subjects, including assumptions formed by perceptions, behaviors, environment, emotional states, values, expectations, and the way a person images the self and others. This perspective is influenced by experience and by the historical events, choices, and social conditioning that make up a person's psychosocial milieu.

The religious dimension of the assumptive worldview integrates both religious belief and human behavior, an approach which is especially relevant to a study of Mexican-American women in relation to Our Lady of Guadalupe. In this population, religion is overtly a part of culture, and for many Hispanics the religious worldview is the only worldview. Additionally, religious and cultural oppression play a major role in the formation of this population's worldview.

In Chapter 4, I examine the social science literature on Mexican-American women and discuss its shortcomings, including the stereotypical interpretations of Mexican-American women, men, and their families, the problems with these uncritical studies and interpretations, and the picture that is emerging from careful critical study.

This chapter focuses on the psychosocial religious reality and the assumptive world of contemporary Mexican-American women, using their history as a springboard. These women are not only the product of a mixture of Spanish and indigenous roots (the Mexican culture, *mestizaje*) but also of the Anglo-American culture which has traditionally dominated life in the United States. Mexican-American women are thus mestizas twice over, ethnically and culturally. In addition we cannot ignore the influence of Christianity itself. Our Lady of Guadalupe as an essentially mestiza figure may serve as a symbol that embodies this multiculturalism.

I chose the historians and sociologists Rodolfo Acuña (1988), L. Grebler, J. Moore, and R. Guzman (1970), and Alfred Mirandé and Evangelina Enríquez (1979) as sources because of their revisionist interpretations. They recount the past through the eyes of the Mexican and the Mexican-American people, rather than through the eyes of those who most benefited from that history. Judith Sweeney (1977) brings a feminist interpretation to historical events. The social scientists used in this study—M. Baca Zinn (1975, 1979), Betty García-Bahne (1977), Sally Andrade (1982), Alfred Mirandé and Evangelina Enríquez (1979), Yvette Flores-Ortiz (1982), and Irene Blea (1992)—represent the various fields that make up an interdisciplinary approach. Their work has refuted that of Mexican Rogelio Díaz-Guerrero (1955, 1975) and those Anglo writers who base their theories on him. In addition, the work of George Bach-y-Rita (1982) is used to underscore the psychological reality of Mexican-American women today. I offer a feminist revision of the stereotype and conclude by highlighting the importance of acculturation.

Chapter 5 summarizes the data about the psychosocial religious aspects of the Mexican-American women in the sample. Here you will encounter the women who participated in the original study. They did more than participate: they opened their hearts and shared their lives. Because of their generosity of spirit and their trust, my life was changed. For those of you who have experienced the presence of Our Lady of Guadalupe in your lives, and have been nurtured by that presence, I want to affirm and validate that source of strength for you. And for those who seek to be consoled, empowered, and given direction, I invite you to contemplate her image.

For my study I purposely selected Mexican-American women who had to some degree been acculturated. I sought to identify the existence and nature of continual Guadalupan devotion and to examine the effects of acculturation. My criteria for acculturation were that the women (1) be Mexican American, (2) be second-generation, (3) be English speaking, (4) have a high school diploma, and (5) have been exposed in some way to the image of Our Lady of Guadalupe. Traditionally, the nucleus group of Guadalupe devotees is lower class, but as it happened the more acculturated group was slightly more affluent. However, I set out to study acculturated devotees, not more affluent ones. I have attempted to retrieve a basic meaning in a new context.

In Chapter 6, I explain how the story of Our Lady of Guadalupe can be understood in light of the psychosocial religious state of the Mexican-American women in this study. This state contributes to the data needed to respond to the following six research questions: (1) What is the assumptive world of the Mexican-American women in this study? (2) What factors influence and inform this assumptive world? (3) Who is Our Lady of Guadalupe? (4) How is Our Lady of Guadalupe perceived by the Mexican-American women in this sample? (5) What is the nature and content of the relationship between Our Lady of Guadalupe and the sample? (6) How does this faith experience of Our Lady of Guadalupe affect the women's overarching assumptive world? I show how exposure to the experience of the apparition can lead to tension and conflict, potentially moving the individual from reflection to change. The story of Guadalupe may enable Mexican-American women to move beyond the model of silent, passive endurance to one of empowerment, defense, and help for the oppressed. These questions cannot be answered adequately by any one of the theorists mentioned previously; thus, using an interdisciplinary analysis, I asked the women to speak for themselves.

Chapter 7 begins the process of theological reflection about Our Lady of Guadalupe. In addition to the influences of conquest and acculturation, Christianity has played a major role in the definition of Mexican-American women's identity because Christianity's belief system has so dominated the cultures of which they have been a part. I used the work of theologians José Luis González (1983), Virgilio Elizondo (1980b), Orlando Espín and Sixto García (1989), Robert Schreiter (1985), Clodomiro Siller-Acuña (1989), and Elizabeth Johnson (1989).

There are three areas in which the understanding and application of the Guadalupe event may offer some theological insights to the larger church: (1) popular religiosity, (2) Guadalupe as symbol of God's unconditional love, and (3) the need for "feminine" metaphors for a more comprehensive understanding of the divine.

In conclusion, the purpose is not only a better understanding of our Mexican-American brothers and sisters. I feel that the image and symbol of Guadalupe itself has something to contribute to all the inhabitants of the Americas by helping us amplify our understanding of who and what God is and how God works in the world. I also believe that the symbol of Guadalupe can be a model for what church needs to be—primarily inclusive. Because I believe she can be a source of comfort, validation, and empowerment, I propose that Our Lady of Guadalupe be given an appropriate place in both theological education and ministerial training to assist those encountering Mexican-American women.

My theoretical framework, a psychosocial religious perspective, is an interdisciplinary construct. My tools and methods are also interdisciplinary composites, using a variety of cognitive as well as affective approaches to elicit a response to something that had never before been asked.

A note on terminology: throughout this book I use the terms "Hispanic" and "Latina/Latino" interchangeably for people of Latin American ancestry, although I personally prefer "Latina" because "Hispanic" is a Eurocentric term. "Mexican American" refers to people of Mexican ancestry born in the United States; "Chicana/Chicano" connotes a certain political awareness or consciousness.

OUR LADY OF GUADALUPE

ONE

Historical Context:
The Spanish Conquest

In each stage of their history, Mexican Americans were confronted with new realities and complex problems. In adjusting to a multitude of circumstances, they have had to adapt and change their customs, values, and beliefs. One reason that their experience is different historically from that of other minority groups in the United States is because they have been made to feel culturally and ethnically inferior by more than one dominant group. Hence, a "layered-on" oppression occurred, which has had an impact on all Mexican Americans but particularly on Mexican-American women today (Vigil 1980:6–7). The roles of women both before and after the Spanish Conquest—such as being the heart of the home, bearing and rearing children, being clean and tidy, dedicating their lives to their husbands, and preserving their respectability in the eyes of the community (Mirandé and Enríquez 1979:15)—are also important because cultural expectations of Mexican-American women date back to Aztec models.

The first of these layers occurred with the imperialist conquest of the so-called New World by Spain. The conquest has been explored by numerous scholars in such diverse fields as theology, history, and anthropology. To appreciate the apparition of Our Lady of Guadalupe and her subsequent psychosocial and religious impact then and now, two aspects of the conquest must be understood: the clash between the Spanish and the Aztec cultures and the subsequent devastation of an entire nation. The role of the United States' "conquest" of Mexico will be developed further in Chapter 4.

The conquest history records that Hernán Cortés began the Spanish Conquest of the Aztec empire in 1519 (León-Portilla 1962:62). Physical contact between the two cultures (usually in the form of rape) began immediately, producing the Spanish-Indian *mestizaje*, the Mexicans. It is impossible to date the end of the conquest period, because the psychological process is ongoing and changes with every new contact.

At the time of the Spanish Conquest, the Aztecs were ruling the Nahuatl peoples of what is now central Mexico. The ancient codices state that the Aztec city Tenochtitlan (what we know now as Mexico City) was founded in the year 1325. A little more than a century later, this formerly destitute wandering people had been able to assimilate the old cultural traditions of the various indigenous people and to achieve complete independence. The Aztecs then began their career as conquerors, extending their rule from the Gulf Coast to the Pacific and as far south as Guatemala. By 1519 the Aztecs ruled over several million people who spoke a variety of languages (León-Portilla 1962: xiv–xxiii).

"Nahuatl" refers to the language, values, and customs shared by a number of the peoples of the Aztec empire. The Aztecs were a demographic subgroup—a dominant one—of the Nahuatl people (León-Portilla 1962:xxxix–xxx). In this book, the terms "Nahuatl," "indigenous," and "Indian" are used interchangeably to refer to the people in this region of central Mexico at the time of the conquest, while the term "Aztec" refers specifically to the dominant group that was in direct conflict with the Spaniards. Although "Aztec" has limitations as an all-inclusive generic term, I have used it here to speak collectively of the various Nahuatl peoples living in the central valley at the time of the conquest.

The Spanish takeover of the Aztec empire was facilitated by a number of factors. First was a certain unrest among the Nahuatl population, dominated by the Aztec people. The Aztecs were the dominant indigenous military group and had developed an aristocracy. They were hated and feared by the subordinate groups, many of which felt that the Aztecs' obsession with human sacrifice had totally perverted the religion (Elizondo 1978:95). Whether the Spaniards were gods or humans, they presented the potential for liberation from this domination (Mirandé and Enríquez 1979:5).

A second factor was that the beginning of the conquest coincided with the ancient Nahuatl predictions that their civilization had lived its time and would come to an end (Elizondo 1980b:41). This "end" was predicted to come about with the return of the god Quetzalcoatl. To the Nahuatl, it was more than a coincidence that these Christians should also come from the east, the direction from which Quetzalcoatl had predicted he would arrive, in exactly the same year he had set for his return (Del Castillo 1977:133). They remembered the word of Quetzalcoatl, who had promised to return; since tradition held that he was a large man, with blue eyes and blond hair, the Spaniard Cortés certainly fit the description.

León-Portilla (1962:4–5) summarizes in detail the good and bad omens that are said to have foretold the arrival of the Spaniards, such as a comet sighted in the skies, an unexplained burst of flames in the temple of Huitzilopochtli, and the damage to another temple by a bolt of lightning. The Aztec leader Moctezuma II addressed Cortés, greeting him as Quetzalcoatl, and welcomed him back to his throne (Meyer and Sherman 1987:113). Thus Quetzalcoatl had returned to redeem the various groups from the captivity of the Aztecs, who had perverted his religion (Elizondo 1978:95).

In addition to deaths caused by warfare, forced labor, brutality, military force, and subjugation, many died from endemic disease: "The diseases brought to Mexico by Europeans wiped out whole towns. These diseases manifested themselves in the form of smallpox, typhoid, measles, typhoid fever and diphtheria epidemics. Because they were isolated from the rest of the world and the Indians had developed no resistance at all . . . certain Calpullis lost 80% of their people through disease . . ." (Vigil 1970:75).

Further factors were the Spaniards' technical superiority, Spain's policy of expansionism, and their evangelical zeal and conviction that the conquest was ordained and supported by *their* God (León-Portilla 1962:6–7). All these brought about brutal violence and the takeover of the economic, political, religious, and social institutions of the indigenous people.

The fall of Aztec society precipitated the fall of the rest of the native world. All the peoples surrounding the Aztec empire, even those who had joined Cortés in fighting against the Aztecs, were overwhelmed by the horror and the violence of the conquest (Elizondo 1978:102).

Aztec Women and the Conquest

The Spanish Conquest of Mexico was a conquest of women as well as a conquest of a people. The seizure of women by force or gift exchange was simply one element in the general enslavement of Indians that took place (Mörner 1967:22).

By understanding the changes that occurred for women as a result of the conquest, contemporary Mexican-American women may be better equipped to cope with the present and to determine their future (Cotera 1976a:8). In other words, their past can shed light on their present psychosocial reality and with this awareness they may be able to change or modify that reality.

The Aztecs maintained a socially stratified society. The family was the most important unit within that structure. Girls were educated by their mothers in so-called feminine duties—sewing, cooking, and embroidery. Education was compulsory for girls of all social classes. The values that were transmitted both culturally and educationally were personal discipline, respect for law and others, love for the good, diligence, honesty, and refraining from greed (Cotera 1976a:20–24).

Although Aztec women were exhorted to stay home, as are Mexican-American women today, they did participate in the work force. Women as well as men took part in business, especially if one of the partners produced goods for sale. Women are shown in the codices as vendors of textiles and featherwork (Hellbom 1967:130) and they worked as bakers, courtesans, *curanderas* (healers), magicians, and midwives (ritual specialists similar to the shamans of other Indian societies). Aztecan women could also "hold property, enter into contracts, take cases to court, and divorce their husbands" (Nieto-Gómez 1975:12). Marriage was regarded as a sacred institution, propagating a noble race.

Before the arrival of the Spaniards, Aztec society incorporated women at all social levels (Mirandé and Enríquez 1979:37–38). Though their roles were rigidly defined by social class and cultural expectations, they were valued in those roles. Women took part in the two important areas of Aztec life: war and religion. They traveled with males in armies into battles (Salas 1990). They were cooks and carriers of supplies. Women participated in religion. Their studies began very early in life. They were educators in the temples in the rituals of the priesthood and midwifery (Blea 1992:25).

Thus, before the arrival of the Spaniards, women in Aztec society were equally valued with men, at least insofar as they contributed to the life of the wider community. Hellbom (1967) provides a comprehensive overview of the place of women in pre-Hispanic central Mexico. She contends (1976:300) that the Aztec woman was on the whole more economically independent than the Indian woman of the post-conquest era.

After the conquest, the existing economic system was destroyed and the Spaniards put in place a colonial system favorable to themselves. Under the policy of *repartimiento*, laborers were to work for wages a limited number of days a year and thus have time for their own needs. But because they had to buy everything they needed and then work off their debt, the people and their children became indebted and eventually enslaved. The Spaniards ruled as lords, and the source of their wealth was Indian labor (Guzmán 1984:5).

With the arrival of the Spaniards came new systems and institutions that limited the roles of women. The new social system displaced women regardless of their race or class. Women were relegated to a universal function during this period: to serve in the home as procreators, housekeepers, wives, and mothers. They were also displaced from the family hearth, the center of the Aztec woman's domestic life, to the establishment of church communities that centered around altars to an alien god (Mirandé and Enríquez 1979:27–38). Indian women who had once reigned as goddesses now wore the facial brands of slavery and were subjected to the imposition of a single, male, Christian god (Blea 1992:36).

Similarly, the Spanish Conquest destroyed the stratified social structure of the Aztecs, a profound trauma for them as a people, but especially devastating for the women (Cotera 1976a:24). Like the men, women were discriminated against because of the color of their skin and their class status, but they were also subject to sexism. The conquest affected the position of women even more since they lost their social status and were relegated to positions of maids to the new masters. Great numbers of them had to assume duties formerly carried out by a servant class, without the prestige or regard that the professional servant class had enjoyed in their culture (Hellbom 1967:269).

After the conquest, women were still involved economically, but in a very different way. In mining communities women worked as forced labor and kept the men alive. They were also used as sexual objects as a means of monetary exchange (Nieto-Gómez 1975:19). Thus women were a necessary part of the colonial economy of Mexico.

The family unit was also affected as Indian men and women were separated and sent to serve in the *encomiendas*. The *encomienda* system was a complex one in which Indian goods, trusteeship of land, and personal services were granted by the crown. For example, a military leader who had served the crown traditionally received a parcel of land (Vigil 1980:60), but a bishop might equally be an *encomendero*. The Indians who were to serve the Spaniards were sent to the *encomiendas* to be "protected" and Christianized. The Spanish *encomenderos* often asked for female domestic servants, who were used as concubines more often than not (Mörner 1967:24). This system was so abusive that even the Spaniards cried out against it early in the colonial period.

Inevitably questions arose among ecclesiastics concerning the justice of the system; a royal letter of August 14, 1529, decreed that all Indians were to serve for a period of one or two years only, not for life. This order was not strictly enforced, and pressure was exerted to allow *encomiendas* to be passed on to *encomenderos*' descendants as inheritances. Thereafter the questions were continually under discussion in Spain and America. The fact remains, however, that the first two decades of Spanish rule were marked by almost unchecked exploitation of the Indians (Hanke 1949:20)—and of Indian women in particular. This oppression is the legacy of contemporary Mexican-American women.

A Clash of Cultures

The clash of cultures between the Aztecs and the Spaniards, vividly described by both the conquistadors and the natives, was something more than an encounter between two expanding nations: it was the "meeting of two radically dissimilar cultures, two radically different modes of interpreting existence" (León-Portilla 1962:xv). To a drastically altered society were added an ethnic mixture and accompanying racist precepts: social class and mobility were determined for the first time in indigenous memory by a person's color and/or features. It was a chaotic time "in which the clash of civilizations occurred in the sharpest form, a period in which native American elements and imported Spanish traits were sometimes fused and sometimes juxtaposed, together giving Mexico its present personality" (Ricard 1966:3).

Elizondo (1978:60–61) identifies the following themes as sources of cultural conflict between the Spaniards and the indigenous people they conquered: land, the soul, the greatest sins, the nature of the person, truth, and the understanding of reality, time, and death.

The Christian Spaniards felt that space-earth had been given to humanity by God and that humans had a right to claim it, to use it for their own good. The Nahuatl people held space-earth sacred, believing it belonged to the gods. Humans could only use it and had to live in harmony with it. The concept of private property was sacrilegious and incomprehensible to them (Elizondo 1978:115).

For the Spaniards, the most important value was salvation, salvation of one's soul in the hereafter and making a name for oneself. For the Nahuatl, the most important value was the salvation of the group and its well-being and preservation. Christianity emphasized salvation of the soul through perfection of the individual character, whereas Indian religion valued the individual only for his or her contribution to collective activities designed to preserve the cosmic order (Madsen 1967:374). The Spaniards' basis for salvation was the sacrifice of Jesus: "one died so that all might live"; for the indigenous, "many had to die that the One [the sun] might continue to live" (Elizondo 1978:16). The Christian Spaniards understood that their salvation came through the sacrifice, death, and resurrection of Jesus Christ. The Nahuatl believed in the salvation of the group, but a growing number called into question the ongoing human sacrifice offered to the sun god. Thus the native and Christian ideas of salvation were very different.

For the Spaniards, the greatest sins were heresy, apostasy, and idolatry; for the indigenous, they were greed, perversion, turning away from elders, and disrespect for human life (Elizondo 1978:114).

For the Spaniards, the person was understood to be an individual, an indivisible unity, whereas the Nahuatl perceived the individual as indivisibly united to the group. "'Rostro y corazón' [face and heart], the Nahuatl image of the individual, appears to be an equivalent of our own modern idea of personality. This concept was completely in accord with the intuitive nature of the thinking of the wise. It was not a definition based on rationalization, but was fresh and full of vitality" (León-Portilla 1963:114–115).

The Nahuatl language used *disfrasismos*, a complementary union of two words or symbols which express one meaning, to communicate the most profound thought or feeling (Siller-Acuña 1981b:12). Thus "the world" was expressed as "heaven-earth"; the human person as "face-heart" or presence and determination; and "God" was expressed as "night-wind," the invisible and the untouchable (Siller-Acuña 1981a: 220). As Don Angel María Garibay has said, this places us before an "anguish" of meanings that attempts to see things from all possible angles.

The Spaniards believed that, through a process of abstraction, the intellect was capable of obtaining truth and communicating it through words. In contrast, the Nahuatl believed that only the heart was capable of obtaining truth. Words were not enough: only through *flor y canto* (flower and song) can truth be obtained and communicated (Elizondo 1978:114–115). The Nahuatl wise men and wise women did not believe that they could form rational images of what is beyond, but they were convinced that through metaphors, by means of poetry, truth was attainable (León-Portilla 1963:79).

Knowledge of reality, for the Spaniards, was accessed through the intellect, using abstractions, definitions, judgments, conclusions, and concepts which were single and linear. For the Nahuatl, knowledge of reality was the result of "seeing" through intuition, symbols, interrelationships, and movements, best expressed through *disfrasismos* (Elizondo 1978:115). This notion of "seeing" is important for two reasons. First, many of the gods of the Meso-American pantheon wore masks so one could not actually see their faces. Second, the seeing is an intuitive vision, which is why intuition and symbols are of utmost importance.

The basis of all reality for the Spaniards was the individual soul or spirit: one God created one soul for each individual. For the Nahuatl, the basic reality was the cosmic community: from one divine couple "emanates everything which is and is sustained through the One Spirit/ soul" (Elizondo 1978:114). In the Nahuatl world all life was dual in nature. This principle of duality, which undergirded all existence, was called Ometeotl.

For the secular Spaniards, the concept of time was not important. Only the present existed: *No hay prisa* (There's no hurry). For the Franciscans, time was crucial because of the urgency to convert native populations before the imminent Second Coming. Time was most important for the Nahuatl: "It is the 'footprints' we have left behind." They believed it was measurable but could be stretched out by actions (Elizondo 1978:115). The measurement of time was one of their main obsessions: they had an accurate calendar of years and months and an astrology based on a complex of days and hours.

For the Spaniards, death was a time of judgment, eternal rest, "now they sleep," reward and punishment. For the Nahuatl, it was a time of awakening from the dreamlike existence of this life; death was simply a different form of existence (Elizondo 1978:116). The Aztecs did believe in eternal life: the soul was immortal and, once having departed this world, it continued to live, in heaven or in hell. But this eternal life was not a sanction: heaven was not a reward, nor hell a punishment. It mattered little how an individual had lived on earth; what mattered was the circumstance of his or her death (Ricard 1966:31).

These differences illustrate how these two groups' values, assumptive worldviews, and *raisons d'être* were diametrically opposed. The two cultures were so different that they were for the most part unable to communicate with each other, although in the early phase of conquest, there were dialogues between the friars and the native elders, and the two societies had some social institutions in common, such as ritual specialists, baptism or purification rites, and confession. The tragedy is that the dominant Spanish culture, rather than integrating Indian society, destroyed it and attempted to replace it. The result was the *mestizaje*, the Mexican people. The rich culture that opposed the Spaniards underwent dynamic evolution, adapting, appropriating, rejecting, and synthesizing. It lives on in Mexicans and Mexican Americans today and has a place in the psychosocial reality of Mexican-American women.

The Devastation of a People

This clash of cultures, coupled with the Spaniards' military superiority and their disdain for the indigenous people, led to the devastation of the Nahuatl and their culture. Those secular and religious individuals who objected were powerless to stop the systemic violence. In their enthusiasm to convert the natives, the clergy lost their humanity even as they pursued divinity.

Physical violence and massacre at the hands of the Spaniards were common experiences, as attested by Aztec paintings from that era that depict Spaniards in the act of dismembering Aztecs. The Spaniards committed some of the most brutal acts ever inflicted upon the people of Mexico (on forced assimilation and prejudice against both Mexicans and Mexican Americans, see Cortés 1974; Arroyo 1980; Sandoval 1983). Intense suffering in the form of hunger and lack of fresh water was caused by Spanish blockades. Abuse of indigenous women was widespread, and the eyewitness indigenous accounts record that the cries of the helpless women and children were heart-rending (León-Portilla 1962:122). As León-Portilla writes (1962: 140), "when the princes were made captives, the people began to leave, searching for a place to stay. Everyone was in tatters, and the women's thighs were almost naked. The Christians searched all the refugees. They even opened the women's skirts and blouses and felt everywhere: their ears, their breasts, their hair. The people scattered in all directions." Elizondo says (1978:117): "Their gods had been defeated, their temples had been destroyed and their women had been violated. They who had considered themselves the chosen people of the gods had been defeated; their honor and glory, their power and their government had disappeared. This traumatic experience of a total conquest would be deeply imprinted in the very soul of the new Mexican people."

The social structure of the indigenous people underwent tremendous upheaval. Aztec society had been made up of a social structure with rigidly defined roles. With the coming of the Spaniards, the Aztec priests and princesses once revered by their people found themselves on the same level as the Aztec peasants (Mirandé and Enríquez 1979:2–12). Land, formerly held in common for the welfare of the people, became a place of slavery where the Indians worked to provide wealth for the Spanish landlords.

The indigenous people were forced into a state of helplessness, powerlessness, fear, anger, and eventually self-hatred. It is only through poetry and song that such devastation can begin to be expressed; the intellect falls silent, unable to make sense of it. The following poems were written by postconquest Aztecs—the sources do not specify whether the authors were male or female—as testaments to the reality of the conquered peoples (León-Portilla 1980:226–228):

Broken Spears

Broken spears lie in the roads:
we have torn our hair in our grief.
The houses are roofless now, and their walls
are red with blood.

Worms are swarming in the streets and plazas,
and the walls are spattered with gore.
The water has turned red, as if it were dyed,
and when we drink it,
it has the taste of brine.

We have pounded our hands in despair
against the adobe walls,
for our inheritance, our city, is lost and dead.
The shields of our warriors were its defense,
but they could not save it.

We have chewed dry twigs and salt grasses;
we have filled our mouths with dust and bits of adobe;
we have eaten lizards, rats and worms. . . .

The Fall of Tenochtitlan

Our cries of grief rise up
and our tears rain down,
for Tlatelolco is lost.

The Aztecs are fleeing across the lake;
they are running away like women.

How can we save our homes, my people?
The Aztecs are deserting the city:
the city is in flames, and all
is darkness and destruction . . .

These are the acts of the Giver of Life. . . .

Flowers and Songs of Sorrow

Nothing but flowers and songs of sorrow
are left in Mexico and Tlatelolco,
where once we were warriors and wise men.

We know it is true
that we must perish,
for we are mortal men.

You, the Giver of Life,
You have ordained it. . . .

Have you grown weary of your servants?
Are you angry with your servants,
O Giver of Life?

The most profound aspect of the conquest was the spiritual devastation of the Aztec people. With the destruction of their pride and their
temples, as well as the killing of their people, came a feeling that the
gods were angry with them and had deserted them. These poems reflect the emerging belief that their gods had ordained this destruction.
The people had nothing to live for: as the Spaniards claimed, their gods
were dead, it was better to allow them to die, too (León-Portilla
1963:183).

At the same time that they experienced the "death" of their own
gods, the indigenous people were urged by the Spanish missionaries to
believe in the God of the Spaniards. Cortés never forgot that the goal
of the conquest was the conversion of "heathen" Indians to Christianity.
A considerable portion, if not the majority, of the Indians of the ancient
Mexican empire in the first half of the sixteenth century were forced to
abandon their ancient religion (Madsen 1967:370, 376).

The people, however, could not accept a religion that asked them to
negate their entire metaphysics, the way they understood reality. They
also could not comprehend that the missionaries, who were admired
and respected because of the simplicity of their lives, came from the
same religion and spiritual origin as the abusive and brutal conquistadors. The Aztec insurgents of the day were fighting not merely against
Spain but against Catholicism. It was evident to them that the two
things were intimately connected (Ricard 1966:265). "The Conquest
was followed by a period of nearly ten years in which the dominant
Aztec reactions to Christianity were Aztec bitterness toward the conquerors and direct conflict between native polytheism and Christian
monotheism" (Madsen 1967:372).

While there were individuals within the ecclesial community who
were supportive and even defended the indigenous population against
the violence of the Spanish conquistadors, they were unable to prevent
the destruction and devastation of the people. The ecclesial community

failed to understand the ways of the indigenous people. Some friars did try to comprehend the Nahuatl mindset, learn the language, and acculturate themselves, but the majority of the dominant culture believed that they were bringing a better way of life to an "underdeveloped" people, a tendency still present today.

Perhaps the best example of the degradation that characterized the conquest is the theological question that occupied the Spanish mind of the time: Do the Indians have a soul? The very humanity of the Indians was questioned by the conquerors (Elizondo 1980b:47–48). If one questions the humanity of an entire people, one is implicitly allowing license to exploit those people and to tame the "animal." Being trained to perform service-oriented tasks is, thus, the most they can hope to accomplish.

Summary

With the coming of the Spaniards, the Aztecs' stratified society was destroyed. The new stratification put the Spanish in the dominant role and everyone else became subordinate. Indigenous men and women alike were oppressed on the basis of race, skin color, and class, but in addition women were oppressed by sexism. Ultimately oppression affects family and community integration.

While all Indians were brutally oppressed by the Spaniards, women were most dramatically affected. This primary experience of oppression serves as the basis for Mexican and Mexican-American women's psychosocial reality. In Chapter 4, a parallel is drawn between the clash of Spanish and Indian cultures during the conquest and that of Mexican and American cultures during the U.S. colonization of formerly Mexican territory.

The fact that the native peoples had a rich culture that collided with that of the conquerors tells us that contemporary Mexican Americans' culture is, in actuality, a mixture of two opposing assumptive worldviews. This opposition is crucial to the understanding of the psychosocial reality of Mexican-American women.

The devastation discussed in this chapter has a particularly strong religious dimension. The Spaniards not only wanted to impose their political power but also their religious belief system. However, in doing so they attempted to obliterate an essential element in the native culture: its spirituality.

Religious principles penetrated the very existence of the pre-Columbian people. Everything was under their domination: public life and private life; every stage of each person's progress from birth to death; the rhythm of time; the arts and even games—nothing escaped (Soustelle 1970:119). This all-pervasive religiosity of the indigenous peoples continues to be a large part of the assumptive world of many Mexicans and Mexican Americans to this very day.

TWO

Our Lady of Guadalupe:
Story, Icon, Experience

In the midst of this clash of cultures, with its devastation and spiritual alienation, Our Lady of Guadalupe appeared at Tepeyac near what is now Mexico City. Her appearance in 1531 predated newspapers and mass media, so it contrasts radically with later appearances such as Lourdes, the story of which immediately spread around the world by rail and steamship. Further, Guadalupe emerged in a society with a huge language gap. At Lourdes everyone spoke French, or at least *patois*, and all pilgrims recited the one and only story, which revolved around the well-known person of Bernadette and the grotto by the river. But at Tepeyac a whole world separated the Indians, who thought in terms of Tonantzin (Our Mother, a goddess both creator and destroyer) and their own traditions, and the Spaniards, who thought in terms of the old shrine of Guadalupe in Estremadura, of its well at the base of the hill, of the old shrines of Europe, and of the whole Catholic tradition of Our Lady in general.

Guadalupan studies have intensified since 1976. In 1981, the 450th anniversary of the event, many forms of investigation—historical, anthropological, sociological, theological, Mariological, moral, pastoral, and even some highly technological—attempted to understand and interpret this event which lives in the people and is conserved as a privileged expression of popular religious practice (Siller-Acuña 1981b: 11). As I present this chapter, I acknowledge that I do so from a position of faith, articulating the position of the marginalized and the poor. I have used those positions that attempt to interpret the story, icon, and experience from a theology of liberation point of view. As mentioned in the preface, whether or not one believes in the reality of the apparition, many Mexican-American women do believe in Our Lady of Guadalupe. To serve this population, it is useful to understand the reality of their belief today and what the story, icon, and experience meant to their ancestors.

What is known—cognitively—about Our Lady of Guadalupe is controversial. There is disagreement over the sources of the story and the origin of the image. I present these discussions, give one version of the story, and conclude with an analysis of what the symbol meant on the affective level to the Nahuatl and Spanish alike.

The Sources of The Narrative

Garibay (1967:821) writes, "According to tradition, on December 9, 1531, the Indian Juan Diego saw the Virgin Mary at Tepeyac, a hill northwest of Mexico City. She instructed him to have the Bishop Zumárraga build a church on the site. Three days later in a second appearance she told Juan Diego to pick flowers and take them to the bishop. When he presented them as instructed, roses fell out of his mantle and beneath them was the painted image of the Lady."

In recent decades, theological study of the Guadalupe devotion has been increasingly based on a document known as the *Nican Mopohua*. This document is the Nahuatl narrative published in 1649 by Luis Lasso de la Vega (chaplain of Guadalupe from 1646 to 1656). The title *Nican Mopohua* is taken from the first phrase of the document (variously translated as "Here it is told" or "In good order and careful arrangement") Although Lasso de la Vega published a good century after the beginnings of Guadalupe, some remarks by Luis Becerra Tanco (1666) have prompted many modern authors to infer that Lasso de la Vega was reproducing a much earlier document by the learned Indian convert Don Antonio Valeriano (1520–1605). Valeriano was a student and later a teacher, a translator, a writer, a Latin scholar, and for forty years the governor of Mexico City (Siller-Acuña 1981b:14). Modern Guadalupan theologians generally accept the *Nican Mopohua* as the literary basis for their study.

Like many aspects of Our Lady of Guadalupe, the authorship of her story is polemical. For believers, the *Nican Mopohua* is for Guadalupe what the Gospels are for Christianity. At the opposite pole are those who tend to see Guadalupe in terms of legend, as a heroine of a folk culture myth. A third school of thought, led by the late Nahuatl scholar Msgr. Angel Garibay, recognizes in Lasso de la Vega's text a plurality of styles, one of which far outshines that chaplain's eloquence. This school, then, sees the *Nican Mopohua* as a composite work, whose loftiest passages—the dialogues and asides and more lyrical description—could only be the work of a master of Valeriano's caliber (Cawley 1992). According to Garibay (1967:821):

> The oldest documentary evidence of this event comes from the interpreter. Since Juan Diego did not know Spanish and Bishop Zumarraga did not know Nahuatl, Juan Gonzalez served as interpreter. Gonzalez was, at 18, a fortune seeker whom the bishop had sheltered, taught, and ordained, and who became a canon of the cathedral. After Zumarraga died, Gonzalez gave up his canonry and devoted himself to the evangelization of the Indians. At the same time he left his papers to Juan de Tovar, [who made a] brief summary of them in Nahuatl. . . . The Tovar summary is of importance as a document based on the evidence given by a witness to the meeting of Juan Diego and Bishop Zumarraga. However, it is not a detailed account. A better-known document is the Valeriano Relation, drawn up between 1560 and 1570. It was written by Valeriano and a group of Indians under the direction of Fr. Bernadino de Sahagun. First used by Miguel Sanchez, the document was published by Luis Lasso de la Vega in 1649. . . . It has two parts: a direct account of the event, [which is] the nucleus of the tradition, and an account of the miracles worked in the sanctuary or through the invocation of the Virgin Mary in this manifestation. The first part, prepared . . . under Sahagun's direction, is arranged in a literary fashion, according to Nahuatl stylistics, but the facts coincide with the Tovar document. The account of the miracles, also written in Nahuatl, is much later and includes events of the 17th century. . . . Among the minor documents are at least fifteen *Anales de los Indios*. These give communal testimony of the most notable happenings in the native world and include many references to the Tepeyac apparitions. While it has been stated that Bishop Zumarraga

made special reports on this event, none are extant; and it is probable that none were ever written. The second archbishop of Mexico, Alonso de Montufar, was a great promoter of the devotion to Our Lady of Guadalupe. In the Provincial Council of 1555, he, along with other bishops, formulated canons that indirectly approved the apparitions.

Students of the origin of the devotions assert that the narration of the apparitions was transmitted, at the beginning and for some time thereafter, in the manner common to the Indians of that time, orally and through "charts" on which they were able to draw the events of history. Only afterward, according to the demands of the circumstances, was the narration written down, first in Nahuatl and later in Spanish. From Indian to Indian, from community to community, the word of what had happened to Juan Diego at Mount Tepeyac began to be told along with the other marvels that took place in the presence of the Virgin of Guadalupe. The deeds rapidly entered into the traditions of the people (Siller-Acuña 1981b:11).

Study of the Image

Smith (1984:3) describes the image of Our Lady of Guadalupe: "Her head is tilted to the right. Her greenish eyes are cast downward in an expression of gentle concern. The mantle that covers her head and shoulders is of a deep turquoise, studded with gold stars and bordered in gold. Her hair is black, her complexion olive. She stands alone, her hands clasped in prayer, an angel at her feet." The image is imprinted on coarse fabric totally unsuitable for such a painting. Despite the coarseness of the fabric and the 450 years since the image first appeared, it has remained as brilliant as ever and is an object of veneration. As a way of exploring the extraordinary image of Our Lady of Guadalupe, this section presents a sample of the artistic, technical, and symbolic elements that make up the image (Fig. 1).

"For those who believe, the explanation is simple. The image of Guadalupe was made supernaturally. No artist painted it, and it was not made with human hands" (Smith 1984:17). Or was it made by human hands? There appears to be both a human and a divine contribution to

Figure 1. The Image of Our Lady of Guadalupe

the image, as parts of the image have clearly been crafted by human hands, while other parts seem inexplicable.

Throughout its 450-year history, many artists and scholars have examined the image of Our Lady of Guadalupe, arriving at a variety of conclusions about its composition. In 1666 a group of artists investigated the image and concluded the following in sworn testimony: "It is impossible for any human craftsman to paint or create a work so fine, clean and well formed on a fabric so coarse as this tilma or ayate, on which this divine and sovereign painting of the most holy Virgin, Our Lady of Guadalupe is painted" (Smith 1984:30).

On March 28, 1666, royal physicians came to examine the painting. What impressed them most was its remarkable state of preservation (Smith 1984:31–32):

The church was situated next to a large lake, Texcoco, which was known to contain a caustic chemical. Moisture-laden breezes off the water carried the chemical into the atmosphere and caused serious damage to another noted painting which hung in a nearby church. The Physicians Royal made a close examination of the back of the tilma. . . . On the back was an oval patch of green, a color that was nowhere to be seen on the front. One observer described the color as comparable to "the leaves of the lilies." . . . When the tilma was held up to the light it was so thin they could see right through it. . . . What was even stranger, the green on the back could not be seen on the front, although the image of the Virgin was clearly perceived from the back.

Although the quality of the image is extraordinary or supernatural, there is an argument for some additions having been made to the image. Vicente Díaz (1985:9) observes in concurrence with the 1648 testimony of Sánchez: "The original image . . . appears embarrassingly to have been painted. . . . Much of the aura of golden rays surrounding the figure has been chipped and fallen away. The angel and the crescent moon at the bottom are in a similar state of decay." Father Mario Rojas and Mrs. Margarita Parente-Martínez, contemporary Guadalupan scholars in Mexico City, suggest that the additions argued for are in fact elements that have been recorded as part of the original description of the image. When Juan Diego told his story to Valeriano, he first told of the dialogue between himself and Our Lady of Guadalupe; there is a second part to that document which describes the contents of the image. The argument of the "no-addition" position is strengthened by this story. However, the Guadalupanas concede that in order to give the image more brilliance at a distance people may have painted over what was already there. Ultimately, their argument states that there were no additions, that the image as-is is miraculous and not made by human hands.

A contemporary study on the human/divine composition of the image has reached conclusions similar to those noted in the seventeenth century. In 1981 Phillip Callahan, collaborating with Jody Brant Smith, utilized infrared photography—an accepted technique in critical studies of old paintings, which examines the undersketching, sizing, and general makeup of the pigments—to examine the image of Our Lady of Guadalupe. They concluded: "The original figure, including the rose robe, the blue mantle, the hands and the face, is inexplicable. There is no way either to explain the kind of color pigments utilized or the maintenance of color and brightness of the pigments over the centuries. Furthermore, when consideration is given to the fact that there is no underdrawing, sizing, or over-varnish, and that the weave of the fabric is itself utilized to give the portrait depth, no explanation of the portrait is possible by infrared techniques" (Callahan 1981:18).

There is disagreement as to whether the image, as it is today, is a combination of work that cannot be humanly explained and work done by human hands in the early years of the image's existence. Nevertheless, every aspect of the image, whether original or added, is significant to the understanding of Our Lady of Guadalupe. The following sections explore each aspect of the image, using interpretations from Nahuatl culture as well as from contemporary art and technology.

The Imagery of Our Lady of Guadalupe

The icon or image of Our Lady of Guadalupe is more than simply a picture. For the people who inhabited central and southern Mexico and parts of Central America before the Spanish arrival, the image of Our Lady of Guadalupe contains codices—ancient symbols and words.

The symbols have a special meaning, particularly to the indigenous, because they were able to decipher the code in that image and because the symbols spoke to their suffering.

The Face

A person's face held great importance for the indigenous people because they felt that through the face one could come to understand the inner person.

> The person was considered to be born faceless and with a nameless heart. It was through education that the child was introduced into the tradition of the group and thus his face was gradually formed, and he received individuality by the unique way in which he assimilated unto himself the tradition of the group. Thus the face could be defined as the embodiment of the self as it had been assumed and developed through education. Face and heart (*rostro y corazón*), then, for the Nahuatl, could then be approximated by our contemporary notion of personality. The face reflected the internal physiognomy of the person. (Elizondo 1980b:18)

Thus, by looking upon the young face of Guadalupe, with mature eyes and a smile of compassion (Elizondo 1980b:83), the Nahuatl saw her as being compassionate. Her face also told the indigenous people that she was not a Spaniard; she was one of their own (see Fig. 2).

Artistically, the face on the tilma is one of the most intriguing aspects of the image of Our Lady of Guadalupe. Callahan (1981:14–15), in agreement with Elizondo, contends that:

> The head of the virgin of Guadalupe is one of the great masterpieces of artistic facial expression. In subtleness of form, simplicity of execution, hue and coloring it has few equals among the masterpieces of the world. Furthermore there are no portraits that I have ever observed which are executed in a similar manner. . . . The expression suddenly appears reverent yet joyous, Indian yet European, olive-skinned yet white of hue. It is a face that intermingles the Christianity of Byzantine Europe with the overpowering natu-

Figure 2. The Face of Guadalupe

ralism of New World Indian; a fitting symbol for all the peoples of the great continent.

Callahan's (1981:14–15) analysis of the face reaches the following conclusions:

1. That the entire face is of unknown pigments and that they are blended in such a manner as to take advantage of the light refraction qualities of the unsized fabric and impart the olive-skinned hue to the skin.
2. That this technique utilizes the rough imperfections of the tilma weave to impart great depth to the painting.
3. That the face is of such beauty and unique execution as to render it inexplicable in terms of present day science.

The Eyes

As with most human images, the eyes of Our Lady of Guadalupe are both intriguing and revealing (see Fig. 3). The eyes of the image are looking down, indicating that she was not a proud creature, "neither did she show the impersonalism of the Mayan gods nor the masked presence of the Aztec gods" (Elizondo 1980b:85).

Between 1950 and 1980, several ophthalmologists analyzed the eyes of Our Lady of Guadalupe. They used infrared photography and a computer to photograph her eyes and amplify them. In this way, they discovered "a human bust" in the eyes of Our Lady of Guadalupe. All of the figures found in the eyes of the dark virgin conceivably could be attributable to "inkblot" speculations were it not for the fact that the same figures appear in both eyes at precisely the positions demanded by the laws of optics and two-eyed physiology (Díaz 1985:14).

To investigate this phenomenon, Dr. José Aste-Tonsmann, a computer engineer, used a process called digitalization. This photo enhancing involves the assignment of numerical equivalents to originally qualitative values; the resulting printout allows evaluation of images too small to be interpreted visually (Smith 1984:xx). The enhancement has revealed images of people in both eyes that are difficult to explain.

Figure 3. The Eye of Guadalupe

It is almost as if when Our Lady of Guadalupe appeared she took a picture of the people who were before her. "She had her eyes cast down looking upon the people and even allowing them to be reflected upon her eyes" (Elizondo 1980b:85).

The most startling discovery in this analysis is the hypothesis about the identity of the images in the eyes of Our Lady of Guadalupe. Previously, it was thought that there was only the image of Juan Diego. Dr. Aste, however, uncovered other images. One is the image of a cross-legged, bare-chested Indian holding his hands in prayer. The muscles of the legs, abdomen, and arms can be seen clearly. The unusually high forehead of the profiled face was typical of the Aztec "Cuacuacultin" priests who shaved their foreheads as a badge of rank (Díaz 1985:xx).

Another image identified was a face, believed to be that of Spanish Bishop Juan de Zumárraga, with a white beard, high cheek bones, and an aquiline nose. The features of the face have been identified as Basque by anthropologists; Bishop Zumárraga was a Basque (Díaz 1985:xx).

One of the most fascinating images discovered by Dr. Aste is the indistinct form of a black woman. This raised questions, since the presence of a black woman in 1531 in Mexico was unusual. Father Maurillo Montemayor, of the Center of Guadalupan Studies, confirms the presence of two black slaves among the household of the bishop (Díaz 1985:xx).

The Hands

Another aspect of the image of Our Lady of Guadalupe that draws attention is her hands (see Fig. 4). Her hands are not poised in the traditional Western style of prayer, but in an Indian manner of offering, indicating that something is to come from her (Elizondo 1980b:1).

Further, the study concluded that Our Lady of Guadalupe's arms were not simply in a position of offering, but were resting on her stomach, in the same way that a woman would place them if she were pregnant (Parente-Martínez 1986:xx).

The examination of her hands, using infrared photography, indicated that the hands have been modified to shorten the fingers and

Figure 4. The Hands of Guadalupe

convert the original hands from elongated fingers to shortened Indian fingers. The gold bracelet and fur cuffs (see Fig. 4) around the wrists have been added to fit a Gothic pattern and the original hands are of unknown pigment (Callahan 1981:13–14). However, one could speculate that such alterations were made in an attempt to clarify the Nahuatl symbology contained in the image for the Spanish. Adding the gold and fur trappings of royalty makes it clearer that Guadalupe is an important figure, almost divine. Shortening the fingers, while more difficult to explain, would make more obvious the Nahuatl understanding that Guadalupe was an Indian, one of them, and not a foreigner.

The Pregnancy

Guadalupe's pregnancy is indicated by another important element of the image—the tassel or maternity band (*cinta*) that she wears around her waist (see Fig. 4). *Estoy en cinta* means "I am pregnant." The skeptics say that the waist tassel was added to the painting some time after the original image was formed (Callahan 1981:9), presenting a dilemma: was the original image of Our Lady of Guadalupe one of a pregnant woman or not? Yet further investigation of the symbolism of the image reveals that below the tassel there is a small flower called *nagvioli*. To the Nahuatl, this flower was a symbol of the sun god. They recognized it as having been on the Aztec calendar. The flower's position on Our Lady of Guadalupe's womb verified for the Nahuatl that she was pregnant (Parente-Martínez 1986). Perhaps the *cinta* was added to make the Nahuatl symbol of the flower clearer to Spanish missionaries.

Other Aspects

Other significant aspects of the image are the stars, the gold sun rays, the moon, and the angel. Each of them relates directly to some aspect of Aztec divinity.

The stars refer to the "luminous skirt wrapped about the feminine aspect of Ometeotl" (León-Portilla 1963:50). The rays of the sun express the presence of the sun god, Quetzalcoatl. The fact that Guadalupe is standing on the moon reminds the Nahuatl of the god of night, the moon god. Finally, Guadalupe's being carried by an angel also relates her to Aztec divinity because royalty and representatives of the deities were carried by others. In addition, being carried by a heavenly creature means that she came on her own and not with the Spaniards (Elizondo 1980b:84).

Examination of these elements offers observations about the pigment and the order in which the additions were made. The stars are of an unknown pigment, and the paint of the sun rays is metallic gold. Both were added around the time that the edges of the mantle were added, long after the original painting (Callahan 1981:7). The moon and angel appear to have been added later than the sunburst, but certainly after the original body (Callahan 1981:9).

The color of Guadalupe's mantle is another aspect of the image that clearly connects her with Aztec divinity. It is turquoise, a blue-green color "reserved for the great God, Omecihuatl" (Elizondo 1980b:1). Analysis has shown that the blue of the mantle appears to be original and of unknown semitransparent blue pigment (Callahan 1981:10). The gold and blue edges of the mantle, however, were added in the late sixteenth or early seventeenth century (Callahan 1981:10).

The most notable aspect of Our Lady of Guadalupe's image is the robe. Elizondo (1980b:3) contends that the color of the robe was the color of the spilled blood of sacrifices, the color of Huitzilopochtli, the sun god who gave and preserved life and was himself nourished with the precious liquid of life blood.

From an artistic viewpoint, the robe of Our Lady of Guadalupe is especially notable because of its unusual luminosity: "It is highly reflective of visible radiation, yet transparent to the infrared rays. . . . It is the most transparent. . . . As in the case of the blue mantle the shadowing of the pink robe is blended into the paint layer and no drawing or sketch is evident under the pink pigment (Callahan 1981:10).

The artistic and technical explanations are a testimony to the extraordinary nature of the image. The description makes clear that the image is not simply a picture, but a story made up of a number of symbols which spoke to the Nahuatl people in the sixteenth century and still speak to twentieth-century people.

The Story

This is the story of the Apparition of Our Lady of Guadalupe in Elizondo's (1980b:75–79) abbreviated version.

Early in the morning of Saturday, December 9, 1531, Juan Diego, a Christian Indian of middle age, was walking to early Mass at Tlatelolco. Suddenly Juan heard very beautiful music. He believed that he was either dreaming or in paradise.

He stopped, looked around, and tried to discover where the music was coming from. He heard a soft voice saying, "Juanito, Juan Dieguito." Without even noticing what he was doing, he began walking up a nearby hillside towards the direction of the call.

When he came to the top of the hill, he saw a lady of glowing beauty. Her dress radiated like the sun and her face had an expression of love and compassion. She said to him, "Juanito, the smallest of my children, where are you going?" He responded, "My dear child, I have to go to your house of Mexico, Tlatelolco, to hear about the divine things which are given and taught to us by our priests, the delegates of Our Lord."

She then spoke to him and made known her will: "Know and understand, you the dearest of my children, that I am the ever holy Virgin Mary, Mother of the true God through whom one lives, Mother of the Creator of heaven and of earth.

"I have a living desire that there be built a temple, so that in it I can show and give forth all my love, compassion, help, and defense, because I am your loving mother: to you, all who are with you, to all the inhabitants of this land and to all who love me, call upon me, and trust in me. I will hear their lamentations and will remedy all their miseries, pains, and sufferings.

"To bring about what my mercy intends, go to the palace of the bishop and tell him how I have sent you to manifest to him what I very much desire, that here on this site below the hill, a temple be built to me." Immediately, he made an inclination, and said to her: "My Lady, I am already on the way to fulfill your mandate."

Juan Diego went quickly to the palace of the Spanish bishop. After a long wait, he was able to see the bishop and gave him the message of the Lady. The bishop was kind to him, but told him to return on another day when he could slowly hear his entire story from beginning to end. Juan Diego left in great sadness because he had failed in his mission.

He went directly on to the top of the hill where he had spoken with the lady, and seeing her, said: "My dear child, I went where you sent me to fulfill your mandate. It was with great difficulty that I entered the room of the bishop. I gave him your message, just as you had told me to do. He received me kindly and he heard me attentively, but he did not believe as true what I told him. He told me to come again and he would hear me out slowly. My dear Lady, I understood perfectly well in the way in which he responded that he believes that perhaps it is an invention of mine that you want them to build a temple here. This I beg you, entrust your mission to one of the important persons who is well known, respected, and esteemed so that they may believe him. You know that I am no-body, a nothing, a coward, a pile of old sticks, just like a bunch of leaves. I am nothing. You have sent me to walk in places where I do not belong. Forgive me and please do not be angry with me, my lady and mistress."

The Lady answered him, "Listen, my son, the smallest of my children, I want you to understand that I have many servants and messengers to whom I can entrust this message, but in every aspect it is precisely my desire that you seek help so that with your media-tion, my wish will be fulfilled. I beg you with great insistence, my son, the smallest of my children, and I sternly command you, once again, to go tomorrow to see the bishop. Greet him in my name and make known my will to him, that he must begin work on the temple which I am asking for. And once again tell him that I per-sonally, the ever holy Virgin Mary, Mother of God, send you."

Juan Diego responded: "My dear Lady, I will gladly go to fulfill your mandate. I will go to do your will. They probably will not listen to me, or if they listen, they will probably not believe me. But in any case, I will return tomorrow afternoon to report to you."

The next day he went from his home to Tlatelolco to the palace of the bishop. Once again it was with great difficulty that he was able to gain an audience with the bishop. This time the bishop asked him many questions—where he saw her, what did she look like, etc.—but he answered the bishop perfectly. He explained with the greatest precision about her figure and everything which he had admired; nevertheless, the bishop did not believe him and told him that his word was not sufficient evidence, that he needed some sign to believe that it was truly the heavenly Lady who was sending him.

Without hesitation, Juan Diego responded: "Tell me what is the sign that you are asking for so that I may go and ask the Lady for it."

The bishop, seeing that he was not disturbed in the slightest, and that it did not change his story in any way, dismissed him, but he immediately sent some of his household to follow him to see where he was going and with whom he was speaking. They started out after him. He went directly to the hill of Tepeyac but when he arrived, they lost track of him. They tried to find him, but they could not and returned to the bishop tired and angered. They begged the bishop not to believe him because he was obviously just inventing the stories.

In the meantime, Juan Diego was already with the Virgin telling her the response of the bishop. Having heard the response, the Lady said to him, "Very well, my son, you will return here tomorrow so that you may take to the bishop the sign which he has asked for. With that, he will believe you and will have no further doubts; and know well, my beloved son, that I will repay you for your care, work and fatigue which you have done on my account. Go and I will await you here tomorrow."

The next day, when Juan Diego was supposed to take the sign so that he might be believed, he did not return. When he had arrived home the previous day, he had discovered his uncle, Juan Bernardino, gravely ill. Juan Diego spent the day searching for a medical person to assist this uncle. Having failed to do so, he promised his uncle that early in the morning he would go to Tlatelolco to call one of the priests to confess him and prepare him for death, because it was evident that it was time for Juan Bernardino to die and that he would not get up from his bed to regain his health.

Very early on the morning of Tuesday, December 12, 1531, Juan Diego rushed to Tlatelolco to get the priest. When he came near the hill of Tepeyac, he thought to himself that it was better not to stop because the Lady might see him and stop him. He did not want to displease her, but he did have to rush to get the priest for his dying uncle. As he was going by the other side of the hill, in order to avoid her, he saw the Lady coming down from the top of the hill, and coming to him, she said: "What is happening, my son, the smallest of my children? Where are you going?"

He became very embarrassed and greeting her, said, "My dear Lady, I hope you are happy; I am going to cause you some affliction. I want you to know that my uncle is ready to die. Now I am rushing to your house in Mexico to call one of the beloved priests of our Lord to go and confess him and prepare him for death. As soon as I have taken care of this, I will return here so that I may take your message. Forgive me, I am not lying to you. I will come first thing tomorrow."

The Virgin answered him: "Hear me, my son, that which scares you and causes you anguish is nothing; do not let your heart be troubled, do not be afraid of that sickness. Am I not she who is your Mother? Your uncle will not die of this sickness; be assured that he is healthy." Juan was greatly consoled and very happy. Then the Virgin told him to go to the top of the hill where he would find various flowers. She told him to cut and gather the flowers and bring them to her. He obeyed immediately and when he arrived at the top, he was astounded to discover numerous exquisite roses of Castille, especially since it was long before their normal time. They had a beautiful aroma and were covered with the morning dew. He immediately cut them and returned to the Lady with the roses. She took them into her hands and rearranged them in his tilma. She then said, "My son, the smallest of my children, this diversity of roses is the proof and sign that you will take to the bishop. You will tell him in my name that he is to see my will in this and he must fulfill it. You are my ambassador and most worthy of trust. I rigorously command you to unfold your mantle only in the presence of the bishop and to show him what you have with you. You are to tell everything. You will say that I told you to go to the top of the hill to cut the flowers, and tell everything that you saw and admired, so that you may convince the prelate to give his help in building the temple that I have asked for."

Immediately after receiving his instructions from the Lady, he set out without haste to the house of the bishop. He was happy and had no doubt that this time he would be believed.

When he arrived at the palace of the bishop, the servants of the bishop came out to see him. He begged them to please tell the bishop that he had to see him, but none of them wanted to listen to him.

They acted as if he were not there. But seeing that he would not go away, that he simply stayed patiently in his place, the servants decided that they had better inform the bishop. Soon the strong aroma of the roses began to spread and the servants also were able to get a few glimpses of what he had with him. They were surprised to see roses of various kinds and of great beauty, and at first tried to take them from him, but he held on all the more. They finally went to tell the bishop what they had seen and that it would be good to see the Indian.

The bishop became very excited, for he sensed that this was the sign that he had been asking for. He immediately asked for Juan Diego to be shown into his study. As soon as Juan Diego came in, he made his reverence to the bishop and began to tell him once again everything that he had seen and admired and also the message of the Lady. He said: "Sir, I did what you ordered me to do, to go and tell my Lady, the Lady of Heaven, Holy Mary, precious mother of God, that you asked for a sign in order to believe me, that you are to build a temple on the site that she is asking for. Furthermore, I told her that I had given you my word that I would bring you a sign and proof of her will. She accepted your request and kindly produced what you asked for, a sign and proof so that her will may be fulfilled.

"Today, very early in the morning, she once again ordered me to come and see you. I asked her for the sign so that you might believe me, as she had told me that she would do. And at that moment she produced the sign. She sent me to the top of the hill, where I had seen her before, to cut the roses of Castille. After I had cut them, I came back down to the bottom of the hill where she took them into her hands, rearranged them, and put them into my mantle so that I might personally bring them to you.

"Even though I was well aware that the top of the hill was no place for flowers, because there are only cactus, mesquites, and other kinds of wild brush, I did not doubt. When I went to the top of the hill, I saw that I was in paradise with all the varieties of roses of Castille, shining with morning dew. She told me why I was to give them to you. That is what I am doing now so that in them you may see the sign which you have asked for and thus you will fulfill her will; also that the trustfulness of my word may be evident. Here they are; accept them."

As he unfolded his tilma, all the roses dropped to the floor and as they did the precious image of the always holy virgin Mary, Mother of God, appeared on the tilma in the presence of the bishop and his household, the image, which has defied time and scientists, and appears just as beautiful today as on December 12, 1531. The same tilma is in the temple built in her honor in Tepeyac, called Guadalupe. As she appeared in their presence on the tilma, they were amazed and fell to their knees. They greatly admired the image and showed by their actions that they truly saw her in their minds and in their hearts.

The Nahuatl Interpretation of the Apparition

I offer this interpretation to add another dimension to understanding Our Lady of Guadalupe. In addition, it gives us an insight into the story, one which would otherwise be lost were it to be given an exclusively Western or Christian reading. It is not my purpose here to compare religions (for further readings on the Nahuatl religion, see León-Portilla 1962, 1963, 1969, and 1980, and Soustelle 1970).

Even with little background about the appearance of Our Lady of Guadalupe, the story is engaging. However, fuller appreciation can be gained by understanding the context in which it was first told and experienced. The following textual analysis is based on the research of Clodomiro Siller-Acuña, a contemporary theologian and anthropologist who combines his academic work in anthropology with extensive pastoral work as a priest among the indigenous peoples of Mexico. His anthropological interest is indigenous peoples, particularly those who speak Nahuatl, and his theological work is based on liberation theology. Since Siller's research is unavailable in English, I have translated it for use in this book.

The original language of the *Nican Mopohua* is Nahuatl. It is important to understand that Nahuatl is a symbolic language which has meaning far beyond words, much more profound, much richer and fuller. It is a simple language, direct, smooth, precise, elegant, resounding, beautiful, significant, and even sublime. As discussed in the previous chapter, another important aspect of the Nahuatl language is the use of *disfrasismos*, a way of communicating the most profound thought or feeling using a complementary union of two words or symbols which express one meaning (Siller-Acuña 1981c:12). Connected with this is the importance of numerology for the Nahuatl people. The numbers four and five are particularly significant.

As Siller notes, the function of a symbol is to accumulate many meanings and various shades of meaning. For example, the symbol flower represents a particular object, the flower, but for the Nahuatl it also has the added meanings of truth, beauty, and authenticity. Because symbols are not the same in all cultures, the flower is not universally a symbol of truth—for example, Shakespeare uses flower imagery to discuss youth and fleeting beauty. To determine the meaning and significance of a symbol within a culture one must turn to the myths of that culture. For an understanding of the *Nican Mopohua*, then, an appreciation of the symbols and myths of Nahuatl culture is essential. Besides offending the Nahuatl people, to neglect the symbolic universe in that culture would falsify and distort the narrative (Siller-Acuña 1981c:12–13).

Myths are the stories that a culture uses to create coherence in its life, values, and symbols. In myths a culture tells its story of origin and its understanding of the major issues of life and death. Another function of myth is to express a culture's whole life—all that it is and all that it values. Myths, then, are not just stories in isolation. They refer to *all* historic moments and not just one. The history of how flower has become a symbol for truth in the Nahuatl culture emerges out of the myth that the truth of all things was brought by the god Quetzalcoatl in the form of a flower, so that humanity could live happily.

The *Nican Mopohua* begins with a statement that sets the historical context of the appearance. The Virgin Mary appears in the setting of the *post guerra*, ten years after the conquest. She associates herself with *El verdadero Dios, por quien se vive* (the true God for whom one lives). This expression is one of the names that the Nahuatl gave to their gods. When the Virgin states that she is from the one true God, the God who gives life, the Nahuatl recognized this God to be their God (Siller-Acuña 1981c:32). The *Nican Mopohua* says that the ever holy Virgin Mary, Mother of God, appeared. The title "always Virgin" is translated into Spanish from the Nahuatl as *doncella entera* (a whole woman). In Nahuatl there existed many words to designate virginity, which underscores its cultural importance. Virginity was highly valued by the indigenous peoples, men and women alike; consequently, they saw Our Lady of Guadalupe as an embodiment of a preconquest value of their culture.

The text states the day, the date, and the time of the apparition: Saturday, December 9, 1531, early in the morning. For the indigenous, *muy de madrugada* (very early in the morning) referred not only to daybreak, but to the beginning of all time. Our Lady of Guadalupe appears early in the morning, just as the day is coming out of darkness and night. This meaningful time defined the Guadalupe event as fundamental, equal in significance to the origin of the world and the cosmos (Siller-Acuña 1981c:37).

As Juan Diego is walking, he hears music. For the Nahuatl, music was one-half of their dual expression of truth, beauty, philosophy, and divinity: flower and song together (a *disfrasismo*) manifested the presence of the Divine. When Juan Diego hears such beautiful and enchanting music, he asks, "Have I gone into paradise? Can I be hearing what I am hearing?" Siller-Acuña notes that the word *canto* (song or music) appears five times. For the Nahuatl, this number five was a symbol of the center of the world (Siller-Acuña 1981c:38).

In Nahuatl numerology the number four symbolizes cosmic totality or completion. In the text, Juan Diego asks four questions. First, "Am I worthy to hear what I am hearing; am I perhaps dreaming?" Second, "I must awaken from this dream. Where am I?" Third, "Perhaps I have entered into the land of paradise that our ancient ones have told us about?" And finally, "Am I in heaven?" Between the point of hearing the music and asking the questions there is a moment of silence. This silence with night is another dual expression that, for the Nahuatl, linked the event with the origins of creation (Siller-Acuña 1981c: 40–41).

Upon hearing the music, Juan Diego looks to the east. The Nahuatl believed that life came from the east, where the sun rises, and it is from this direction that Our Lady of Guadalupe speaks. The east is the place of the sun, one of the symbols of God. When a priest climbed up to the temple dedicated to the sun, he looked to the east, with the west at his back. As a result, because of the explicit mention of the placement, Mount Tepeyac is represented as a symbolic base for a temple. The temples of the Indians were constructed atop artificial mounds; so when Juan Diego looks toward the top of the hill toward the east, it is implied that Tepeyac is functioning symbolically as a temple (Siller-Acuña 1981a:226–227). This hill was the ancient site of the Nahuatl mother goddess, Tonantzin.

At this point, Guadalupe calls out to Juan Diego in the diminutive form, "Juan Dieguito," which has been interpreted as an expression of maternal love and delicacy. Siller (1981c:42) says that the term "Juan Diego" in its diminutive form had the suffix -tzin in Nahuatl. This form designated reverence. Similarly, he points out that the text does not report that Our Lady of Guadalupe appears to Juan Diego, but rather that he encounters her. He sees her as a woman of nobility. But here the text makes an important distinction. It says that Our Lady of Guadalupe is standing up. Nobles, whether Aztec or Spaniard, received people sitting down. Sometimes they were seated on a pedestal or in some designated place. This seated position showed not only that the noble presided over the people but, in the experience of the conquest, dominated the people. In this case, the nobility that Juan Diego sees in this woman is not domineering (Siller-Acuña 1981c:43). And Our Lady does not treat Juan Diego as one of the conquered ones; she restores his dignity.

As Siller observes, just as Our Lady of Guadalupe restores dignity to Juan Diego in her dialogue with him, her presence elicits a response from the earth and from the world. The text says that the flowers and ground glow like gold. Everything is bright and emerald-like. This signifies that this event affected the world and in many ways produced new life: not just for people, but for the land as well.

One of the descriptions of the Lady is that she is covered with the radiance of the sun. For the Nahuatl, the sun was a symbol of God. A person's clothing was dyed a certain color and displayed certain objects or symbols that told others who that person was, who had sent that person, or where the person came from. The fact that Our Lady of Guadalupe is covered by the rays of the sun informed the indigenous that she had something to do with God and that God formed part of her experience and personality (Siller-Acuña 1981c:44).

One of the most important lines in the text is the one in which Our Lady of Guadalupe identifies herself. Early in the text, Our Lady of Guadalupe indicates that she is (1) the Mother of God, who is the God of truth; (2) the Mother of the Giver of life; (3) the Mother of the Creator or Inventor of men and women; (4) the Mother of the One who makes the sun and the earth; and (5) the Mother of the One who is far and close. In this passage, Our Lady of Guadalupe implies that she is the Mother of the ancient gods of the Mexicans by, in essence, stating the five names of the gods that were known to the Nahuatl, using Nahuatl duality and phrases. She gives the names of their gods: "the God of truth" and "the God who gives life." The third and fourth names are names that the Nahuatl understood to be the operative essence of God. The last one implied the cosmological and historical dimension of their God (Siller-Acuña 1981c:49).

Siller (1981a:218) points out that *Dios Inninantzin* (Mother of God) is an expression half-Spanish and half-Nahuatl and suggests that the use of Spanish may be part of a mechanism of dialogue intended to widen the communication from Nahuatl to Spanish. The phrase *Inipalnemohuani, nelli Teotl Dios* means True God, Author of Life: Inipalnemohuani, the one who gives us life, is one of the names that the Nahuatl gave to God many years before hearing the Gospel. This name expresses a content whose reference is anthropological—it does not say who God is; rather, it explains what God does for humanity. *In nelli, Teotl* means God with roots, True God, and is also an ancient expression that tells of the essence of the God (Siller-Acuña 1981a:220–221).

Our Lady of Guadalupe says that she is:

—*Inninantzin in huelnelli Teotl Dios*, "Mother of the Great Truth."
Note that the words Teotl (God) and Dios (God) are both
capitalized.

—*inninantzin inipalnemohuani*, "Mother of the Giver of Life."

—*inninantzin in Teyocoyani*, "Mother of the Inventor of Humanity."

—*inninantzin in Tloque Nahuaque*, "Mother of the Lord of near and
close by," which means that all things find room in God.

—*inninantzin in Ilhicahua in Tlalticpaque*, "Mother of (the Lord) of
Heaven and Earth." (Siller-Acuña 1981c:48–49)

In the next part of the text, the Virgin tells Juan Diego that she wants
a temple to be built for her. Previously, Juan Diego has told the Virgin
that he is going to her house in Mexico-Tlatelolco, referring to a church
where he attends mass and religious instruction. Our Lady of Guadalupe, however, says that she wishes her house to be at Tepeyac (Siller-
Acuña 1981c:49). This site is of great significance. The hill called Tepeyac had previously been the shrine of Tonantzin, an earth goddess
and one of the major divinities of the Aztec people. The name "Tonantzin" designated Cihuacoatl, in the same way that "Our Lady" desig-
nates the Virgin Mary in the Christian religion (Lafaye 1976:212–213).

Given the context of this apparition, the indigenous people would
make strong connections between Our Lady of Guadalupe and their
own divinity and religious system. It was very natural for the Aztecs to
associate Guadalupe with Tonantzin since both were virgin mothers of
gods and both appeared at the same place (Madsen 1967:378).

During the second apparition, Juan Diego addresses the Virgin as
Señora, la más pequeña de mis hijas (Lady, the smallest of my daughters).
By referring to the Virgin in this manner, he is implying that she, too,
is poor and depreciated in the same way that he is. Juan Diego suggests
to the Virgin that she send someone "who is of greater importance,
who is known, who is respected, and who is esteemed." (The use of
four terms to describe the desired envoy, as noted, is consistent with
Nahuatl numerology; four represents totality and completion.) He believes that he is not taken seriously because he is an Indian.

Juan Diego then asks forgiveness from the Virgin for any pain he
may have caused her by his failing to convince the bishop of her mes-

sage. His self-hatred and sense of unworthiness exhibited in this passage are a tragic result of the conquest, wherein the Aztec people took on a "victim mentality," leading to a loss of a sense of their own self-worth. Juan Diego believes that it is his fault that he is not accepted (Siller-Acuña 1981c:61).

But the Virgin absolutely refuses to choose another messenger. She reaffirms her desire that he be the one, even though she has "many servants and messengers." At the same time, she does not negate or deny the oppression that Juan Diego is experiencing. The Virgin is very insistent and uses such phrases as *con rigor te mando, te ruego,* and *mucho te ruego* (I command you and I beg you).

This is a conversation between equals. Our Lady of Guadalupe is according him the dignity and respect of a person who has a right of choice. The conversation with Juan Diego is concluded when she states, "And once again, tell the bishop that I send you, the ever Virgin, holy Mary, Mother of God, it is she who sends you." Juan Diego reaccepts and embraces this mission. He is still concerned with not wanting to cause the Virgin any pain and, at the same time, is manifesting a commitment, because he says with much joy and energy, "I will go and complete your order" (Siller-Acuña 1981c:64).

Juan Diego returns to the house of the bishop. Once again, there are difficulties. He subjects himself to distrust, humiliation, and disbelief for the sake of the mission. When the bishop finishes interrogating Juan Diego, he states that he cannot build the temple on the Indian's word alone. He sends Juan Diego back to ask the Virgin for a sign. The bishop also directs his own people to follow Juan Diego, but they become lost and cannot find him (Siller-Acuña 1981c:65).

Siller points out that, when Juan Diego is speaking with the bishop, he refers to the Virgin as the "always Virgin, Holy Mary, Mother of our Savior the Lord Jesus Christ." Siller (1981c:69) suggests that this is a theological reflection on the part of Juan Diego. With the return of the self (Juan Diego's restored dignity) comes the ability to theologize.

In the next section of the text, Juan Diego finds that his uncle, Juan Bernardino, is sick. Siller notes that a common life-threatening disease at the time was smallpox, introduced by the Spaniards. It was a disease that the Indians did not know how to cure.

Juan Diego is caught in a dilemma. Siller (1981c:76) speaks in some detail regarding the important role of the uncle: "The sickness of the uncle came at a crucial moment in the mission of Juan Diego. . . . For us perhaps it would have been more important if the mother or father of Juan Diego was sick . . . but for the majority of the Meso-American people, the uncle played a social role of capital importance. Uncle referred only to the brother of the mother and it was the uncle who willed his inheritance to the nephews and not to his sons. . . . The uncle was the maximum expression of respect that one could give an adult. . . ."

Juan Diego is convinced that the sad news of his uncle's nearness to death will cause the Virgin grief. When he does meet her, even though he tries to avoid her, he begins by saying, "I am going to cause you affliction" (Siller-Acuña 1981c:79).

Guadalupe's response to Juan Diego's concern is expanded to include all sickness and anguish: "Do not fear this sickness, or any other sickness or anguish" (Siller-Acuña 1981c:82). This is followed by five rhetorical questions: "Am I not here, your Mother? Are you not under my shadow and protection? Am I not your foundation of life? Are you not in the folds of my mantle, in the crossing of my arms? Is there anything else that you need?" (The number five would indicate to the Nahuatl that some reference was being made to the center of the world.) In these questions, Guadalupe reveals herself as someone who has authority. Siller (1981c:83) states that the Mexicans understood authority as someone with the ability to cast a large shadow, because the one who is greater than all the rest must shelter or protect the great and small alike.

Juan Bernardino is cured, and this is the first miracle on the part of the Virgin. It produces healing not only for the uncle, Juan Bernardino, but for Juan Diego and the whole Nahuatl people. It is important to note that there is a discrepancy in the literature as to whether there were four or five apparitions depending on whether or not the appearance of the Virgin to Juan Bernardino, not recorded in the narrative, is considered one of the apparitions. The healing and the miracle of the uncle also extends itself to Juan, who "felt much consoled and was left feeling contented" (Siller-Acuña 1981c:84).

The Virgin orders Juan Diego to go to the hill and to look for some roses, cut them, gather them, and bring them to her. At a time when roses are not in season and do not bloom, they are not only fresh but fragrant. Flowers, as explained above, were a sign to the Nahuatl people of truth and of the presence of divinity. Siller (1981c:86–88) offers an interesting interpretation. He says that Juan Diego brings truth (i.e., the flowers) to the "Lady from Heaven." She touches the flowers and makes herself present in them, remaining within the logical symbolic culture of the Indian.

The servants in the bishop's palace try to take away what Juan Diego is holding in his tilma, but he has been ordered not to show the flowers to anyone except the bishop. Symbolically, Siller sees this action as the dominant culture's attempt to take the truth away from the Indian. For Juan Diego, the conquerors and dominant culture have already taken his land, his goods, his city, his form of government, and his reasons for being and acting. Now they want to take away his truth, which is all he has left. Siller (1981c:93) states that, given the Guadalupan event, it is no longer possible to take the truth away from the indigenous people; in fact, it is Juan Diego, an Indian, who brings the truth to the Spanish bishop.

Once again, Juan Diego tells his story to the bishop. According to Siller, in the process he implies that by doubting him and asking him for proof of a sign the bishop is, in fact, questioning and demanding a sign from the Virgin. Juan Diego says that the Virgin "sent me up to this hill to get flowers, but I knew it was not the season, yet I did not doubt." After making this statement, Juan Diego hands over the proof—the roses—and asks the bishop to receive them.

As the flowers fall from the tilma of Juan Diego, the fifth apparition occurs: the image of Our Lady of Guadalupe imprinted on the tilma. When the bishop and those around him in the room see this, they all kneel, admire it, and repent for not believing. The first thing that the bishop does upon his conversion is to take the tilma into his private chapel. He also offers hospitality and orders his assistants to follow Juan Diego so that he can designate the place where the temple is to be built. The Virgin tells Juan Diego's uncle to give his testimony about his healing to the bishop; thus the image is not separated from the act of healing. The image is an expression of compassion and the relief of Nahuatl suffering. "The image must be connected to the healing and restoration of the dignity of the poor" (Siller Acuña 1981c:104–106).

The Impact of the Story

The significance of this story is twofold: (1) it was the foundation of Mexican Christianity and (2) it provided a *connection* between the indigenous and Spanish cultures.

The appearance of Our Lady of Guadalupe was the occasion for the conversion of the indigenous people and was, therefore, the foundation of Mexican Christianity. The real turning point in the conversion of the Aztecs to Christianity came with the miraculous appearance of the Indian Virgin of Guadalupe in 1531. This event brought about "the emotional acceptance of a new faith, which has been aptly called Guadalupinist Catholicism" (Madsen 1967:377).

Only six years after the apparition of Our Lady of Guadalupe, nine million Aztec people had been baptized into the Christian faith (Elizondo 1980b; Madsen 1967). In the sixteenth century, the Virgin of Guadalupe came to be a symbol of the new Indian Catholicism as distinguished from the foreign Catholicism of the conquerors. The Aztecs adapted Catholicism to their own religious concepts by a process of fusional syncretism. Guadalupinist Catholicism spread rapidly in central Mexico and became the focal point of Aztec culture (Madsen 1967:378).

In addition to prompting conversion, Our Lady of Guadalupe's apparition also provided a link between the indigenous and Spanish cultures. When the Spaniards came and followed Juan Diego, after the miracle of the apparition and the flowers, they went to the home of Juan Diego's uncle to question him. They asked him if the Virgin had given a name. He said, "She calls herself 'Tlecuauhtlacupeuh.'" To the Spaniards, this sounded like "Guadalupe," and they were quick to associate it with the Guadalupe of Estremadura, Spain. A large number of the conquistadors were from the province of Estremadura and quite naturally were devoted to the local patroness. It should be noted as well that the devotion to Our Lady of Guadalupe in Estremadura was reaching its peak at the time of the first contacts between Spain and the New World (Ascheman 1983:87). But the Nahuatl language does not contain the letters *d* and *g*; therefore Our Lady's name could not have been "Guadalupe" (Escalada 1965:13).

The Nahuatl understanding of "Tlecuauhtlacupeuh" is *La que viene volando de la luz como el águila de fuego* (she who comes flying from the region of light like an eagle of fire; Echeagaray 1981:21). The region of light was the dwelling place of the Aztec gods, and the eagle was a sign from the gods.

To the Spaniards, it sounded like "Guadalupe" and reminded them of their Virgin at home. To the natives, it sounded like "Tlecuauhtlacupeuh" and referred to a sign that had come from their gods. The name that each heard brought them to see, in the apparition, something each understood and valued, which would inevitably bring them together and be a unifying force. The symbol of Our Lady of Guadalupe has had various manifestations: it affirmed the humanness of the indigenous populations, it provided a symbolic means of forging a new culture and polity out of Spanish and Indian elements, and today it serves to bring together disparate groups who otherwise would never know one another.

In summary, at the time Our Lady of Guadalupe appeared to Juan Diego, the Aztec nation found itself in a situation of subordination, alienation, suffering, and oppression. "The image of Our Lady of Guadalupe cannot be understood without the story that gives it life. Nor can the story be understood without the cries and sadness of the Indians and of all the poor of Mexico and Latin America. It is from there that it gathers meaning" (Concha Malo 1981:385–386). Whether the apparition proved to be of benefit to the indigenous people or not is a point of controversy to this day. Nevertheless, Our Lady of Guadalupe occupies a place so central to Mexican culture that any consideration of the Mexican people in general, and Mexican-American women in particular, must include reference to her.

THREE

Insights from the Experience of Juan Diego, First Perceiver of Our Lady of Guadalupe

For Mexican Americans, Our Lady of Guadalupe is a symbol of both cultural and religious identity. For a people who were stripped of everything, she restores to them their dignity, their humanity, and their place in history. Virgilio Elizondo contends that only a divine intervention could have turned around the devastation caused by the conquest. She "who comes from the region of light on the wings of an eagle" restores dignity and life to a people who were dead.

The religious perspective is crucial in this work for two specific reasons. First, Our Lady of Guadalupe is a religious experience, image, and story. Although the contemporary Mexican-American woman has not experienced a firsthand vision of Our Lady of Guadalupe, the apparition is the primordial experience that is kept alive in the cultural and psychological memory of the community. This cultural and psychological memory lives in the Guadalupe image in Mexican-American homes, and Mexican-American women share in the memory of the originating experience. Some internalize the memory so that it becomes for them a personal religious experience.

A second reason for employing a religious perspective is that, as an integral part of the human experience, a religious perspective demands to be included in the total identity of the Mexican-American woman. Religion is not separate from those human characteristics that constitute the psychosocial dimension, but rather considers all those characteristics in relation to whatever one may consider the divine (James 1958:42). Thus the two dimensions—psychosocial and religious—are interconnected. Joining these two dimensions makes possible an understanding of how the religious image of Our Lady of Guadalupe can affect the Mexican-American woman as an individual member of a particular culture.

Only recently have we realized the impact and the importance of images in shaping character and personality. Historian Margaret Miles (1985:147) contends that contemporary culture minimizes the importance of images in shaping a person's values and that self-image, values, and longings are shaped by "the visual objects of one's habitual attention." We select and develop a repertoire of images, chosen both because they attract and because we receive from them visual messages that help us to visualize—to envision—personal and social transformation (Miles 1985:148–149).

According to Miles, images we select have two functions. An image either *expresses* a valued aspect or quality of our experience or *compensates*, offering alternatives or supplements to the intrinsic value of the individual's experience. For example, Our Lady of Guadalupe expresses a Mexican-American woman's values of being female, a mother, brown-skinned, mestiza. Her image compensates when a woman feels herself lacking and petitions her for strength, endurance, patience, or compassion. Humans need images that represent—that make present—aspects of human possibility we have known perhaps only momentarily or can only imagine (Miles 1985:148–149).

The dimensions that make up our humanity—the psychosocial dimension, religiosity, experience, stages of development—are so intrinsically linked that they cannot be separated. It is no longer possible to speak of any one of them alone, to talk solely of a psychosocial dimension, a religious dimension, or a developmental dimension. Rather, to speak of one is to imply the others; for this reason, I have used an interdisciplinary psychosocial religious approach which also acknowledges the developmental nature of reality.

The Psychosocial Dimension

Human beings are social creatures, and as such their worldview and behavior are molded by the standards of the groups to which they belong (Frank 1961:6)—our worldview cannot be divorced from cultural influences.

The psychosocial dimension of a person includes interior or intra-psychic life: perceptions, emotional states, and feelings of well-being (Frank 1961:27). These, in turn, are formed by and help form a person's environment and interpersonal relations. To be able to function, according to Jerome Frank, each individual must impose an order and regularity on the welter of experiences impinging upon her. To do so, she develops out of her personal experiences a set of assumptions, the sum of which can be termed her "assumptive world": "This is a short-hand expression for a highly structured, complex, interacting set of values, expectations, and images of oneself and others, which guide and in turn are guided by a person's perceptions and behavior and which are closely related to emotional states and feelings of well being. . . . The more enduring assumptions become organized into attitudes with cognitive, affective, and behavioral components" (Frank 1961:27).

Personal assumptive worlds vary, as do experiences and self-images. How we see ourselves and our surrounding world, the values we attach to what we see, and our resulting behaviors all join to form the psychosocial dimension.

Culture plays an important role in this assumptive world. The Mexican-American culture, with its multiple identities, unique foods, music, history, and religious traditions, is central to the psychosocial reality of Mexican-American women. Because of its cross-cultural nature, that reality, that experience, that dimension is very different from the psychosocial realities of either Mexican or American women.

To understand Mexican-American women, we must appreciate their assumptive world, their psychosocial reality. Furthermore, to understand the effect of any religious experience on a person, we must understand how this experience is perceived, is valued, and how it motivates behavior—in other words, how it fits into that person's assumptive world and psychosocial reality.

The psychosocial dimension is often considered the primary and exclusive avenue by which individuals understand their world. This dimension is spoken of as containing an assumptive worldview, which includes intrapsychic life and interpersonal relations. In my own psychosocial religious perspective, I also include assumptions as formed by perceptions, behaviors, environment, emotional states, values, expectations, and the way a person images the self and others, as well as how this assumptive world is influenced by historical events, choices, and social conditioning.

This psychosocial dimension is not a different component from the religious dimension but is inherent in it. The religious dimension of the sphere of human experience integrates belief, faith, and behavior in relation to the divine. Given this intrinsic link of the psychosocial and religious, questions previously considered religious must be asked within this broader perspective. Thus the psychosocial religious perspective is one that examines the nominally religious within the broader context of human experience. Within the religious dimension, this study focuses on Our Lady of Guadalupe as both a religious and cultural symbol.

A Working Understanding of Faith and Religion

Although faith may be "engendered by a religious tradition" (Fowler 1981:9–12), it does not automatically involve traditional concepts of religion and belief. Rather, says Fowler (1981:14), faith is an active concept, a way individuals make meaning: "a universal feature of human living . . . involves a resting of the heart, in accordance with a vision of transcendent value and power . . . is not a separate dimension of life . . . and gives purpose and goal to one's hopes and stirrings."

Faith is not static but is instead an ongoing process: "Faith is a person's or group's way of moving into the force field of life. It is our way of finding coherence in and giving meaning to the multiple forces and relations that make up our lives. Faith is a person's way of seeing himself or herself in relation to others against a background of shared meaning and purpose" (Fowler 1981:4).

I use the term "religion" to mean an integral part of the human experience that enables us to see ourselves and the world in a particular context: one of hope and community. It is used here not in any Marxist or Freudian sense of escape or dependency, with an aim to take us away from the experience of being human. Neither is it used with any particular persuasion in mind or any organized form of institutional worship, structure, or hierarchy. Rather, "religion" is used here as "the feelings, acts, and experiences of individual[s] in their solitude, so far as they apprehend themselves to stand in relation to whatever they may consider divine. . . . Religion, whatever it is, is [one's] total reaction upon life" (James 1958:42, 45).

This definition implies that religion cannot be separated from human emotion and human life—religion is integral to the human experience. While the Divine or the religious object may vary from person to person and from culture to culture, the *emotion* that is directed toward that object or that divinity is a person's natural emotion directed to a religious object (James 1958:40). James's definition of how an individual experiences whatever that person considers divine is useful in addressing the question: "What does a Mexican-American woman think and feel when she stands before the image of Our Lady of Guadalupe?" Because Our Lady of Guadalupe lives in the realm of popular religiosity, not official religiosity, I define her devotees' religious experience in terms of the individual rather than the institutional. (See Chapter 7 for a full discussion of popular religiosity.)

That religion is not a separate and isolated consideration in human life is best described by William James (1958:40):

As concrete states of mind, made up of a feeling plus a specific sort of object, religious emotions of course are psychic entities distinguishable from other concrete emotions; but there is no ground for assuming a simple abstract "religious emotion" to exist as a distinct elementary mental affection by itself, present in every religious experience without exception.

As there thus seems to be no one elementary religious emotion, but only a common storehouse of emotions upon which religious objects may draw, so there might conceivably also prove to be no one specific and essential kind of religious object, and no one specific and essential kind of religious act.

Thus, as touched on in the previous chapter, religious yearning is a feeling, or in James's words, a psychic entity.

An Understanding of Faith Development as Applied to Juan Diego

It has taken scholars over 450 years to uncover much of the symbolism in the image of Our Lady of Guadalupe and the theological significance of her apparition. Our Lady of Guadalupe is a complex "event," combining the symbolism and iconography of her image and the chronicle of her deepening relationship with Juan Diego and the entire Nahuatl people.

When symbolic/mythic language is used, as happens in the *Nican Mopohua*, the person, things, and events are "synchronized": the past, the present, and the future are signified in one single symbol-myth. Thus, Juan Diego represents all the poor who lived before, who were alive at the time, and who were to live afterward, and not simply the historical Juan Diego (Siller-Acuña 1981a:219). Understanding Juan Diego's marginalization is useful in comprehending the marginalization of contemporary Mexican-American women.

Juan Diego was one of the first converts to Christianity in Mexico. His name before the coming of the Spaniards was Cuauhtlatoatzin, "he who speaks like an eagle," that is, he who explains the wisdom of the Knights of the Order of Eagles or he who explains the wisdom of God (the sun). The eagle is the symbol of the sun, which in turn is a symbol for God (Siller-Acuña 1981a:222). His name suggests that he may in fact have been one of the elders or wise men in the Nahautl culture.

According to the narrative of the apparition of Our Lady of Guadalupe, Juan Diego—a member of the oppressed and conquered Nahuatl people—met the Virgin on a hill at Tepeyac, outside of present-day Mexico City. But who did Juan Diego understand this woman to be?

The text of the *Nican Mopohua* shows that he referred to Our Lady of Guadalupe as "my dear child" (two times), "my lady" or "dear lady" (five times), "lady and mistress" (one time), "heavenly lady" or "lady of heaven" (two times), "Holy Mary" (one time), and "Precious Mother of God" (one time). In addition, given her physical appearance, Juan Diego most likely perceived Our Lady of Guadalupe as a member of his race (a *morenita* or dark-skinned woman).

The relationship between Our Lady of Guadalupe and Juan Diego is one of familial respect. Our Lady of Guadalupe not only speaks to Juan Diego in his own language, but she uses the suffix -*tzin*, which denotes respect and love. Both Our Lady of Guadalupe and Juan Diego address each other in familial terms, right from the beginning. She addresses him as "Juanito," "Juan Dieguito," "the smallest of my children," and he addresses her as "my dear child" and "my daughter."

Juan Diego's first encounter with Our Lady of Guadalupe does not elicit fear but peace, such that he feels he is in paradise. She herself sets up the context or content of what the relationship will be: "to give forth all my love, compassion, help, and defense, because I am your loving mother."

Martin Lang (1983) provides a useful insight into their affective relationship by connecting systems of meaning and what he terms "bonding." He believes, and rightly so, that religion is not just an intellectual exercise, but rather that in order to have a meaningful religious system there must be emotional and passionate elements: the religious devotee has to love someone (Lang 1983:7).

Bonding, according to psychological literature, begins with the parent-child relationship and is basically concerned with "belonging." This belonging moves from bonding with parents, to bonding with brothers and sisters, to bonding with community. This bonding links together people who love and care for each other (Lang 1983:41). At the root of this caring is *trust*; it is a precondition for bonding. I believe that Juan Diego manifests some kind of emotional attachment or bonding to the image of Our Lady of Guadalupe.

This notion of trust as the prerequisite for bonding echoes the pioneering work of James Fowler (1981) in the area of the psychology of human development and the stages of faith. As there are stages of development in psychology and biology, religious development can also be studied in stages. One particularly useful understanding of these stages is Fowler's schema of faith development. Although the stages are sequential, Fowler (1981:274) does not argue for the superiority of one stage over another: "Each stage has the potential for wholeness, grace, and integrity and for strengths sufficient for either life's blows or blessings."

Fowler draws from the disciplines of theology and developmental psychology to identify meanings and values at the center of life. The development of faith begins with a prestage that he calls Undifferentiated Faith. This stage is characterized by "the quality of mutuality, and the strength of trust, autonomy, hope, and courage (or their opposites) . . . [which] underlie all that comes later in faith development" (Fowler 1981:121). The trusting relationship with the person or persons providing primary love and care for the infant is crucial, for it will mark the individual for the rest of his or her life.

For Fowler, the stage of Undifferentiated Faith parallels the first Eriksonian stage of psychosocial development as the basis for all future human growth. In this stage basic trust and the relational experience of mutuality with the one(s) providing primary love and care emerge (Fowler 1981:120). In the initial meeting between Juan Diego and Our Lady of Guadalupe, Juan Diego evidences this trust and bonding when he accepts who the Lady says she is: "the ever holy Virgin Mary, Mother of God."

Thought processes and the use of language trigger the transition to an Intuitive-Projective Faith (Stage One), which is fantasy-filled imagination influenced by "examples, moods, actions, and stories of primally related adults" (Fowler 1981:133). This stage fosters the ability to correlate the child's intuitive understandings and feelings toward life with powerful images and stories. "In league with forms of knowing dominated by perception, imagination in this stage is extremely productive of long-lasting images and feelings (positive and negative) that later, more stable and self-reflective valuing and thinking will have to order and sort out" (Fowler 1981:133).

Juan Diego quickly moves into what Fowler terms Stage One or Intuitive-Projective Faith—"the ability to unify and grasp the experience-world in powerful images and as presented in stories that register intuitive understandings and feelings toward the ultimate conditions of existence" (Fowler 1981:133)—by speaking to the Lady and recognizing that she is the same person he has learned of from the priests, "the delegates of the Lord."

When Juan Diego meets the Virgin a second time, he relates the failure of his mission. He states that the bishop believed that her message was "an invention of mine." This shows that Juan Diego is beginning to "clarify the distinctions between what is real and what only seems to be" (Fowler 1981:134), the transition to the next stage of growth. As thinking processes develop, the ability to distinguish between what is real and what only seems to be signals the transition to the next stage of faith development.

Mythic-Literal Faith (Stage Two) is marked by the acceptance by the individual of the "stories, beliefs, and observances that symbolize belonging to his or her community" (Fowler 1981:149), as well as the literal interpretation of those beliefs and symbols. Contradictions in these stories lead to a reflection on their meaning, which creates the need for a more personal relationship on the part of the individual with whatever is perceived to be the ultimate unifying power. This felt need, this tension, is the sign of readiness for the next stage.

Juan Diego believes and accepts the Lady's story and message, which is an indication that he has reached Fowler's second stage, Mythic-Literal Faith. He then refers to himself as "nothing" and "no one" and begs the Lady to choose someone else as her messenger, very clearly echoing what Fowler (1981:150) terms an "abasing sense of badness due to apparent disfavor of significant others," an obvious tension and ambiguity in his relationship to the Lady.

The Lady reassures Juan Diego that, despite what he thinks of himself, he is to be her messenger. When the bishop still does not believe him, he asks what sign the bishop desires. The narrative relates that the bishop saw that Juan Diego "was not disturbed in the slightest and did not change his story in any way." This, again, is indicative of Fowler's second stage and the transition to the next stage—the contradictions faced by Juan Diego lead him to reflect on their meaning, "creating the need for a more personal relationship with the unifying power of the ultimate environment" (Fowler 1981:15).

Fowler (1981:162) writes: "In Stage Three, Synthetic-Conventional Faith, an individual is aware of having values and normative images. He or she articulates them, defends them, and feels deep emotional investments in them, but typically has not made the value system, as a system, the object of reflection." This stage leads the individual outside of the family in search of authority figures and sources of meaning. The questions of identity and personal outlook are confronted in this stage, although both are linked to others' expectations and evaluations. Because of this link, contradictions in authority sources, experiences, or perspective lead to the realization that an individual's beliefs and values are relative to a particular group or background. This realization signals a transition to Stage Four.

Before the third apparition, Juan Diego experiences a crisis, one that leads him into the third stage of faith. When Juan Diego's uncle falls ill, he stays at home with the family instead of going to meet the Virgin.

He avoids the hill for fear of meeting the Lady, but she appears to him anyway.

This scene accurately depicts Fowler's third stage of Synthetic-Conventional faith, which is described as occurring outside of the family, set up by a tension between traditional authority figures and the individual's own identity. Juan Diego is torn between loyalty to his family (his uncle) and loyalty to the Lady. He fears her authority, yet he has enough of a sense of self that he makes his own decision to attend to his uncle.

As Juan Diego explains his uncle's situation to the Lady, and his reason for not meeting her as promised, there is an indication that he is already on his way to the fourth stage of growth. Through his dialogue with Our Lady of Guadalupe and her response to his situation, Juan Diego deals with what Fowler (1981:173) terms "contradictions between valued authority sources, experiences or perspectives that lead to a critical reflection on how one's beliefs and values have formed and changed, and how 'relative' they are to one's particular group or background."

Individuative-Reflective Faith (Stage Four) is a stage in which the individual "begins to take seriously the burden of responsibility for one's own commitments, lifestyle, beliefs, and attitudes" (Fowler 1981: 182). There is a great deal of tension at this stage: individuality versus being defined by the group and self-fulfillment or self-actualization as a primary concern versus service to and being for others. To resolve the tension and to discover an identity, both in faith and as a person, many of the myths and former belief systems are repressed, and critical reflection takes place.

This tension leads Juan Diego to Stage Four. The Lady assures Juan Diego of his uncle's regained health and tells him to collect flowers from the top of the hill. Since flowers in the Nahuatl culture symbolize both truth and beauty, Juan Diego is thus forced to integrate the religious faith of his past and of his people with the new message and culture of the Lady and the bishop. This felt need for integration is described by Fowler as the transition to Stage Five.

Stage Five, Conjunctive Faith, is most characterized by the reworking and reclaiming of the past, embracing polarities and integration. "Importantly, this involves a critical reflection of one's social unconscious—the myths, ideal images, and prejudices built deeply into the self-system by virtue of one's nurture within a particular social class, religious tradition, ethnic group, or the like." The result of this stage is "the capacity to see and be in one's or one's group's most powerful meanings, while simultaneously recognizing that they are relative and inevitably distorting apprehensions of transcendent reality" (Fowler 1981:198).

Placing the flowers in his tilma, Our Lady of Guadalupe instructs Juan Diego to go to the bishop with her message. This is a fitting image of Fowler's Stage Five—Conjunctive Faith—in which there is "the integration of all the images and symbols that were repressed in order to attain Stage Four, in which symbolic power is reunited with conceptual meaning, and in which there is a reclaiming and reworking of one's past" (Fowler 1981:197). Arriving at the bishop's palace, Juan Diego does not allow himself to be dismissed. He has become a person; he has reached adulthood. Carrying the symbols of the Virgin's message of love and justice, Juan Diego personifies the "emerging strength" of this stage: "The recognition of living and acting between an untransformed world and a transforming vision and loyalties" (Fowler 1981:198).

The sixth and final stage of faith development is Universalizing Faith: "Heedless to the threats to self, to primary groups, and to the institutional arrangements of the present order, Stage Six becomes a disciplined, activist *incarnation*—making real and tangible—of the imperatives of absolute love and justice of which Stage Five has partial apprehension" (Fowler 1981:200).

Juan Diego is the central figure in the final scene: speaking before the bishop, relating the apparitions of the Lady, and spilling the flowers onto the floor as the fifth and final apparition of Our Lady of Guadalupe takes place—the image of the Mother of God on the tilma of the Nahuatl Indian. This final scene of the narrative illustrates the sixth stage of maturity and selfhood.

This incarnation turned symbol is the end result of the deepening relationship of Juan Diego and Our Lady of Guadalupe. Without denying who he is—indeed, embracing who he is—and with the support and encouragement of his connectedness and relationship with the Lady, this Nahuatl Indian enters the inner confines of the established order and brings to it a message of hope and promise, of love and justice, which causes the establishment to act, to try to change the way things are.

The Religious Worldview of Mexican-American Women

Inherent in those cultures that served as influence for the Mexican-American woman are religious worldviews, demonstrating that what is psychosocial is also religious. These worldviews—or assumptive worlds, to use Frank's terminology—include sixteenth-century Spanish Catholicism and the indigenous Aztec religion. The legacy of Mexican-American women is the Spanish Conquest, which was motivated, facilitated, and sanctioned by religion. Religion motivated the Spaniards to seek not only wealth for the Spanish crown but souls for God. Religion facilitated the conquest through missionaries who assimilated the Indians and through a church structure that controlled them. Religion also sanctioned the conquest because the Spaniards believed that they were doing the will of God, as shown in Chapter 1. The assumptive world of sixteenth-century Spanish Catholicism clashed with that of the indigenous people.

Henceforth, a religion forged from the combination of sixteenth-century Spanish Catholicism and Indian religiosity would influence the faith of Mexicans and Mexican-Americans. "Manifest destiny," which motivated the Anglo-American colonization of the Southwest, had religious overtones. Consequently, for survival, Mexican-Americans retreated into a form of religious expression that was (and is) separate from the Anglo-dominated religious institutions. For example, life-cycle ceremonies such as celebrating one's fifteenth birthday and the *compadrazgo* system are uniquely Mexican-American. Interwoven with the religious belief system is the extension of meaningful social bonds.

There is literature that addresses the religious development of Mexicans, but none on Mexican Americans, let alone Mexican-American women. We can surmise, however, that there exists a Catholicism influenced by indigenous religion that provided Mexican Americans with a set of assumptions and behaviors with which to make order out of chaos. This form of Catholicism has enabled Mexican-American women to endure suffering to interpret their experience. This religious inheritance has also formulated their development thus far. Therefore, Mexican-American women's psychosocial religious development has been brought about as well as hindered by this legacy of a culturally construed Catholicism.

As in most traditional social orders, it fell to Mexican-American women to be the primary carriers of the religious belief system. The very nature of the hierarchy of the Roman Catholic church and of its traditional teachings has called for women to be subordinate to men, but this system has not precluded them from playing an active role in the practice of popular religiosity. It is mainly the women who have been expected to socialize their children into the cultural belief system of Mexican Americans and to instill in them the religious belief system, including the teachings of the Roman Catholic church as they have understood them (Williams 1990:22–23). Chapters 5 and 6 articulate some of their beliefs.

Within the population of Mexican-American women, there are varied perceptions of, reactions to, and influences from Our Lady of Guadalupe. First, in the population I used for my study, religion is overtly a part of culture. For many people in the Hispanic community, and in general for people who have been similarly marginalized on many levels, the religious worldview is their only worldview. They understand everything within a religious context. Mexican-American women have been marginalized as women, as mestizas, as Chicanas; thus religion is a significant dimension of their human experience.

Second, for this population, religious and cultural oppression plays a major role in the formation of its assumptive world. The history of the Mexican-American woman is a legacy of conquest and resistance, shaping the uniqueness of her perceptions, emotional states, images of self, values, gender roles, and expectations—all of which affect her relationship with Our Lady of Guadalupe.

Third, because the relationship of the Mexican-American woman with Our Lady of Guadalupe exists within the larger relationship that individuals have with whatever they may consider divine, we can study this relationship within the context of stages of faith development. However, no understanding of faith development, particularly that of women, would be complete without the insights of Carol Gilligan (1982). Her work is significant for having elevated to a scientific level the discussion of the ways in which women arrive differently at decisions, relate differently, and women's epic of attachment, relationality, and care. Prior to Gilligan most of our understanding of developmental stages, psychological or religious, had come from the perspective of male experience.

With a more inclusive understanding of humanity, we can address complex relationality in Hispanic culture and religion. In Hispanic culture, everything is interrelated, interconnected, and interdependent, and people identify who they are in relationship to others. In Hispanic religion, the types of relationships between people also apply to the relationships between people and the Divine. The saints are Jesus's friends and they are friends of mine; Jesus is my brother, God is my father, Guadalupe is my mother. Gilligan's framework supports this understanding of relationality in terms of women. For Hispanics, relationality is even more prominent, and it operates on three levels: the cultural (human), the religious (divine), and the complex (interrelationship between human and divine). Our Lady of Guadalupe is part of Mexican-American women's cultural milieu as well as part of their faith experience.

FOUR

The Experience of
Mexican-American Women

What do I mean by "experience," and whose experience is it? Mexican-American women are a heterogeneous group in which the identification of acculturation factors is critical. Are we considering first-, second-, or third-generation Mexican-American women? Were they born here or in Mexico? Are they urban or rural dwellers? What is their socioeconomic status, level of education, migration process? The sum total of these factors will identify whose experience is being discussed.

Despite Mexican-American women's diversity, a number of elements may or may not bind them together. One common element is that, in general, Mexican-American women primarily identify themselves in relation to others, unlike the Western way of thinking of oneself first as an individual and defining oneself through work and roles. Mexican-American women do not separate the fact that they are someone's sisters, daughters, mothers, and friends from who they are and what they do. Other elements include the desire to (and belief that we have the right to) maintain our cultural heritage, which we have maintained despite five hundred years of "influence." This heritage includes our language, customs, and ways of perceiving the world and acting in that world.

Throughout history, both in Mexico and in the United States, this right to cultural maintenance has been consistently denied by dominant cultures. "We had learned about the greatness of the American experience and we hold it in great reverence. What we had not studied was the cruel injustices involved in the process of nation-building

[Christianizing, civilizing]: the massacres of the natives, the slave trade, the systematic impoverishment of the Mexican inhabitants of the Southwest" (Elizondo 1992:40). At the base of all these dynamics is the racism, ethnocentrism, and classism deeply ingrained in United States culture.

Nuestra Realidad

There is a word for experience in Spanish, but it is not used the same way the word "experience" is used in English. When we want to talk about experience in Spanish we talk about la realidad—reality. Reality is a synthesis of experiences which are part and parcel of the totality of that person in a given moment. It entails a psychosocial history that has an impact whether the individual is conscious of it or not. Many factors in the lives of any two women may be the same, but the historical and cultural context and therefore the interpretive framework may be different.

What makes up the experience of Mexican-American women? Words that come to mind are "conquest" and "resistance," "borderlands," "born and/or raised in the USA." And yet another group of words accompanies the first, words like "integrity," "anger," "pain," "economically and politically marginalized," and "multiple identities." Other women may have multiple identities in terms of their roles, but here I mean something profoundly metaphysical: a woman from a dominant culture does not have to learn another culture's point of view to survive, but Mexican-American women must know the ways of the dominant culture. Many people, because of the various roles they play, know what it is like to live multiple identities in terms of roles. Here is a description of what it is like to cross between cultures that are metaphysically different from Gloria Anzaldúa's Borderlands (1987:78–81): "Indigenous like corn, like corn, the mestiza is a product of crossbreeding, designed for preservation under a variety of conditions. Like an ear of corn—a female seed-bearing organ—the mestiza is tenacious, tightly wrapped in the husks of her culture. Like kernels she clings to the cob; with thick stalks and strong brace roots, she holds tight to the earth—she will survive the crossroads." This constant crossing becomes the most ordinary thing in Mexican-American women's lives. Although they cross back and forth between these dual identities, they sometimes feel so terribly unaccepted—orphaned. Some do not identify with the Anglo-American cultural values and some do not identify with the Mexican-American cultural values. Mexican-American women are a synthesis of these two cultures with varying degrees of acculturation, and with that synthesis comes conflict. One woman told me how it feels to her: "Sometimes the Latina in me doesn't understand or is in contradiction to the Anglo-educated side of me. Sometimes I feel like one cancels out the other. And I feel like nothing." Mexican-American feminists claim that when they know they are "more than nothing," they call themselves the name for whichever group they most strongly identify with: mestiza when affirming both Indian and Spanish heritage or Chicana when referring to political consciousness—that is, people who are aware that they were born or raised in the United States. As another example, because I have my roots in Latin America, I usually refer to myself as a Latina. But because I am U.S.-born, I identify myself as a Chicana. Even in this naming, there is no one word which says it all.

The struggle of the mestiza is, above all, a feminist one. Mexican-American women have been raised within a culture and a church which have never taught Mexican-American literature, history, customs, traditions or foods. We have had to study about everyone else but never about ourselves. We now need to take that time to study ourselves and our origins because "history is not merely the record of the past but the life source of the present and the hidden energy of the new future" (Elizondo 1992:39).

After having examined the apparition of Our Lady of Guadalupe and Mexican history for the origins and legacy of Mexican-Americans, I move now to contemporary Mexican-American women, the group from which the women in this study are drawn. The present chapter describes elements in Mexican-American women's struggle to identify self: colonization by the United States, the roots of their psychosocial religious worldview, their role in the family, and the impact of acculturation.

Just as the symbolic significance of Our Lady of Guadalupe draws its meaning from the backdrop of the Spanish Conquest of Mexico, so does her significance in the present draw its meaning from yet another conquest: the U.S. takeover of Mexico's northern territories. On February 2, 1848, the Treaty of Guadalupe Hidalgo (the Magna Carta for Mexican Americans, intended to guarantee their rights and privileges) was signed at the basilica in Mexico City. Conquest is the ground of Mexican history, and of Mexican-American history. The Mexican-American woman's story is an integral part of that history; without her it would be false and truncated. By the same token, her history is fundamental to the history of women (Sweeney 1977:99–100).

The situation of Mexican-American women in U.S. society brings additional elements to bear on the meaning of Our Lady of Guadalupe for these women. This chapter provides a brief overview of relevant historical, sociological, and psychological information necessary to understand the Mexican-American woman, with information on the sample in this study and its major findings.

The terms "Chicana" and "Mexican-American woman" are used interchangeably here. Prior to the 1960s, "Chicana" was used in a derogatory manner to identify women of Mexican-American descent in the Southwest. The name had historically been a pejorative term applied to lower-class Mexicans and farm workers. Working-class people themselves, however, had always used it playfully to refer to each other (Acuña 1988:338). With the advent of the civil rights movement, Chicanos adopted the term to reflect their biculturalism and their political struggle to be recognized as neither Mexican nor American (Flores-Ortiz 1982), but rather as a new *mestizaje* that is still in the process of being articulated.

A Legacy of Oppression: Colonization

Social science literature about the Mexican-American woman contends that she is subjected to three basic forms of oppression: the sexism that comes with being a woman, being a member of a historically subordinated group, and sexism within her culture (Pesquera and Segura in press:2). This oppression *within* the culture results from the conflict of values between Spanish and indigenous cultures (cf. Chapter 2). Second, the oppression *outside* Chicano culture is exerted by the dominant culture of the United States.

The necessity of examining historical periods is obvious when one considers the Chicana's legacy as a member of a colonized people. All Chicanos are colonized people, who have their roots in warfare and sexism, a creation of the imperial conquest of one nation by another through military force (Alvarez 1976:38). Their colonial heritage has had an enormous impact on their lives, but the particulars of that impact are especially profound in the lives of Mexican and Mexican-American women today.

The period from 1519 to 1821 was a transitional one for Mexico, moving it into a Hispanicized society with an ethnic mix of indigenous, European, African, and Asian components. This *mestizaje* gave way to a "racial" stratification. The Spanish women who arrived in the mid-1500s came to hold the highest, most valued position. Next in status came the *criollas*—Spanish women born in the New World—and then the mestizas, or women of mixed Indian and Spanish blood. The Indian woman came to hold the lowest social position (Blea 1991:40). Whereas in the beginning of the conquest there was tension and violence among indigenous people, Africans, and Spaniards, by the mid-1800s parents had become willing to give their daughters in marriage to the Spaniards so that the next generation of women would have a chance for a better life. This improvement, they felt, was attainable through marriage or relations with the Spanish male, seeking the same status for them that the Spanish woman enjoyed (Cotera 1976b:31). No matter what rung of the hierarchy women were on, the colonial period in Mexico did nothing to increase the status of women. In fact, women were channeled into very limited and submissive roles as daughters, wives, and mothers.

The second form of colonization of the Mexican people resulted from the loss of northwestern Mexico to the United States, a conquest which resulted in the emergence of the Mexican-American people. The conquest took the form of a treaty: the Treaty of Guadalupe Hidalgo incorporated into the United States forty percent of northern Mexican territory as a result of the U.S. war with Mexico in 1848. The colonization of the Mexican people had begun in 1821, as Europeans and adventurers from the United States entered the northern borderland of Mexico to seek their fortune. "The period from 1821 to 1910 saw increasing Anglo-American penetration into Mexican affairs, culminating in the Mexican-American War from 1846 to 1848. After 1848 the inhabitants of the Northern Mexican provinces were cut off from Mexico and gradually assumed their own identity as a separate people. Chicano historians thus identify the post-1848 period as the crucible of Chicano history" (Sweeney 1977:103).

Unlike the Spaniards, who sought treasures for both God and country, the Anglo-Americans came primarily for economic development. The United States invaded Mexico in the mid-nineteenth century during a period of dramatic change. Rapid technological breakthroughs transformed the North American nation from a farm society into an industrial competitor. The battles with Mexico, symptoms of this transformation, stemmed from the need to accumulate more land and to prove the nation's power by military superiority (Acuña 1988:5). There is some evidence from correspondence between Thomas Jefferson and James Monroe that the United States had intended to take the Southwest long before U.S. settlers started moving into Texas (Alvarez 1976:33).

Although the U.S. war with Mexico was chiefly for land (Hernández, Haug, and Wagner 1976:39–40), religious beliefs again played a role. The Anglo-Americans were Christian, but as Protestants did not share Mexico's Roman Catholic perspective:

> Manifest destiny had its roots in Puritan ideas which continue to influence Anglo-American thought to this day. According to the Puritan ethic, salvation is determined by God. The establishment of a City of God on earth is not only the duty of those chosen people predestined for salvation, but it is also the proof of their state of grace. This belief carried over to the Anglo-American conviction that God had made them custodians of democracy and that they had a mission. . . . They were predestined to spread its principles, . . . establish its power, . . . expand westward. . . . Many citizens believed that God had destined them to own and occupy all of the land from ocean to ocean and pole to pole. Their mission,

their destiny made manifest, was to spread the principles of de-
mocracy and Christianity to the unfortunates of the hemisphere.
(Acuña 1981:12–13)

"On February 2, 1848, the Mexicans agreed to the Treaty of Guadalupe Hidalgo, in which Mexico accepted the Rio Grande as the Texas
border and ceded the Southwest (which incorporated the present-day
states of California, New Mexico, Nevada, and parts of Colorado, Arizona, and Utah) to the United States in return for $15 million" (Acuña
1988:18).

[Mexicans in the new U.S. territories] shall be incorporated into the
Union of the United States, and admitted as soon as possible, . . .
to the enjoyment of all the rights of citizens of the United States. In
the mean time they shall be maintained and protected in the enjoyment of their liberty, their property, and the civil rights now vested
in them according to the Mexican laws. With respect to political
rights, their condition shall be on an equality with that of the inhabitants of the other territories of the United States. . . . The same
most ample garanty [sic] shall be enjoyed by all ecclesiastics and
religious corporations or communities. . . . This guaranty shall embrace all temples, houses, and edifices dedicated to the Roman
catholic [sic] worship. . . . All grants of land . . . in territories previously appertaining to Mexico . . . shall be respected as valid. . . .
(Treaty of Guadalupe Hidalgo, 1848, articles 9 and 10, in Miller
1937:241–243)

At the close of the Mexican-American War in 1848, the United States
had acquired California, Arizona, and New Mexico, and over two million Mexicans who inhabited that land (Hernández, Haug, and Wagner
1976:41–43).
    The war and its treaty left a legacy of hostility that would not easily
be overcome (Meyer and Sherman 1987:351). The treaty was not honored by the United States. The Anglo-American conquest transformed
Mexicans from a position of citizenship, owners of their own lands, to
a colonized people. This taking of the land brought about almost total

disruption of a way of life. Power and control of major social institutions shifted from the Mexican to the Anglo-American. Chicanos found themselves a landless and impoverished people, exploited economically and politically (Mirandé and Enríquez 1979:68).

As a result of the U.S. acquisition of this land, the Mexican residents became a dominated people, rendered politically and economically powerless. The development of a Mexican-American culture that differed appreciably from the society of Mexico as well as that of the majority Anglo-American society was fostered by the virtual exclusion of the newly created Mexican Americans from the economic and social systems of mainstream U.S. society. On paper, Mexican Americans were designated U.S. citizens; in reality, they were relegated to a second-class status in their "new" country (Williams 1990:21).

Mexican Americans may have sought to assimilate into Anglo-American culture by removing themselves from Mexican heritage and highlighting their Spanish-American heritage, using the rationale that as descendants of the Spanish conquistadors they were somehow in the upper echelon of the hierarchy (Acuña 1981:48–54). From the few studies made on the role of Mexican women on the frontier, one theme that emerges is intermarriage, apparently the same dynamic which functioned between Indian women and the Spaniards. Intermarriage with Anglo-Americans was based on economic necessity. "The chance offered by intermarriage was perhaps the only one available to Mexican women, but even that decision was made by the male head of the family based on class interest and material factors that operated in an Anglo-dominant society" (Acuña 1988:33).

Intermarriage provided upward mobility for the mestiza, as it had for the Indian woman. Perhaps more important, women on the frontier experienced higher status and relative freedom, primarily as a response to severe conditions. The status and freedom may also have been a result of early intermarriage between some of the most prominent settlers and the Pueblo Indian women, who had more freedom than their Spanish sisters (Blea 1992:45). Thrown into a new set of circumstances, they began to evolve new modes of thought and action in order to survive, making their culture different from the culture of Mexicans in Mexico (Hernández, Haug, and Wagner 1976:38).

In contrast to the classical Spanish Conquest, the U.S. conquest in the Southwest was an *internal colonization* in which contiguous territory was acquired. While classical colonization is recognized formally and legally, internal colonization has an informal existence. Thus Chicanos today are not formally colonized. They constitute an internal colony within the territorial boundaries of the United States. The internal colony is a de facto one, with formal and legal equality, but is informally excluded from the legal-political system. Chicanos are powerless, lacking control over critical social institutions which have direct impact on them (Mirandé and Enríquez 1979:9).

These two forms of conquest suffered by the Mexican people have striking similarities. Both the Spaniards and the Anglo-Americans imposed their culture by force onto another people. With that imposition also came the attitude of looking upon the conquered people, their contributions, and their culture as inferior. Both the Spaniards and the Anglo-Americans gained power over the Mexican and Mexican-American people by military force and advanced technology. Both rendered the Mexicans economically and politically dependent and powerless, and both construed their mission as divinely ordained (Mirandé and Enríquez 1979:68).

What makes the experience of Mexican Americans unique compared to all the other ethnic populations that migrated to this country is their psychohistorical experience and their subsequent subjugation—all taking place in what the indigenous peoples considered to be their own land (Alvarez 1976:42).

In general, what impact does colonization continue to have on Chicanos and Chicanas? Structurally, it produces powerlessness and lack of control over those institutions which have a direct impact on them, such as schools, the political system, and businesses (Mirandé and Enríquez 1979:68–70). Besides the oppression of physical colonization, there is also an oppression brought about by *psychological colonization*. A conquered population characteristically exhibits feelings of inferiority, lack of self-worth, hostility, apathy, apparent indifference, passivity, and a lack of motivation in relation to the goals of the dominant society (Guerrero 1987:24).

The oppression experienced by these conquered people was especially felt by the Mexican women, who, along with their families, became a conquered group for the second time, as their colonization status changed from Spanish-Mexican to Anglo-Mexican (McWilliams 1968:52).

For Chicanas, internal colonization coupled with racism produces an even deeper sense of marginality in an Anglo-dominated society. In addition to sharing the consequences of being a colonized people as are the men in their culture, they also suffer from the oppression of being women, with the added burden of internal oppression by a cultural heritage that tends to be dominated by males (Mirandé and Enríquez 1979:12) and that insists on rigid role expectations. The women suffer the most socioeconomically, which may heighten their feelings of powerlessness, low self-esteem, and identity confusion.

A Legacy of Oppression: Sexism

Sexism is the oldest form of economic exploitation and colonization, and the Chicana, like most women, is a victim of a sexist history (Gonzales 1980:229, 231). Like other women, the Chicana has traditionally and historically moved from her parents' home to the home of her husband. This same conditioning may foster emotional dependence and a concern for the needs of others before her own needs. The Chicana specifically is expected to move easily into the family role of wife and mother (García-Bahne 1977:41). Should she attempt to move away from this expected role, she may be labeled aggressive, uncaring, or neglectful. The Chicana is faced with these difficulties that many other women share, coupled with living one set of values at home and having to confront or include a different set of values outside of the home.

During the Americanization phase (and this is still the case today), Mexican-American women lived two lives: they were Americans in school and other public places and Mexicanas in their homes and Chicano communities. Many engaged in a struggle between what was taught at home and what was taught in school, for their mothers were of a different generation, a different country, a different historical period (Blea 1992:53).

It is true that within the Mexican-American culture the Mexican-American woman is burdened by machismo (Mirandé and Enríquez 1979:12). Men who show machismo are alleged to boast a great deal about their male conquests and to refuse to do "womanly" things such as dishwashing, cooking, diaper-changing, or minding the children. One way of understanding this concept is that machismo is an over-compensation for a feeling of inadequacy as a man within a racist system (Casavantes 1976:10). And what is a Chicano man supposed to do?—provide for, protect, care for, and defend his family. When these needs are truncated and reinforce feelings of inadequacy, this overcompensation may take the form of excessive fighting, drinking, or bragging about conquests (Casavantes 1976:11), and thus may render the family or relationships dysfunctional.

To compensate for their feelings of inadequacy, the men of these defeated people respond by being machos. Unable to protect them from the rape and plunder that accompanied the conquest, males developed an overly masculine and aggressive response to their women (Mirandé and Enríquez 1979:241). Thus, rather than being innate to the culture, machismo is a response to the dominant culture's oppression (see Urrabazos 1986).

U.S. social scientists inevitably conclude that machismo produces maladaptive, pathological responses. In the hands of these researchers, social science becomes a tool for legitimizing deeply ingrained though unfounded assumptions about Mexican culture, which in turn have been applied to Chicanos (Mirandé and Enríquez 1979:109–110).

What is the stereotypical role of the Mexican-American woman vis-à-vis this concept of manliness? Her role is that of the submissive, naive, rather childlike "sainted mother," whose purity is preserved by her husband's refusal to bring the world and its sins into the home (Grebler, Moore, and Guzmán 1970:363). Additionally, the oppression of the Mexican-American woman in her culture is usually downplayed by the general oppression experienced by her colonized people (Sutherland 1970:423–424). As a consequence, the women not only experience their own feelings of inferiority, but also bear the brunt of their men's inferiority.

However, Chicana scholarship suggests that Chicano culture is not as male-dominated as the original researchers would have had us believe. Research by Lea Ybarra (1982a, b) and M. Baca Zinn (1975, 1976) contends that relations between the sexes are more egalitarian—perhaps more egalitarian than in the dominant Anglo-American culture. Irene Blea (1992:29) further argues that "the more urbanized and Americanized [i.e., Anglicized] the Chicanos become, the lower the status of their women falls."

The Roots of the Psychology of Mexican-American Women

There is no psychology *per se* of the Mexican-American woman. There is, however, limited psychological literature, which is predominantly based on the writings of Mexican males about Mexican women, stereotypical studies of women, men, and families. When I began my investigations in Chicano Studies, the writings of Octavio Paz (1961) and Rogelio Díaz-Guerrero (1975), both out of a Mexican psychoanalytic model, were widely quoted, and they are still taught as definitive classics. U.S. social scientists have applied these theories on Mexican culture and built on this information, applying it to Mexican Americans. While Díaz-Guerrero's contemporary research is much more nuanced, U.S. social scientists continue to use his earlier works.

Díaz-Guerrero (1975:37) wrote of the inherent inferiority complex in the Mexican culture, which he viewed as a direct result of the conquest: "When Mexico was born, it found itself in the civilized world in the same relation as the child before his elders. It appeared in history when a mature civilization held sway, a civilization that only half understood an infantile spirit. From this disadvantageous situation was born the sense of inferiority that was ingrained by the Conquista, by mestizaje or cross-breeding, and even by the disproportionate magnitude of nature." Further, his research on mental health indicated that, in Mexico City, "forty-four percent of the female population over eighteen is 'neurotic'" (Díaz-Guerrero 1975:10). According to Díaz-Guerrero (1975:9–10), the role of women in the Mexican family is primarily that of self-sacrificing mother yielding to the supremacy of the father.

Literature on the life and thought of Mexicans (Paz 1961) also contributes to a degrading feminine image in Mexican culture as well as in Mexican-American culture. As in Western culture, where women are categorized as either a disobedient Eve or a virginal Mary, the Mexican and therefore Mexican-American woman is permitted two roles: that of Malinche, traitor and mistress of Cortés the conqueror or that of Our

Lady of Guadalupe, pure and passive, who prepares the way for hu-
mankind salvation (Gonzales 1980:231). "However, in the case of the
Chicana where historical events have produced . . . major physical
and psychological conquests—the colonial experience, . . . contemporary economic instability, . . . the scapegoat attitude and its resul-
tant characterizations allowed the Chicana are exaggerated" (Gonzales
1980:229).

Women are viewed as unworthy of confidence, and as violated, submissive, passive, and even masochistic. This degradation of the feminine image in Mexican culture, and the view of women as untrustworthy and traitorous, can be traced back to the story of Malinche.
"Octavio Paz, Samuel Ramos, Carlos Fuentes, and many other writers,
both Mexican and foreign, have made this one woman, Doña Marina
(La Malinche) the symbolic object of all their negative feelings about
the Conquest and mestizaje" (Cotera 1976b:32).

Malinche: The Archetype of the Feminine

Malinche was an Indian woman who served as Cortés's translator,
counselor, and mistress. It is alleged that because of her brilliant mind
and her wide knowledge of the realities of the times she helped Cortés
to overthrow the ruling Aztec empire. In this respect she can be considered a *conquistadora, coronela,* or *soldadera* (Salas 1990:160).

Another indictment of Malinche is that she was allegedly a whore. It
was through active volition on her part—sexual transgression—that
she became the violated mother who then symbolically gave birth to
her illegitimate child—the Mexican people. She was the beginning of
the mestizo nation, its mother—she initiated it with the birth of her
mestizo children (Del Castillo 1977:141). Malinche thus emerges as an
infamous emblem of female transgression and treachery (Mirandé and
Enríquez 1979:31). Paz (1961:86) suggests that Malinche's sexual
transgression derives precisely from passive volition on her part, an
openness and willingness to be violated: "It is true that she gave herself
voluntarily to the conquistador, but he forgot her as soon as her usefulness was over. [Malinche] became a figure representing the Indian
women who were fascinated, violated or seduced by the Spaniards.

And as a small boy will not forgive his mother if she abandons him to search for his father, the Mexican people have not forgiven La Malinche for her betrayal."

Modern interpretation of the story of Malinche centers around the theme of the unworthiness of women. To this day a woman is called Malinche if she associates with and adapts to the values of the dominant culture and thus "sells out" to foreigners (Mirandé and Enríquez 1979:27). The following are stanzas from a popular Mexican song:

> The curse of offering foreigners
> Our faith, our culture,
> Our bread, our money,
> Remains with us . . .

> Today, at the height of the twentieth century,
> Fair-haired ones [foreigners] keep arriving,
> And we open our homes to them
> And we call them our friends . . .

> Oh, curse of Malinche!
> Sickness of the present,
> When will you leave my country?
> When will you free my people?
>
> (Mirandé and Enríquez 1979:247)

A Chicana feminist interpretation challenges all of these characterizations of Malinche (Del Castillo 1977; Mirandé and Enríquez 1979). It contends that Malinche was barely fourteen and did not give herself to this man to bring about the downfall of a people, nor did she subject herself to these sexual transgressions voluntarily. Malinche, whose Nahuatl name was Malinalli, was not originally a slave but actually came from a noble family. Her mother remarried, giving birth to a son, and the inheritance that by rights should have gone to Malinalli went to the son. Malinalli was given to a group of Mayan traders who then sold her to Tabascans; it was the Tabascans who made a gift of her, as a slave, to Cortés, when she was fourteen years old. Cortés gave her the Christian name Doña Marina. The title "Doña" indicates respect (Mirandé and Enríquez 1979:26). She was honored by the Spaniards because she gave them good advice on how to successfully relate to the Mejica (Aztecs) using both diplomacy and force (Del Castillo 1977).

In reviewing historical literature, it is clear that Malinche was a gifted young woman from an aristocratic background. Juana Armanda Alegría (1975) suggests that Malinche's obedience to Cortés was not based on weakness or passivity; rather, her compliance was an intelligent response to an alienating experience. Additionally, her participation in the conquest has been interpreted as arising out of a strong religious conviction. The religious beliefs of the time were centered on the return of the god Quetzalcoatl and the destruction of the Aztec empire. According to Del Castillo (1977:141), Malinche, "knowing" this salvific history, participates in the ending of one era and the beginning of a new one: "A careful look at what is known about her and her times seems to indicate the immense probability that Doña Marina's participation in the conquest of Mexico was a manifestation of her faith in a godly force—the prophecies of Quetzalcoatl. It is because of this faith that she sees the destruction of the Aztec empire, the conquest of Mexico, and as such, the termination of her indigenous world as inevitable."

What emerges from the reinterpretation of Malinche is a female historical figure, lifted out of her proper time and place, made into a cultural scapegoat who was blamed for a tragic clash between cultures, and whose misrepresentation is still used to suppress women in their own culture (Mirandé and Enríquez 1979:31). Mexican literature holds up Doña Marina as the sole cause of the people's downfall, referring not to her competence but rather to her "treachery." This mistrust of women is carried over into social science stereotypes of Mexican-American women.

In summary, the Mexican woman historically has been depicted as treacherous, passive, and willingly violated (i.e., Malinche). An alternative view is a young woman who was able to assess her situation and able to act according to a value system that acknowledges and honors her understanding and worldview as well as concern and compassion for the people around her. As a product of two forms of colonization and of sexism, Mexican-American women are rendered politically and socioeconomically powerless. Symptoms of low self-esteem, identity confusion, and feelings of powerlessness are not innate to culture or gender but may be attributed to the larger political and systemic oppression and devastation, as opposed to being gender-identified. Mexican-American women are still able to find ways of consciously or unconsciously resisting assimilation and total annihilation by the dominant culture. They do this by attempting to maintain their cultural values and forming complex relationships—interdependent, extended-family relationships.

The Role of Mexican-American Women in the Family

Mexican-American women's role has been stereotypically limited to the family. Therefore, the family is the most central arena for placing and understanding the Chicana. Most of our understanding about the Chicana in the family comes from studies done in Mexico by Díaz-Guerrero in 1975, which have been applied universally to Mexican-Americans. These studies paint a pejorative and pathological picture of the Chicana family.

Beginning in the 1970s, researchers such as Miguel Montiel (1970) have critiqued social scientists for their uncritical acceptance of, for example, the concept of machismo, which has become the way to explain all of the pathologies found in the Mexican and Mexican-American family. Further, these family studies are infused with psycho-analytic concepts and paradigms that attempt to establish a model Mexican personality type characterized by a pervasive feeling of inferiority and a rejection of authority (Mirandé and Enríquez 1979:109).

Díaz-Guerrero (1975) is a primary example of this uncritical acceptance and furtherance of the concept of machismo, explaining the dynamics of Mexican family life through this all-encompassing concept. These uncritical studies of the Mexican family studies have substantially influenced psychoanalytical formulations of Mexican-American families in the United States (Mirandé and Enríquez 1979:109).

Stereotypically, then, the man is the lord and master of the Mexican-American household, with the woman relegated to an insignificant, subordinate position. The rigidity of the family is assumed by social scientists to have negative effects on the personality development of children, and the authoritarian household is not thought to engender achievement, independence, self-reliance, or self-worth (Mirandé and Enríquez 1979:110). In contrast, "recent bodies of literature on decision-making in the Mexican-American family suggests [sic] that Mexican-American families are showing an increasingly egalitarian trend to this decision making" (Blea 1992:83). Blea further argues for the need to consider the role of class in these decision-making processes. In a study she conducted involving wives in the working and professional classes, she found that the two classes of women were alike in that they took the lead in suggesting and/or creating new roles for themselves; the difference was that "the professional women, even the most traditional among them, had already achieved a personal and social identity that working class women were still struggling to construct" (Blea 1992:116).

Although social scientists have correctly identified the social organizations of the Chicano family in terms of its patriarchal-authoritarian principles, they have incorrectly assumed this to mean that women are insignificant (Baca Zinn 1976:20). M. Baca Zinn (1976:21) and Michelle Zimbalest Rosaldo (1974) both identify and recognize women's informal and often recognized power. Chicano social organization appears to people outside the culture to be rigid and patriarchal, but women do have power within the private sphere of the home. Olivia Espín (1992:142) says, "Latin women experience a unique combination of power and powerlessness which is characteristic of the culture."

Familiarity with the Chicano culture makes us aware of the relational character of the people. Independence at the cost of giving up the cultural value of interdependence and relationship to others is simply not a Mexican-American goal. The same is true of self-reliance and self-worth: personality is defined by the community of which the individual is a part. Identity is defined in relationship to others: not to belong to a group is not to exist.

Achievement, independence, self-reliance, and self-worth are values that are promoted in U.S. society. For the Mexican American, questions are raised: Achieve what? Whose values? At what cost? The Mexican-American understanding of achievement is captured by the word *educado*, to be educated and to know how to treat people. Given the poverty of most Mexican Americans, the doors of most institutions are

closed and there are few Chicano role models for the American definition of achievement.

The Mexican-American family does, however, have certain distin-
guishing characteristics, some of which have existed since pre-Columbian times. There is much more emphasis on the family, both immediate and extended, than is found among Anglo-Americans. As in Aztec
society, the needs of the collective frequently take precedence over
those of the individual, and achievement and success are measured
according to the contribution made to the family (Mirandé and Enríquez 1979:107).

The family (including good friends and godparents—*compadres*) is
the single most important unit in Mexican-American life. It is the basic
source of emotional support and growth. It is within the family that
Chicanos learn the cultural values of cooperation and mutual aid. For
example, resources are pooled so that one person may go to school or
buy a house, and everyone pitches in to help.

The positive values and characteristics of the Mexican-American
family can be summarized as follows: it is stable and resilient, providing needed warmth and support in an otherwise hostile and unreward-
ing environment (Mirandé and Enríquez 1979:111). The family facili-
tates achievement through its extended network of support, wherein
grandparents and other elders are more likely to be seen as affectionate
than as authoritarian.

The mother is recognized as an important figure in the home, especially by the children, such that she often takes precedence within the
home over the father, exercising great influence that is characterized
by warmth and affection toward the children (Mirandé and Enríquez
1979:112–114). Norma Williams (1990) challenges this overgeneral-
ization by discussing the Mexican-American family's traditions and
changes with emphasis on the impact of class on family dynamics.

In addition, this influence in the home leads to a position of power
when one takes into account the *Mexican* understanding of the concept. In the Mexican socioculture, power is bestowed, traditionally,
upon those you love: your nuclear family, the extended family, your
relatives, friends, and so forth. In the Mexican socioculture of love,
final decisions are made in terms more of affiliation than of power.

Power is primarily in the hands of the father; the mother also has power in terms of love and respect. Power and love are almost never completely separated from each other. There is not a significant differentiation between these two patterns of interpersonal interaction (Díaz-Guerrero 1975:xvi). The extent to which this holds true for Mexican-Americans depends on their degree of acculturation.

The Chicana's influence filters into her relationship with the children, giving rise to a closely knit group of mothers and children. If there is a persistent image of the woman in Chicano culture, it is that she is a strong and enduring figure. The family is undoubtedly the most important institution for Chicanos, and the woman in turn is the backbone of the culture. Although the woman is largely relegated to the home, her domestic role is not passive. She is charged with essential familial functions: reproduction, transmission of cultural values and beliefs to the next generation, and provision of needed warmth, support, and affection for family members who must survive in a hostile environment (Mirandé and Enríquez 1979:116). Chicanas' ideas of success may extend beyond biological motherhood and servitude to include respect, good health, having a family, and "valuing human beings regardless of age, gender, or race" (Blea 1992:90).

The powerful social control in which the Chicana finds herself is perhaps the greatest obstacle to her breaking away from the traditional role. In addition, she must deal with the conflict of meeting traditional expectations and developing her capabilities (García-Bahne 1977:44), which may or may not lead to goals outside the familial.

Betty García-Bahne (1977:44) understands the man's sense of responsibility for leadership and provision of resources as reflecting "a need for accountability of the most employable members of the family to assure the well-being (financial, health) of all family members." This expectation puts an overburdening responsibility on the male as head of the family and undermines the woman's worth as capable of contributing income or making decisions.

García-Bahne also examines the stereotypical value of the self-sacrificing mother, who puts aside her own needs for the gratification of her children. The woman thus directs what limited resources there are toward the assurance of the health and care of the next generation. Although her activity has maintained the family system, she has done so at a great cost to her own personhood. It places her in the home and induces guilt if she does not adhere to that norm, even to the extent of neglecting her own body. According to García-Bahne (1977:44), a mother's needs are secondary to children's, furthering her secondary status within the family.

García-Bahne's final concern is that the values of modesty and reserve expected of the Chicana may perpetuate obstacles for her in asserting herself regarding a career or education and may block the development of any assertive skills. This in turn may interfere with her economic independence, and she herself may come to the point where she believes she needs to be protected. Originally, this ideal may have been promoted for the protection of violation of women under conditions of exploitation and oppression (García-Bahne 1977:113).

While García-Bahne looks for logic behind the stereotypes, Baca Zinn (1976:25) offers a more empowering interpretation, identifying the traditional role of the woman as the very source of her influence: "Traditionally, the Chicana's strength has been exercised in the home where she has become the pillar of family life. It is just this role that has brought her leadership and her abilities to the larger community. . . . It is the Chicana who goes to her children's school, . . . makes the long trip to the social security office, . . . [and] fights the welfare bureaucracy for her neighbor's family."

In summary, social scientists have highlighted that the traditional Mexican cultural ideal, for the female, is total devotion to the family. She is encouraged to be nurturing and warm and responsive to the needs of her family. In turn, she is respected, revered, and recognized as an important figure. Though she may not have the same type of prestige as a man, she appears to have equal power in the home (Mirandé and Enríquez 1979:113).

The accuracy of portrayals of the Chicana as a submissive, passive, baby-making entity is an empirical and conceptual question for contemporary social scientists (Andrade 1982). Williams (1990:83) calls into question both the stereotype of the machismo-dominated patriarchy and that of an egalitarian relationship between husbands and wives.

Problems with the Portrayal of Mexican-American Women
in the Social Sciences

As noted, traditional social science literature portrays the Chicana almost exclusively in a maternal role, assigning her a lowly status in the culture, while at the same time expecting her to be nurturing, warm, and responsive to the needs of her family. She is described as passive, masochistic, and self-sacrificing, as well as strong, enduring, and the backbone of the culture.

The problem with some of these conclusions is that most social science formulations of the Chicana ignore socioeconomic, political, and specific historical factors: many Chicanas are heads of households, are not paid enough, may be in the United States without documentation, or may be refugees. Another flaw is that almost all of the studies investigated lower class samples, thus confounding ethnicity with socioeconomic status (Andrade 1982:229). Consequently, general statements are made about Chicanos that perhaps are only really applicable to the class that was studied.

It is important to recognize that demographic, cultural, economic, and psychosocial variables contribute to differences among Chicanos. Mexican-American women are the products of two cultures: a traditional Mexican culture wherein the Chicana is relegated to the home, and the U.S. culture that encourages the participation of women in society. Thus Mexican-American women are influenced by two cultures and are in transition between the two. "As Chicanas endure economic social stress, urbanization, the women's movement, the impact of the media, the Chicano movement, and so on, their values change" (Blea 1992:91). Income, urbanization, experience, and education all influence an individual's assumptive worldview.

Social science must recognize certain limitations when studying a cultural group as complex and heterogeneous as Mexican-American women. As with the term "Hispanic," to speak of Mexican Americans in the United States is to refer to "an amalgam of millions of persons from a variety of . . . religions and political and cultural experiences who are through historical circumstances or political or individual design, a permanent and vital segment of our population and who are striving to improve their status in this society while maintaining their dignity and identity in both cultures" (Conference of the Educational and Occupational Needs of Hispanic Women, 1980, cited in Gibson 1983:7).

Some of the differences among Chicanas can be traced to social and geographic factors. For example, these women live in rural and urban settings. Uneven economic development has contributed to social inequality, resulting in social stratification as well as different patterns of child rearing (Montiel 1970). There are also different political and religious outlooks. Consequently, to speak of the Chicana as a member of a homogeneous group is misleading. Her cultural roots lie in Mexico, which is in itself a pluralistic country with distinct cultural groups. Yet social science has not always recognized the pluralistic nature of Mexican culture.

Andrade (1982:231) argues that not enough attention in the research on Mexican-American women has been given to the interaction among the forces of gender, ethnicity, race, social class, and social economics. She further suggests that attention must be focused on alternative theoretical and methodological approaches to the study of the Chicana's values, roles, and behaviors.

Whether social science descriptions are valid or not, images created by this literature often are internalized as cultural truths. Social science research must be critical and the difference between a cultural trait and an Anglo-American fabrication must be made clear (Andrade 1982: 231). Andrade (1979:68–69, citing Baca Zinn 1979) agrees with Baca Zinn, who states that "the most serious methodological flaw in Chicana research is that of reducing family dynamics to crude accounts of cultural values"—those of dominant male, submissive female, and poverty. "While cultural ideals and norms are important dimensions of families, they do not by themselves determine, nor explain family organization" (Baca Zinn 1979:69).

The Impact of Acculturation

In addition to understanding the social science literature (and the critique of that literature) about the Mexican-American woman's role in the family, to further understand the Chicana, we must explore the impact of acculturation, a major source of stress for the Chicana.

Acculturation has been defined as a complex process of psychological and cultural change resulting from the contact of two different cultures, with one group of people being dominant and the other forced
to modify or adapt some of their original cultural patterns and to ab-
sorb some of the dominant culture's in order to accommodate to a new
environment. This process can be prolonged and quite painful (Flores-
Ortiz 1982; Gibson 1983:121).

As previously stated, social science literature treats the Chicana as
part of a homogeneous group and the importance of differences related
to the level of acculturation is overlooked. It has been suggested that
acculturation may be the multifaceted cause of many intergenerational
and socioeconomic problems and it is most visible in the conflicts that
arise between spouses. It arises specifically between a wife who has
acculturated and who may even consider herself "liberated," and her
husband who retains some, if not all, of the traditional values from the
country of origin.

Because of its limited scope, the traditionally linear and unidimen-
sional model of acculturation has been called into question by Yvette
Flores-Ortiz (1982). She proposes a circular, multidimensional process
that takes into account a number of factors which may be orthogonal
(uncorrelated) and thus merit individual attention. These factors
include:

1. *Generation:* How long has this particular family or person been in
the United States? Being forced to adhere to traditional cultural values
in a context where they are not accepted, valued, or understood is
stressful. An additional difficulty for the Chicana is that she may live
out the traditional values at home, while being forced to abandon or
reject these values temporarily to succeed in the dominant culture.
This tension is intensified because she has no role model. She is fac-
ing a new situation without the guidance of the previous generation's
experience.

2. *Religiosity:* What is the religious belief system of this particular
person or family? What role does it play? The more one is acculturated,
the more tension one experiences in the realm of religion. An example
is the tension surrounding Our Lady of Guadalupe. The older Mexican
women might focus on Our Lady of Guadalupe's maternal and self-
sacrificing aspects, while a younger Chicana would either reject or re-

interpret the symbol to match her contemporary experience. Moreover, another limitation of social science literature is that it ignores the role of religion in the lives of these women. Chicanas' marginalization from social and political structures may include organized religion. Studies indicate that as Hispanic Americans become more assimilated into the American society and more affluent, religion will become less important in their lives (Gallup and Castelli 1987:143). Therefore, we might suspect minimal involvement in organized religion and a more active role in popular devotion. This area needs research.

3. *Cultural Awareness:* To what extent does the person have knowledge of and participate in cultural rituals, such as *quinceañeras* (fifteenth birthday celebrations), *compadrazgo* (relationship with godparents), and devotion to Our Lady of Guadalupe? A strong cultural awareness may serve to increase or decrease stress. Stress is increased because cultural awareness forces an individual to face the inherent racism in the dominant culture, such as when her child is rejected for being "darker" than other children; when she faces discrimination due to language, accent, color, or cultural expressions; or when she is punished for speaking Spanish in school or told that earning an A in English is impossible because her surname is Díaz. But cultural awareness may serve to decrease stress by providing a stable sense of one's identity: knowing that her culture derives from an ancient and great civilization; being afforded the opportunity to choose the best from both cultures and languages; and having the advantage of the extended family, with its support systems and celebrations.

4. *Language:* What is the person's language preference? What is the degree of bilingualism, fluency in either or both languages? Monolingual Spanish speakers clearly have difficulty in functioning in a society which is monolingually English. Not so obvious is the stress of being bilingual—the stress of moving back and forth between the different worlds that each language represents. The persistent use of Spanish reflects in part the historical isolation of large segments of this population, but it is probably reinforced by the recency of mass immigration and by the continuous arrival of newcomers from Mexico. Higher-income people and those living in mixed neighborhoods are more likely to speak English (Grebler, Moore, and Guzmán 1970:583).

5. *Ethnic Identity:* What is a person's ethnic identity or loyalty as

determined by chosen values? Stress is produced in a mestiza's attempt to create a bicultural identity, which involves maintaining the richness and value of her culture of origin while integrating the positive values from the dominant culture. Most Hispanic women, despite their heterogeneity, do share some common concerns, among them the desire to maintain their language, their cultural identity, and their commonality of experiences as a minority group within the dominant culture (Gibson 1983).

Chicanos differ widely among themselves in terms of bilingual capabilities, skin coloring, and economic status. All of these factors have some effect on the development of the individual. Generally, the dominant society's strategy is to play against a people's differences, to define them as stereotypes or as an ideal. The dominant society manipulates a certain culture's elements to maintain its position of power, as occurred recently in Oakland, California, during a discussion about not allocating funds for nursing and health to Hispanic elders. Why not? Because "the family would take care of them." The cultural ideal of the extended family and respect for elders was being manipulated in order to justify a lack of resources and facilities for Hispanics.

This overview has been presented to provide the historical sociopsychological background of the Mexican-American woman, a discussion of those forces which still have an influence upon her attitudes, behaviors, and reactions. Chicanos are a colonized group and are affected in unique ways by their historical reality, regardless of whether they are conscious of it or not. We have seen, through the story of Malinche, that the conquest of a people was blamed on a woman. The Chicana has been victimized by history, by sexism, and by racism. In its description of the Chicana, social science literature is erroneous and incomplete because it does not take into consideration historical, socioeconomic, and political factors. Particularly misleading are those studies that rely most on the existing literature. It is possible that a study originally conducted in Mexico to support predominating beliefs could have been cited in the 1960s and again in the 1970s to the extent that a myth prevails in the literature that may have never existed empirically in the United States.

Furthermore, social science tends to perpetuate the stereotypes that maintain the Chicana's oppression. Although she has been characterized as oppressed, the Chicana has, at the same time, survived that oppression while maintaining her commitment to her value system.

The picture of the Chicana that results from this historical and social science review is in contradiction with her reality. Social science almost inevitably depicts Chicanos pejoratively and as pathological, for those images reinforce and legitimate their lowly status. The lack of achievement is more readily attributed to some deficiency in their culture or family life than to their status as an oppressed internal colony. The myth of the Mexican-American family, then, is useful for blaming the problems and oppression of Chicanos on themselves and their culture rather than on prejudice, discrimination, colonization, or the dominant Anglo-American culture (Mirandé and Enríquez 1979:115–116).

Newer historical and social science literature, however, views the Chicana as the sustainer of cultural, linguistic, and religious values and the foundation of the family; in all, a strong and enduring figure (Mirandé and Enríquez 1979:116–117). As Williams (1990:23) writes, "Mexican-American women have played an active role in the home. . . . They have cared for the children and carried out a variety of tasks, not just in the household but at times also in the fields. Under these circumstances, they could hardly have been the passive and weak beings that social scientists' stereotypes have made them out to be."

FIVE

Methodology and Research Findings

Methodology

My purpose was to investigate the experience of Mexican-American women in relation to Our Lady of Guadalupe, to determine if a relationship existed and, if so, to establish the nature of it. My methodology was to select a sample of Mexican-American women and (1) to discover what their perceptions of Our Lady of Guadalupe were and (2) to identify themes that described their relationship to Our Lady of Guadalupe.

The history, story, and symbols surrounding Our Lady of Guadalupe have been established. My next step is examining the influence of this symbol on a particular sample of Mexican-American women.

The Sample

The criteria for inclusion in the study were that the women be (1) of Mexican-American origin; (2) Roman Catholic with Our Lady of Guadalupe as part of their religious experience; (3) English-speaking and acculturated into North American society; and (4) young, married mothers.

(1) That they be Mexican American: At the time of the study, Mexican Americans represented sixty percent of all Hispanics in the United States (this has increased to sixty-three percent: National Council of La Raza 1992), but then and now there is a dearth of material on Mexican Americans, especially on Mexican-American women and their religious experience. I sought to rectify this imbalance.

(2) That they be Roman Catholic, with Our Lady of Guadalupe as part of their religious experience: This was determined by asking each participant if Our Lady of Guadalupe was an important symbol in her life. It was necessary that Our Lady of Guadalupe be part of their religious experience because of the focus of my study.

(3) That they be English-speaking and acculturated into North American society: Dynamics of acculturation may or may not affect perceptions of Our Lady of Guadalupe. The study focuses on women who were born or raised in the United States and who are of Mexican descent. As a way of ensuring a similar level of acculturation within the sample, the criteria specified that these women be English-speaking and have some level of high school education. The San Francisco area was chosen because it is urban and multiethnic.

(4) That they be young, married mothers between the ages of 22 and 30: This age bracket was chosen as a framework to embrace the median age of Hispanics, which was 23.5 at the time of the study and because women within this age bracket are usually married and mothers (U.S. Department of Commerce 1988; the median age has increased to 26.2: National Council of La Raza 1992:3). I chose mothers because of their central role as transmitters of cultural and religious values in a bicultural context (Secretariat for Hispanic Affairs 1986), and to explore the significance of Our Lady of Guadalupe's maternity for young Mexican-American mothers.

The sample was gathered by inviting individuals from various ministries in the Catholic church (e.g., catechists, youth, parishioners) to identify women who met these criteria. The selection of the sample was necessarily limited geographically; while the size of the sample was small, it met the requirements for an exploratory study such as mine.

I contacted coordinators of religious education and pastoral ministry and requested their help in recruiting participants. Potential participants were informed about the research and invited to take part in the study. If they met the criteria and were interested, they were given my telephone number and name. No monetary incentives were offered. Women recruited through group contacts or through personal contacts were then asked to suggest other potential participants. Presentation of the study, whether in person or by telephone, also included a brief description of the confidentiality involved. Once the subject was identified, met the criteria, and was contacted, a date was set for the interview.

The interview lasted between one hour and an hour and a half and was conducted at a place most convenient to the subject, usually at her home. All subjects were asked to sign a "Consent and Participation Agreement" form. To preserve their confidentiality, I have changed their names.

After introductions, I explained that the study was concerned with researching Mexican-American women and religion. I then administered the following: (1) the Demographic Questionnaire, (2) the written reflection articulating the subject's feelings, thoughts, or experience of Our Lady of Guadalupe, (3) the Adjective Check List, and (4) the taped interview.

The Instruments

The Demographic Questionnaire

The Demographic Questionnaire was developed to identify the social, cultural, and economic status of the women in this sample. The purpose of this instrument was (1) to identify the psychosocial profile of the sample, (2) to determine whether their level of acculturation was a factor in influencing their comments about Our Lady of Guadalupe, and (3) to determine if, in fact, these women would identify Our Lady of Guadalupe as someone who was important to them.

The questionnaire was analyzed by dividing it into four sections: (1) socioeconomic status; (2) participation in cultural and religious organizations; (3) most important religious holidays, symbols, and beliefs; and (4) highest-ranked religious and cultural holiday.

The questionnaire was used to gain some basic sociocultural information about the participants and to ensure that the sample approached an average sampling of Mexican-American women. The demographic questionnaire consisted of twenty-seven questions in three parts (Appendix A-1). The first part dealt with general demographics: age, marital status, number of children, income, generational level as Mexican American, birthplace, ethnicity of parents, ethnicity and religion of spouse, and number of years in the San Francisco Bay Area.

The second part asked seven questions to explore the level of religious and cultural participation: (1) With what other organizations or groups of a Catholic nature are you affiliated? (2) With what other organizations or groups of a Mexican-American nature are you affiliated? (3) List the activities of a Catholic nature in which you are now involved. (4) List the activities of a Mexican-American nature in which you are now involved. (5) If you have children, please list the organizations or groups of a Catholic nature to which they belong. (6) If you have children, please list the organizations or groups of a Mexican-American nature to which they belong. (7) At what age did you get involved in church-related activities?

The third part of the questionnaire asked about specific religious attitudes: What do you consider to be the most important—(1) church holiday, (2) symbol, or (3) belief, and why?

The last two questions asked the participant to rank the most important religious and cultural holidays. These questions were asked to discover what their religious priorities were and whether Our Lady of Guadalupe would be reflected in their responses. I based items for this questionnaire on the instrument developed by Sam Tabachnik (1985), with modifications. The information provided by the Demographic Questionnaire may offer clues as to how some acculturation factors (e.g., marital status, socioeconomic status, education) may have affected this sample.

The Written Reflection

The purpose of this instrument was to elicit unbiased responses from the women in terms of what they thought, felt, or experienced when they looked at the image of Our Lady of Guadalupe. I instructed them to write down their responses, which I later examined for aspects of the psychosocial religious reality of these women.

To elicit a maximum amount of material, both oral and written reflections were requested from the sample. Each participant wrote a reflection of Our Lady of Guadalupe prior to being interviewed, so as to attain an unbiased initial response to the image. The participants were shown an image of Our Lady of Guadalupe (the same image, which I brought) and asked to free-associate the following: "Tell me what you see. Tell me what the image means to you." They were then given time to write whatever reflections or feelings they had upon looking at the image. In order to help them center themselves, instrumental indigenous flute music was used ("Music can move us, . . . can inspire our most exalted religious feelings and ease our anxious and lonely moments": Rosenfeld 1985:49).

The purpose of the written reflection was to provide an opportunity for the sample to articulate in an open and free manner what Our Lady of Guadalupe meant to them. Information that emerged from these reflections was analyzed using basic thematic concerns in conjunction with the overall analysis of the taped interviews.

Adjective Check List

The Adjective Check List (ACL, developed by Gough and Heilbrun 1965) consists of 300 adjectives and adjectival phrases commonly used to describe a person's attributes. While the ACL is normally used as a tool for self-description, according to the manual developed by the test designers it can also be used to describe legendary or historical persons.

Following the written reflections, the participants were asked to complete the ACL. I explained that the ACL has been used to describe the subject, but for the purpose of this study, they were to check off the adjectives that described Our Lady of Guadalupe.

Computerized analysis of the ACL was utilized to identify and tabulate the two highest-ranked clusters (positive and negative scales) attributed to Our Lady of Guadalupe.

The Taped Interview

The last part of the interview was taped to document the women's oral commentary on their written reflection. The participants were asked to elaborate on what they had written; they themselves stated that they spoke better than they wrote. These commentaries were examined and later categorized into themes.

I examined the taped interviews using a structure for analysis developed by George DeVos (1973). A cultural anthropologist, DeVos developed a framework that integrates the disciplines of psychology, anthropology, and sociology. Though trained originally as a social scientist, DeVos (1973:xi) became critical of social science generalizations that left out "the intense reality" of personal experience. Pursuing his interests in culture and human psychology, he focused on the cultural psychology of the Japanese. As a way to develop a method for demonstrating conclusions, he began to do work in psychological testing, specifically Thematic Apperception Tests (TAT). He utilized the Rorschach inkblot test as a means of systematically comparing the perceptual patterns and the intrapsychic adjustment patterns of the American-born Nisei with those of their immigrant parents (DeVos 1973: xiii). I used DeVos's categories to organize the themes emerging from the taped interviews. These categories were particularly useful because his framework has been used cross-culturally.

DeVos (1973:1), along with Frank, James, and myself, agrees that no theoretical conclusions can ignore the influence of personality variables that are the transmitted heritage of different cultural traditions. Human behavior is influenced by both social structure and cultural patterns, and both are modified by political, educational, and economic institutions.

I was mindful that DeVos's categories are often interpreted along gender-defined lines, thus perpetuating myths and stereotypes regarding gender-specific attributes. The objective of utilizing this instrument was to categorize the perceptions of Our Lady of Guadalupe held by the sample. Therefore, no gender-specific bias should be applied to the following interpretations.

Using these categories, I grouped participants' statements under instrumental or expressive behavior. Given the projective nature of this task, a response might have fit within a number of categories. However, a decision was made to assign the statement to that category which most clearly reflected DeVos's definitions.

In *instrumental behavior*, the action is perceived by self and others as a means of achieving a goal or to meet a standard by which behavior is judged (DeVos 1973:23). In this category, action behavior is noted, that is, there is a consequence to the act. The five dimensions under this category are Achievement, Competence, Responsibility, Control, and Mutuality. It is implied in each of these categories that an action occurs which results in an outcome (for example, an individual acts in order to achieve).

In *expressive behavior*, feelings are examined. The feelings may be associated with the act itself, the situation, or the relationship, but it is the particular feeling involved which is examined. The five dimensions in this category are Harmony, Affiliation, Nurturance, Appreciation, and Pleasure. Note that the instrumental and expressive behaviors are not separate entities; rather, we find a complex network of attitudes and expectations in which various instrumental and expressive motives are inextricably intertwined (DeVos 1973:23). In other words, the affective and instrumental natures can be examined as parts of a whole.

In summary, the transcribed interviews were organized in the following manner: (1) the projective statements were subjectively placed under the appropriate category, guided by DeVos's operational constructs; (2) a list was made regarding who the initiator of the action was and who the recipient was, giving insight into how active Our Lady of Guadalupe was in these women's lives—and in which areas of their lives she was active; and (3) a percentage for the participants' responses to each theme was determined. The findings are discussed below.

Findings of the Demographic Questionnaire

General Demographics

The Demographic Questionnaire was developed to describe and identify the social, cultural, and economic status—the psychosocial dimension—of the women in this sample. The data gathered from this questionnaire both locate the women in their psychosocial religious context and provide information about their cultural and religious orientation.

Twenty women were chosen for this study. The Demographic Questionnaire elicited information about respondents' age, marital status, number of children, ethnic and religious background of spouse and parents, income of respondent and that of respondents' family of origin, educational level, birthplace, length of residence, and generation. The findings are described below; the raw data are presented in Table 1.

Age: All participants were between 23 and 30 years of age, with the mean age being 26.9.

Marital status: Eighty percent of the participants were married ($N = 16$), fifteen percent divorced ($N = 3$), and five percent were partnered ($N = 1$).

Spouse: The spouses of the women were Catholic except for one. Forty-five percent ($N = 9$) of the spouses were Mexican, thirty percent ($N = 6$) were Mexican-American, fifteen percent ($N = 3$) were Latin American or Central American, and ten percent ($N = 2$) were of European descent.

Number of Children: The number of children was between one and four. Forty percent ($N = 8$) had two children, thirty-five percent ($N = 7$) had one child, fifteen percent ($N = 3$) had three children, and ten percent ($N = 2$) had four children. The mean number of children was two. The age range of the children was between eight months and ten years. In total, the sample reported having forty children, fifty-five percent male and forty-five percent were female.

Educational Level and Occupation: Mean years of education for this sample was 12.1 years. Forty percent of these women ($N = 8$) were involved in full-time employment outside of the home; five percent ($N = 1$) were involved in part-time employment outside of the home; while fifty-five percent of the sample ($N = 11$) had no employment outside the home. Of those employed full- or part-time outside the home, the types of employment represented were travel agent, lead foreman, babysitter, cashier, aerobics teacher, administrative secretary, bookkeeper, dental office assistant, dental office manager, receptionist, typist, and clerk.

Family of Origin Income vs. Present Income Per Year (including Spouse and Partner): To examine whether these women had experienced economic mobility, two questions were asked regarding income. One was the request for the combined income of the participants' family of origin. The second question was the present income per year including income of both participant and spouse. The data showed that forty-five percent of the sample ($N = 9$) had stayed within the same economic income category as their family of origin, while forty percent ($N = 8$) showed upward mobility and fifteen ($N = 3$) demonstrated downward mobility on the economic ladder.

Birthplace, Length of Time in the San Francisco Bay Area, and Generation: Eighty percent ($N = 16$) of the women were born in the Bay Area, fifteen percent ($N = 3$) were born in Mexico, and five percent ($N = 1$) were born in Southern California. Those born in Mexico identified themselves as Mexican Americans, most likely because all their formal education had been North American and they had lived a major part of their lives in the United States. Eighty-five percent of the sample ($N = 17$) were second-generation (born in the United States to Mexican parents), while fifteen percent ($N = 3$) were first-generation (who emigrated from Mexico to the United States).

Ethnic and Religious Background of the Parents of the Sample: All of the respondents' parents were Catholic. Ninety percent of the mothers ($N = 18$) were Mexican and ten percent ($N = 2$) were Mexican American. Eighty percent ($N = 16$) of the sample's fathers were Mexican and twenty percent ($N = 4$) were Mexican American.

The salient features of this sample included homogeneity in terms of generation, education, and adherence to religious and cultural roots. Only three out of the twenty women were first-generation Mexican-Americans. The rest were second-generation. The three that were first-generation, however, identified themselves as Mexican Americans and had been in the United States for twenty to twenty-eight years.

Homogeneity was further expressed by the fact that (1) all of the women's self-identification was Catholic, (2) all of their parents were Catholic, and (3) ninety-five percent of the men they married were Catholic. Catholicism is both a cultural and a religious phenomenon. The sample population can be contrasted to the larger Mexican-American population: today approximately eighty percent of Mexican Americans are Catholic.

The U.S. Census figures for March 1989 show that the mean number of persons in Hispanic families was 4.05, but do not indicate the mean number of children. The mean number of children in this sample was

Table 1. *General Demographics*

#	Age	Marital Status	Spouse Ethnicity	Catholic	Education	Occupation
1	26	M	Mx	Y	12	Housewife
2	27	M	Mx	Y	12	Trav Agt
3	30	M	A/I	Y	12	Housewife
4	26	D	MA	Y	11	Foreman
5	28	M	Mx	Y	12	Housewife
6	23	M	Mx	Y	9	Housewife
7	26	M	Mx	Y	13	Housewife
8	27	M	Mx	Y	12	Housewife
9	30	M	MA	Y	12	Housewife
10	28	M	MA/A	Y	12	Housewife
11	28	M	MA	Y	14	Hw/Csh/A
12	30	D	N	Y	12	Housewife
13	28	D	Mx	N	12	Adm Secty
14	25	M	Ita	Y	12	Bkkpr
15	26	M	Mx	Y	12	Dent Asst
16	24	M	MA	Y	14	Dent Asst
17	29	M	Mx	Y	12	Reception
18	28	M	CR/I	Y	13	Housewife
19	25	P	MA	Y	12	Housewife
20	24	M	ElS	Y	12	Secretary

Marital Status		Income	
M	Married	1	under $5,000
D	Divorced	2	$5,000–10,000
P	Partnered	3	$10,000–15,000
		4	$15,000–20,000
		5	$20,000–30,000
		6	over $30,000

resent come	Family Income	Birthplace	Mother/Father Eth/Cath	Residence	Generation
5	5	Oakland	Mx/C-Mx/C	26	2nd
4	4	Oakland	Mx/C-Mx/C	27	2nd
5	3	Alameda	Mx/C-Mx/C	30	2nd
3	5	Calif	Mx/C-Mx/C	26	2nd
4	4	Union City	Mx/C-MA/C	28	2nd
5	5	Fremont	Mx/C-Mx/C	23	2nd
3	2	Pittsburgh	Mx/C-Mx/C	26	2nd
5	5	Mexico	Mx/C-Mx/C	25	1st
6	4	Walnut Cr	Mx/C-Mx/C	30	2nd
4	4	Martinez	Mx/C-Mx/C	28	2nd
5	5	San Diego	Mx/C-Mx/C	10	2nd
2	3	Alameda	Mx/C-MA/C	30	2nd
5	2	Oakland	Mx/C-MA/C	28	2nd
5	4	Martinez	MA/C-Mx/C	25	2nd
6	3	Oakland	Mx/C-Mx/C	26	2nd
4	4	Oakland	Mx/C-Mx/C	24	2nd
5	3	Oakland	Mx/C-Mx/C	29	2nd
6	4	Mexico	Mx/C-Mx/C	28	1st
2	3	San Pablo	MA/C-MA/C	25	2nd
5	5	Mexico	Mx/C-Mx/C	20	1st

Ethnicity		Occupation	
Mx	Mexican	Csh	Cashier
A/I	Anglo/Irish	AI	Aerobics Instructor
MA	Mexican American		
MA/A	Mexican American/Asian		
N	Nicaraguan		
Ita	Italian		
CR/I	Costa Rican/Irish		
ElS	El Salvadoran		

two. At first glance, this number appears to be relatively low, given the importance in Hispanic culture of having children. The lower mean number of children may be due to the age of the sample or to acculturation factors.

Additional demographic factors were the following: (1) the median age for the sample was 26.9, a bit higher than the median age given by the U.S. Census's figure of 23.5 (U.S. Department of Commerce 1988), and (2) fifty-five percent were housewives, with the remainder breaking into the work force with full- or part-time, white-collar, traditional employment (e.g., cashier, bookkeeper, or receptionist).

The variables of median age, level of education, and occupation are important to keep in mind as we proceed to the remaining findings. This study defined acculturation in terms of educational attainment and generational level, focusing on women who were born or raised in the United States, of Mexican descent, English-speaking, and having some level of high school education. The sample was homogeneous in terms of these variables. Because of this, we would expect fewer differences across the variables. Literature on acculturation suggests a correlation between educational level and higher levels of acculturation, so we would expect that this sample is a relatively acculturated and homogeneous one. Roberto González and Michael LaVelle (1985:176) contend that a correlation exists between religiosity and level of acculturation: "The vast majority (83%) of Hispanic Catholics consider religion to be a very important part of their lives. . . . First-generation Hispanic Catholics (87.2%) are more likely than second- and subsequent generation Hispanic American Catholics (76.8%) to consider religion a very important part of their lives. . . . First-generation Hispanic Catholics are also stronger in religious belief than second- and subsequent generation Hispanic American Catholics."

Organizations of a Catholic or Mexican-American Nature

This next section presents findings on the level of affiliation with cultural and religious organizations on the part of the sample. The level of participation in an organization may reveal the values that are inherent in an individual's psychosocial religious developmental identity.

Table 2 presents the religious and cultural affiliation of the sample. Table 3 shows the types of religious participation and the number of respondents that belong to each type. Appendix A-2 lists these organizations.

As seen in Table 2, fourteen out of the twenty respondents indicated involvement with an organization of a Catholic nature. In addition, seven belonged to two or more organizations. Those most frequently mentioned were youth groups ($N = 6$), marriage encounter ($N = 4$), Bible study groups ($N = 3$), cursillos (little courses) ($N = 2$), choir ($N = 3$), and catechism ($N = 2$).

Table 2 also presents the cultural organizations to which the sample belonged. Seventy percent ($N = 14$) of the respondents indicated no affiliation with Mexican-American organizations or groups. Twenty percent ($N = 4$) of the respondents belonged to one organization, and ten ($N = 2$) belonged to two or more. One respondent indicated belonging to the Hispanic Marriage Encounter, which is both a religious and cultural affiliation. Religious groups such as cursillos, encuentros, and Guadalupanas were created specifically for the Mexican and Mexican-American parishioner. Twenty percent ($N = 4$) had participated in a Mexican-American organization during their high school years.

The respondents were also asked to list those activities of a Catholic or Mexican-American nature in which they and/or their children are currently involved (Appendix A-2). Eighty percent of the respondents ($N = 16$) indicated that their children were not involved in any activity of a Catholic nature; none of them indicated involvement in any organization of a Mexican-American nature.

Finally, the respondents were asked at what age they had become involved in church-related activities. The ages ranged from 11 to 25 years. Twenty-five percent ($N = 5$) of them indicated their participation as adults (18–25 years), primarily in such activities as Bible study, catechism, and cursillos. Thirty-five percent ($N = 7$) began their involvement as teenagers (13–17 years) in such activities as youth groups, encounters, and retreats. Only ten percent ($N = 2$) began their involvement as children (11–13 years), primarily as catechists' aides.

Table 2. *Affiliations of a Catholic and Mexican-American Nature*

#	Affiliation Groups/Org.: Catholic	Affiliation Groups/Org.: Mex-Amer	Involvement Activities: Catholic	Involvement Activities: Mex-Amer	Children's Involvement: Catholic	Children's Involvement: Mex-Amer	Age Began Church Activity
1	Bible Study Cursillo Youth Group	N/A	Bible Study	N/A	N/A	N/A	15
2	Youth Group	N/A	N/A	N/A	N/A	N/A	17
3	Catechist Marr Enc	N/A	Mar Enc Cat Train	N/A	CCD	N/A	11
4	Youth Group Bible Study	N/A	N/A	N/A	N/A	N/A	24
5	Bible Study	May Club	N/A	N/A	N/A	N/A	16
6	N/A	N/A	N/A	N/A	N/A	N/A	N/A
7	Choir	N/A	N/A	N/A	N/A	N/A	13

8	N/A	N/A	N/A	N/A	N/A	N/A	N/A
9	CCD Teach	N/A	Teaching	N/A	CCD	N/A	25
10	N/A	N/A	Bible Study	N/A	CCD	N/A	25
11	Parish Cursillo Choir	Mex-Am Club	N/A	N/A	N/A	N/A	22
12	Enc Juv	N/A	N/A	N/A	Cath School	N/A	17
13	N/A	N/A	N/A	N/A	N/A	N/A	N/A
14	N/A	N/A	N/A	N/A	N/A	N/A	N/A
15	Marr Enc Youth Group	League Lat Soccer	Marr Enc	N/A	N/A	N/A	16
16	N/A	N/A	N/A	N/A	N/A	N/A	N/A
17	Marr Enc Choir	MECHA	N/A	N/A	N/A	N/A	16
18	Marr Enc	SSUC	N/A	N/A	N/A	N/A	17
19	Guadalupanas 200 Club	HS Chicano	HS Chicano	N/A	N/A	N/A	23
20	Enc Juv	N/A	N/A	N/A	N/A	N/A	16

Table 3. *Number of Participants with Catholic Affiliations*

Organization/ Activity of a Catholic Nature	Number of Responses by Participants	Percentage of Participant Response
Youth Group	6	30
Marriage Encounter	4	20
Bible Study	3	15
Catechist	2	10
Cursillo	2	10
Lector/Parish/Euch Minister	1	5
Choir	3	15
Guadalupana	1	5
200 Club	1	5
None	6	30

Note: Percentages exceed 100% because of multiple responses by some participants.

Most Important Holiday, Symbol, and Belief

The respondents were asked to list their most important holiday, symbol, and belief. Table 4 summarizes the results, the holiday, symbol, and belief for each participant. Fifty-five percent ($N = 11$) of the respondents stated that Christmas was the most important holiday. Forty percent ($N = 8$) cited Easter, with only five percent ($N = 1$) stating that Our Lady of Guadalupe was the most important holiday. Appendix A-3 outlines the reasons given by the respondents for choosing a specific holiday, symbol, or belief.

The most important symbol listed was the cross or crucifix, cited by seventy percent ($N = 14$) of the respondents. Other symbols mentioned at five percent ($N = 1$) were water, the Eucharist, the presence, picture of Christ, baby Jesus, and God. Fifty-five percent ($N = 11$) indicated that the most important belief was God and Jesus. Others men-

Table 4. *Most Important Church Holiday, Symbol, and Belief*

Partic-ipant	Church Holiday	Symbol	Belief
1	Christmas	Sign of the Cross	Communion
2	Christmas	Cross	Our Lady of Guadalupe
3	Feast of OLG	Cross	We are saved/part of a community Inherit kingdom through Christ
4	Easter	Water	Jesus Christ is alive
5	Christmas/Easter	Sign of the Cross	Jesus Christ
6	Easter	God	God
7	Resurrection	Cross	Jesus died for our sins
8	Christmas	Baby Jesus	Jesus Christ born into the world
9	Christmas	Cross	Prayers
10	Easter	Christ Picture	Life after death
11	Holy Week	Eucharist	Holy Spirit
12	Christmas	Crucifix	God is savior and father creator
13	Christmas	Cross	Jesus died on cross and rose
14	Christmas	Crucifix	God
15	Christmas	Cross	God willing to forgive
16	Holy Week/Easter	Cross	Mary and Jesus
17	Christmas	Cross	Mass
18	Easter	Presence	God loves us
19	Christmas	Cross	God is there
20	Easter	Crucifix	Ten Commandments

tioned one time each were Our Lady of Guadalupe, Communion, the Holy Spirit, being saved, the Ten Commandments, mass, prayers, life after death, and Mary and Jesus.

Highest-Ranked Religious and Cultural Holidays

The women in the sample were given seven religious and seven cultural holidays and asked to rank them in order of importance. Table 5 presents the highest-ranked religious and cultural holidays. (Appendix A-4 lists the holidays in ranked order by respondents.)

Two religious holidays emerged as important: forty percent ($N = 8$) cited Easter and forty percent ($N = 8$) cited Christmas. Fifteen percent

Table 5. Highest-Ranked Religious and Cultural Holidays

Participant	Church Holiday	Cultural Holiday
1	Christmas	Día de las Madres
2	Christmas	Día de las Madres
3	Easter	Día de las Madres
4	Easter	Día de las Madres
5	Christmas	Cinco de Mayo
6	Easter	Cinco de Mayo
7	Easter	Día de los Muertos
8	Our Lady of Guadalupe	Grito de Dolores
9	Christmas	Día de las Madres
10	Easter	Cinco de Mayo
11	Easter	Día de las Madres
12	Christmas	16th of September
13	Good Friday	Día de las Madres
14	Christmas	Cinco de Mayo
15	Christmas	Día de las Madres
16	Easter	Día de las Madres
17	Good Friday	Día de los Muertos
18	Good Friday	Cinco de Mayo
19	Christmas	Día de las Madres
20	Easter	Cinco de Mayo

($N = 3$) stated that Good Friday was the most important. Only five percent ($N = 1$) cited the feast of Our Lady of Guadalupe.

Fifty percent of the sample ($N = 10$) stated that Mother's Day (Día de las Madres) was the most important cultural holiday, followed by ($N = 6$) Cinco de Mayo (May 5th), the celebration commemorating the defeat of the French by the Mexican Army in 1862. Ten percent ($N = 2$) stated that Día de los Muertos (November 2, All Souls' Day) was the most important cultural holiday. Ten percent ($N = 2$) indicated that the 16th of September (or Grito de Dolores, the beginning of Mexican independence from Spain) was the most important cultural holiday.

The feast of Our Lady of Guadalupe was mentioned only once. It was celebrated as a memorial until 1989, when it was raised from an optional memorial to a feast of the church; its formerly unofficial status may be one reason that it was not ranked as an important church (i.e., institutional) holiday. Responses to this question also may have been affected by use of the word "holiday" instead of "feast day" or "holy day". It was only later in the study, in the informal interviews, that Our Lady of Guadalupe emerged as important in the lives and religiosity of the sample.

The highest ranked religious holiday and the highest ranked cultural holiday were Christmas and Mother's Day, respectively. When asked why Christmas was the most important holiday, the usual response was, "Because Jesus was born." The highest ranked religious holiday, therefore, appears to reflect a traditional Christian response, while the Mother's Day response reflects a traditional cultural response (United States, Mexican, and Mexican American).

Findings of Written Reflections

The women in the sample were shown an image of Our Lady of Guadalupe and instructed to free-associate, writing what they felt or thought when looking at the image. The purpose of the written reflection was to provide an opportunity for the sample to articulate in an open and free manner what Our Lady of Guadalupe meant to them. Information that emerged from these reflections was analyzed using basic thematic concerns in conjunction with the overall analysis of the taped interviews.

The following are directly transcribed responses by some of the interviewees when I asked them to free-associate what came to mind when they looked at the image of Our Lady of Guadalupe.

Ruth: The *virgen de* Guadalupe is a lovely lady to me. She plays an important role in my life. She gives me strength. I see in her a strong woman. I would like to be a good mother and have a nice family—she has it all.

Yolanda: She's a mother symbol for all
       She is strength Hope Optimism
       She is here with me
       She is my life (she's always been there)
       She's beautiful (she's ours los latinos)
       She's special

Edyth: I think she was a virgin that was very concerned about her people (Mexican) people feel a lot of respect for her.

Carolina: "Our Lady of Guadalupe" she is everyone's Lady of Guadalupe as to say she is the mother of the world or a Mexican Mother waiting, caring, unselfish. I can't really relate as much as I would want to maybe because growing up my mother or family did not introduce or encourage me to know her and love her. Personally I think she reaches the really oppressed! I have not made a bond with her, she is a symbol to me and has not become real and active part in my life.

Beatrice: Our Lady of Guadalupe to me is very kind, understandable person. I believe in her and trust in her. When I see her picture or pray to a statue of her I have I really feel that she hears me and understands what I am saying or feeling. She is very kind and sweet in her looks, a very understanding person and I have asked her for help many times and will always love her and trust in her. God Bless Her!

Irene: I've never really had an experience with Our Lady of Guadalupe but I know she is Mary, the mother of God who was sent by Him to a Mexican town and she brought with her a message from God. She is "La Patrona" of the Mexican faith. The Mexican population rely very heavily on her.

Monica: The Lady of Guadalupe is something I believe in since my younger years. I look up at her statue and I think how beautiful and very peaceful she looks. Now she is someone who I still think is very beautiful and peaceful looking. I can speak to her for comfort and for help and feel relief and peace inside. She is the Mother of our father Jesus Christ whom I also speak to for help and comforting. Just seeing her statue or pictures means relief inside my soul. A peaceful deep feeling inside. It's comforting to be able to have her to look upon.

Julia: Our Virgin de Guadalupe represents to me everything we as a people should strive to be. Strong yet humble, warm and compassionate yet courageous enough to stand up for what we believe in no matter how tense the pressure. Above all obedient to God's will.

Rosío: My Lady is someone who can speak to God for me, she has more leverage. She is the Queen of the Church. She is holy. I pray to the Virgin and to God separately.

Catalina: Our Lady of Guadalupe means that she is a considerable loving mother-type because of the way she was thoughtful enough for the "children" to look upon us and come to us in an image that we are familiar with. La Virgen Morena, to make us feel comfortable and to come and remind us of a love and a spirit that does exist.

The most frequent themes that emerged from these written reflections are Our Lady of Guadalupe as a *mother-type* (fifty percent, $N = 10$), as *someone to be prayed to* (thirty percent, $N = 6$), as one who *brings comfort and peace* (twenty-five percent, $N = 5$), and as someone who is *strong and/or gives strength* (twenty percent, $N = 4$).

Computer Analysis of the Adjective Check List Clusters

A computerized analysis of positive and negative attributes was utilized to identify and tabulate the two highest ranked clusters attributed to Our Lady of Guadalupe.

Tables 6 and 7 report the standard scores of the prominent clusters on the ACL. The purpose of the ACL was to obtain an objective self-

Table 6. *Major Clusters of Adjective Check List*

Partic-ipant	Ideal Self	Nurtur-ing Parent	E1 (+) Nurtur-ance	Affilia-tion	Self-Control	Adapted Child	E2 (−) Aggres-sion	Critica Paren
1	67	53	53	58	58	36	46	52
2	65	63	63	2	56	41	39	40
3	72	57	57	57	52	36	52	47
4	58	63	63	60	62	36	52	47
5	55	56	56	51	53	47	34	32
6	56	47	47	51	49	48	40	37
7	62	62	62	64	63	37	33	39
8	57	51	51	54	54	47	45	47
9	60	60	60	58	45	36	40	42
10	58	58	58	52	49	48	46	45
11	58	50	50	49	49	46	46	46
12	59	58	58	53	58	42	37	39
13	59	55	55	60	54	44	41	38
14	63	56	56	55	49	45	44	40
15	57	67	67	67	67	37	35	35
16	62	62	62	61	64	38	32	31
17	56	54	54	52	53	49	45	37
18	56	46	46	52	46	52	51	48
19	59	63	63	54	66	44	35	40
20	60	58	58	52	60	42	34	34

report of these women's perceptions of Our Lady of Guadalupe. These perceptions are essential in discerning the relationship of Mexican-American women to Our Lady of Guadalupe. The ACL is a list of 300 adjectives, normally administered by clinicians to help people articulate descriptions of themselves, but it was not used here to measure Mexican-American women's own psychosocial identity. Although its use was problematic in that the women were not familiar with all the words, it did yield a list of common adjectives used to describe Our Lady of Guadalupe.

The computer analysis showed two basic clusters with five categories

Table 7. *Two Major Clusters: Attributes of*
Our Lady of Guadalupe

Cluster I Positive Attributes

Scale	Standard Score of Subjects
Number 24 Ideal Self	60 +/− 4.24
Number 30 Nurturing Parent	57 +/− 5.41
Number 10 Nurturance	57 +/− 5.65
Number 11 Affiliation	56 +/− 4.96
Number 21 Self-Control	55 +/− 6.67

Cluster II Negative Attributes

Scale	Standard Score of Subjects
Number 33 Adapted Child	43 +/− 5.13
Number 15 Aggression	41 +/− 6.03
Number 29 Critical Parent	41 +/− 5.79

(For further definition of terms see Appendix B-1)

in the first and three in the second cluster. One cluster consisted of what Our Lady of Guadalupe is seen to be, that is, qualities attributed to her. The second cluster describes qualities that are not attributed to Our Lady of Guadalupe.

Under the first cluster, those characteristics that the women affirmed, Our Lady of Guadalupe received the highest number of adjectives relating to *the ideal self*. This finding indicates that Our Lady of Guadalupe has great personal worth for Mexican-American women. The women view Our Lady of Guadalupe as their ideal self, which they strive to be.

The next highest rated adjective was *the nurturing parent*. This scale indicates attitudes of support, stability, and acceptance associated with the concept of a nurturing parent. The adjective ranked third was *nurturance*, described as the ability to engage in behavior that provides maternal or emotional benefits to others. The fourth adjective was *af-filiation*, seeking and maintaining numerous personal friendships. The fifth one cited was *self-control*, that is, the extent to which self-control is imposed and valued.

The adjectives that were least attributed to Our Lady of Guadalupe can be divided into three main categories. First, Our Lady of Guadalupe is not seen as conforming or being subordinate, as indicated by the low score she attained under the category of *adapted child*. The adapted child identifies those adjectives that indicate attitudes of def-erence, conformity, and self-discipline associated with the concept of an adapted or very dutiful child. Second, Our Lady of Guadalupe was not described with those adjectives that address *aggression*. That is, Our Lady of Guadalupe does not engage in behaviors that attack or hurt others. Third, Our Lady of Guadalupe was not seen as a *critical parent*. These adjectives identify attitudes of evaluation, severity, and skepti-cism associated with the concept of a critical parent.

In summary, for the women in the study, Our Lady of Guadalupe scores high in nurturance, personal worth, and affiliation, which rep-resent qualities valued by women in traditional Mexican and Mexican-American cultures (i.e., nurturance, relationality, self-sacrifice). Our Lady of Guadalupe was not seen as aggressive or conforming by the sample, as indicated by the low score she received in these areas. These Mexican-American women ambivalently perceived Our Lady of Gua-dalupe as being meek and strong-willed, independent and dependent, assertive and shy—all at the same time. I address these seeming con-tradictions in the following chapter.

Findings of Taped Interviews

Another instrument used to identify Mexican-American women's per-ceptions of Our Lady of Guadalupe was the interview. I directed the participants to expand on their comments recorded in the written re-flections. As discussed earlier in methodology, DeVos's scoring system was used for scoring self and social attitudes according to ten basic motivational concerns. Five of these dimensions are primarily *instru-mental* (Achievement, Competence, Responsibility, Control/Power, and Mutuality), and five are *expressive* (Harmony, Affiliation, Nurturance,

ble 8. *Instrumental Behavior*

	Category	Total Responses	OLG as Active	Partic-ipant as Active	Active Agent	Recip-ient	Percent
1	Achievement	45%	40%	5%	OLG	P	5
					OLG	O	30
					P	OLG	5
					OLG	Jesus	5
2	Competence	70%	55%	10%	OLG	P	25
					OLG	O	30
					God	OLG	5
					P	OLG	10
3	Responsibility	25%	15%	10%	OLG	O	15
					P	OLG	5
					P O	OLG	5
4	Control/Power	50%	40%	10%	P	OLG	10
					OLG	O	25
					OLG	P	10
					OLG .	God	5
5	Mutuality	60%	30%	25%	P	OLG	25
					OLG	O	15
					OLG	P	15
					O	OLG	5

A   No statement of theme given
G   Our Lady of Guadalupe
Other
Participant

Appreciation, and Pleasure) in motivation. Comments were further examined to ascertain who the initiator or "actor" in this dynamic represented.

As Table 8 indicates, Our Lady of Guadalupe is viewed as instrumentally *active*, specifically in the areas of Competence (fifty-five per-

Table 9. *Expressive Behavior*

	Category	Total Responses	OLG as Active	Partic-ipant as Active	Active Agent	Recip-ient	Percent
1	Harmony	30%	15%	15%	P	OLG	15
					OLG	O	5
					OLG	P	10
2	Affiliation	80%	35%	45%	OLG	P	20
					OLG	O	15
					P	OLG	45
3	Nurturance	75%	55%	20%	OLG	P	35
					P	OLG	20
					OLG	O	20
4	Appreciation	60%	20%	30%	P	OLG	30
					OLG	P	5
					OLG	O	15
					O	OLG	5
					God	OLG	5
5	Pleasure	25%	20%	5%	P	OLG	5
					OLG	P	10
					OLG	O	5

KEY
N/A No statement of theme given
OLG Our Lady of Guadalupe
O Other
P Participant

cent, $N = 11$), Control/Power (forty percent, $N = 8$), Achievement (forty percent, $N = 8$), and, to a lesser degree, Responsibility (fifteen percent, $N = 3$). The one category that reflected the participant as initiator was Mutuality (twenty-five percent, $N = 5$).

In contrast, the primary active agent under expressive behavior (Table 9) was the participant, particularly in regard to the theme of Affiliation: forty-five percent ($N = 9$) of the respondents initiated this particular behavior; thirty percent ($N = 6$) initiated Appreciation; and fifteen percent ($N = 3$) experienced Harmony. However, for the theme of Nurturance, Our Lady of Guadalupe was found to be the active agent (fifty-five percent, $N = 11$). This was also true for the category of Pleasure (twenty percent, $N = 4$). In both instances the participant was the recipient of pleasure and nurturance individually, as opposed to the group. (See Appendix B-3 for a listing of the women's statements that were categorized under each of DeVos's basic motivational concerns.)

Summary

As mentioned in the preface, a person's or a group's faith in a symbol simultaneously reflects both the believer and the symbol. In spite of—and because of—their history as a twice-conquered people, Mexican American women have the ability to acculturate and endure. But to what extent could Our Lady of Guadalupe be said to have an empowering impact on their lives, if at all? In my study, I asked the Mexican-American women themselves, using an interdisciplinary approach and Our Lady of Guadalupe as a sort of Rorschach inkblot test, to tell me what they saw in her.

SIX

Analysis: Six Questions

E arlier in this book, I asked, "How can I best represent what the women in my research have revealed to me?" In writing this chapter, I was torn between representing them in a neat, logical, grammatically correct profile or allowing the reader to witness the thought processes and feelings of women attempting to articulate that which had never been voiced.

Feminist methodology places—accurately, I believe—a great emphasis on women's experiences as an important source of scholarship. It is crucial to understand and appreciate the challenging process of articulating what we most cherish. Because what we most cherish is usually held in "protective custody" deep within us, we sometimes lose or forget what has been our source of strength—our own voice.

In this chapter I integrate my analysis with the thought process and feelings (sometimes contradictory) of the women interviewed. What I am engaged in is nothing less than the reclaiming of our voice. In raising their voices, I raise my own. I am fortunate to have had a role as midwife in this process.

No matter what discipline one is working in, professionals and scholars must evaluate their theories as applied to living, breathing people with unique psychosocial histories and experiences. As I have already indicated in Chapter 4, the factors of acculturation must be considered. We can no longer speak of "the" experience of a given people because within a group (such as Mexican Americans), we find a heterogeneous group—we must ask again: How long have they been here? Under what conditions did they come? What are their socio-economic statistics, their education? What level of language and cultural proficiency do they have? What is their religious orientation? Are they from rural or urban areas? All of these factors combined give us a much clearer and more adequate picture of the people of whom we are speaking.

Because the focus of this research was to try to identify insights or perceptions that a specific group of people had in relation to Our Lady of Guadalupe, I tried to keep my study group as homogeneous as possible: they were all married, they all had children, they were all second-generation, they all spoke English, and they all had a high school diploma. I am not so much interested in a comparative study as an exploratory study asking Mexican-American women what they think or feel about Our Lady of Guadalupe. I utilized the responses to answer my own research questions.

1. What is the assumptive world of the Mexican-American women in this study?
2. What factors influence and inform this assumptive world?
3. Who is Our Lady of Guadalupe?
4. How is Our Lady of Guadalupe perceived by the Mexican-American women in this study?
5. What is the nature and content of the relationship between Our Lady of Guadalupe and the sample?
6. How does this faith experience of Our Lady of Guadalupe affect the women's overarching assumptive world?

1. What is the assumptive world of the Mexican-American women in this study?

The way these women come to make meaning of their world, or their overall assumptive world, is powerful and has at its core what I term complex relationality. Complex relationality refers to the way in which women's experience is grounded in interpersonal relations and extends itself even into the realm of divinity. This assumptive world is organized, structured, and logical. The logic of relationship is complex, a web of inter-relation and connection that is pervasive in their lives.

Twenty-six year-old Ruth says of Our Lady of Guadalupe, "I love her and she is part of my culture; she is our *madre*."

In working with this population, we cannot afford to be reductive. This assumptive world is a cultural religious assumptive world, centered in complex relationality. Its core, where meaning is made, is characterized by the communal, the interpersonal, values, cultural memory, and consistency.

While this multidimensional system has experiential and affective elements, it also has a logical/cognitive component to it. In this assumptive world nothing is expendable. The focus is experiential and oriented to the immediate or personal needs of these women, that is, family and local issues (which may be followed later by global issues, the environment, etc.). However, every need brings with it all that has come before. What addresses immediate personal needs is not merely immediate and personal. Rather, a whole culture and symbolic system addresses the need, whatever it may be—planning a family, marital harmony, finding a job—and for these women the system works. The way this multidimensional assumptive world operates is illustrated in the following discussion with Yolanda.

Author: Who told you about Our Lady of Guadalupe?
Yolanda: This goes back when I was a little girl so we were raised up and this was one belief taught us by our parents and especially by my mother. That is where I found out about her.
Author: Do you remember what she told you about her?
Yolanda: She told me that if you believe in her nothing could go wrong in that the "crianza" [belief], which she was taught to pass on to us.
Author: Have you found that to be true?
Yolanda: In my own personal experience, I think that I have her like a torch in my life.
Author: What does that torch do for you?
Yolanda: It keeps me going. It keeps me active. More when I am down. I see that she's always been there for me. I've never felt abandoned by her, whereas, other saints perhaps, or Jesus or God I

felt. . . . I know maybe it's not fair to put her above God or Jesus, whatever, but sometimes I find myself doing that.

In this exchange are elements of ritual (in the form of prayer), symbol (as transmitted by cultural memory), the personal (woman's response to Our Lady of Guadalupe), and the interpersonal (family involvement).

The assumptive world of these Mexican-American woman is one which entails struggle and limitations, less in terms of economic poverty than in terms of marginalization. On a personal level, they struggle for identity, self-worth, appreciation, being a better mother, being financially secure, and for the welfare of their children. Those who work outside the home must balance the double burden of maintaining a job and a household at the same time, along with the pressures of changing roles. This level of survival is the root of their assumptive world of struggle, centered on the traditional role of mother and nurturer. If these women do not live up to what is expected of them (an expectation that may come from the culture, family, or themselves), their assumptions about who they should be may result in guilt; the struggle to live up to these expectations may produce anxiety.

Author: Do Mexican mothers identify with her?
Carolina: Yeah, they do a whole lot. I guess because she understands everything that they are going through and it seems like they don't get enough credit for what they are doing and only Our Lady of Guadalupe knows what they are going through and what's their goals, and trying to raise a family and trying to accomplish something. There's too much unselfishness in regards to mothers and Latino women and they're always worrying about what if someone else, or the man in their life or their children.
Author: So you think they need to balance their care for other people with their care for themselves?
Carolina: They need to care for themselves more than they do for whoever surrounds them. But, in turn, you know, I guess there is a balance that can be accomplished, but it's a hard one. Because you

do get into that and caring about yourself, and you lose yourself and I find a lot, I don't know, maybe it's because you can never speak to any of these people on how their true feelings. It's just, yes I'm doing what I'm doing and I guess they see what they've accomplished in their children, but when their children are gone or grown or. . . . That was their role though, I guess, that they did feel satisfied with that.

Author: Do you think that Latina women are satisfied with being mothers?

Carolina: They feel satisfied in any area they might want to accomplish as long as they're appreciated and told, you're doing good, I appreciate you, it's important what you're doing, you're a person, you're a human being, I care about you. It doesn't matter what area they're in, as long as they know what they're doing, and that's what they want to be doing and someone in their life is appreciating what they are doing, being their kids, husband, or family. Out of their own choosing.

Author: Do you think Our Lady of Guadalupe chose what she wanted to do?

Carolina: Yes, definitely. She has a purpose too, and she does it out of love and a million of other things that you can't imagine what is in her head or what. There's so much love there that there is no way of putting a guideline on what kind of love—it's just—you can't imagine.

Although most of the women of the study do not have the luxury of theological reflection, there exists a religious dimension within their assumptive worlds. The women in my study are all Roman Catholics, with Catholic parents and (for the majority) Catholic spouses. They put their world together with vague concepts about God, the divine, and the holy, which—as the interviews indicate—help them cope. The world is given some sense through their belief system. Their concepts of the sacred are simple and relational, and their religious formation is basic, consisting mainly of knowledge of their catechism (rudiments learned through question and answer format). They state that Christmas, Easter, and Jesus are important events or images to them. The focus on Jesus, God, and Mary on the part of these women supports my study and the study done by *Religion in America* (1987) which attested to the fact that these entities are important for Hispanics in general. But it is with Our Lady of Guadalupe that they have daily conversations. Twenty-four-year-old Monica tells me that she can speak to Our Lady of Guadalupe for comfort, help, relief, and peace. When I asked her what kinds of things she talks to Our Lady of Guadalupe about, she responded, "About my day. About my little girl. About my husband. About my family. Mainly just about family, close family and friends."

> *Author*: When you look at her, you say, you feel peaceful inside.
> *Monica*: Yeah, I feel a relaxed feeling, some of my worries can kind of go away, things that I've had on my mind can just disappear for a while. Just like when I go to church, you know, I can just sit there and just feel really relaxed, no worries, just talk. It's like a conversation. Yeah, just really, really peaceful.

The sample was characterized by minimal involvement in organized church and cultural activities. Of the women who had been involved with the Catholic church, most had first been involved as teenagers. They may have become involved because church activity was the only acceptable outlet for girls and was culturally encouraged. The women's lack of involvement in Mexican-American and church organizations may be correlated with their being too busy surviving, the lack of political activity in school, and cultural gender issues. Or perhaps they were never asked to join. The vast majority (eighty-eight percent) of Hispanic Catholics across the nation are not presently actively involved in their parishes. Furthermore, approximately six out of every ten had never been approached to become involved (González and LaVelle 1985:178). Most of them started off active in the church as youths, but as young adults became less involved. Then, as they had children of their own, they sometimes returned as catechists.

The majority of Hispanic Catholics are not actively involved in parish-oriented activities; rather, their activities are much more within the realm of popular religiosity. They attend mass and perhaps register their children in a program. One reason for Mexican Americans' disinterest in church may be that bicultural services and education are not provided. Or if they are offered, people do not have access to them, not simply because of inconvenient locations, but for cultural reasons, such as wanting to bring their children along but not having childcare provided.

Usually the cultural activities are political in nature: once Mexican Americans organize, the organization assumes a political consciousness, in that they have come together to maintain their culture. Women who have been exposed to college usually become interested in Chicano organizations such as MECHA (Movimiento Estudiantil Chicano de Aztlán).

Most of the women in the sample were also not associated with Mexican-American organizations, perhaps because they are working mothers and have been working from an early age. Further, participation in Mexican-American political groups may not be encouraged and/ or supported, and acculturation may also play a role.

There is, however, a deep faith statement that the women make surrounding the story, image, and experience of Our Lady of Guadalupe. The context is simple, but the faith is very complex and relational. Our Lady of Guadalupe makes tangible this religious devotion: a replica of the tilma can be touched, the image can be seen, and the story can be shared with others. Yolanda states, "I look at her and I know that by just going to mass and just touching the frame of where she's at I feel that strength comes to me that keeps saying, 'Yolanda, you can do it, don't worry. I will always be here.'"

The relationship that emerges from this religious and cultural transmission of the story of Our Lady of Guadalupe has reciprocity as one of its elements. There's an exchange—something mutual happens. The women pray to her, light candles, and leave flowers before her image, and they believe that she responds. The story of Our Lady of Guadalupe is a story about a caring God. The image, story, and experience of Our Lady of Guadalupe tell the people that God has not given up on them, affirms them, and is present for them. Moreover, Our Lady of Guadalupe herself is there for them, protects them, and loves them. Although the people's faith may appear uncritical, their faith is salvific because it helps give meaning to their lives.

The image of Our Lady of Guadalupe is a symbol of power for a population in a seemingly powerless situation. Unlike the dominant culture's traditional equation of power with action, for the Mexican-American woman prayer is power. She is inspired, strengthened, given encouragement and hope. Her logic is simple: in the end, all is going to be well. After all, the women conclude, consider what happened to Mary. Her son was crucified, suffered, and died. But he rose from the dead! Therefore, things will be well, despite the torment, pain, alienation, loneliness, confusion, and suffering. This analysis of the meaning of Our Lady of Guadalupe is supported by several statements recorded in the women's interviews. A sampling of their remarks follows:

Catalina: She brings me comfort, sometimes because, ever since I had my children I feel she knows what I mean. She knows how I feel and I can talk to her woman to woman, mother to mother.
Irene: When I'm alone, when I need someone to talk to, when I need help, I go to her—although I don't really talk to her as much as I should. When I pray to her I feel like she's really listening to me; I feel more at ease and I feel like everything is going to be all right. I don't think she ever turns anyone away.

This was the exchange between myself and Edyth:

Author: Why were you drawn to Our Lady of Guadalupe?
Edyth: Because she was Mexican and I'm Mexican.
Author: Anything else?
Edyth: She is a woman.
Author: What does that mean? Why is that important?
Edyth: Because I'm a woman.
Author: So you relate to her?

Edyth: Yeah, I think she feels, as a mother, she feels the things that I feel.
Author: And what is it that you feel?
Edyth: All the pain and suffering in the world, and all those things.
Author: And do you think she understands and hears you?
Edyth: Uh huh. Yeah, certain things that are more female problems, I kind of pray to her more, because I think she'll understand more than . . .
Author: Like what kind of female problems?
Edyth: Like when the kids get to you and sometimes the husband doesn't understand how you get real tense and upset over any little thing and how you need your own piece of time for yourself.
Author: What makes you think she would understand?
Edyth: I don't know, I just think she's listening to me when I talk to her.

How then can we summarize the response to question 1: What is the assumptive world of the Mexican-American women in this study? The overarching assumptive world cannot be separated from its religious dimension. Both have, at core, the values of hope, family, importance of life, and the ability to endure suffering, in particular that of straddling two cultures and not belonging to either one.

Assumptions are tied to beliefs. For these women, the world is ordered. There is a God. God cares for them. God works through Mary/Our Lady of Guadalupe. More importantly, Mary is accessible. She is approachable, and because we can approach her, we can approach God.

Rosío: She has more leverage. . . . Well, I pray to the Virgin like I say the "Our Father," but I speak to the Virgin, you know, like as if she's my mother. . . . Okay—in school—okay, like if someone would ask for something to God directly, maybe he would be more stronger and say, "No, I'm not going to give in to this, you do it this way," or whatever. But then you talk to Mary to talk to God, that's his mother and he gives in to her, you know. He has that love for her when she asks him for something, that he'll bend and he'll give in.

Lest the reader assume that Rosío's family of origin shaped her belief, I asked, "Were your parents like that? Was your mom the one who interceded for you?"

Rosío: No, my mom was the boss.
Author: Your mom was the boss. Did your father intercede for you?
Rosío: No.

Julia theologizes in the following manner in answer to my question, "What do you think is the greatest gift Our Lady of Guadalupe brings?"

Julia: She's always been there for me, but then again she's always been there for God, she's always represented him. Some people don't like the idea or the image that portrays a woman representing a man, but that's the way it's always been. She's like an activist. Always representing him, because she has supposedly appeared in . . .
Author: What is it about God that she represents? What aspect of God does she represent?
Julia: I guess his hope for the world. He doesn't give up on it. Because when you think of God—if I was God I'd get upset, just get rid of everybody, not put up with it because there are so many things taking place, if you talk about it, all at once every day, every day. I mean, it blows my mind to think that God is that tolerant of us. Because when you think of God you can't think of him on human terms. It's impossible to think of him on human terms. When you think of him on human terms, then you realize, "Hey, if I was God I wouldn't be that tolerant."

Catalina said that Our Lady of Guadalupe comes to remind us of a love and a spirit. I asked her to explain.

Catalina: The love of the spirit that I'm saying is this: that she came to remind us the God does exist. That Jesus exists and to me it's almost as though she came and reminded us of that love and that spirit that does exist. For us as something that we shouldn't forget.

These examples illustrate how Our Lady of Guadalupe lies within Mexican-American women's religious dimension, which itself lies within their overall assumptive world.

2. What factors influence and inform this assumptive world?

Many of the factors shaping Mexican-American women's assumptive world—education, economic status, marital status, generation, religion, language of proficiency and preference, age, and so on—are results of acculturation (see Chapter 4). All of these factors contribute to the development of their personal assumptive world.

For the women in this study, their biculturalism is significant. That most of them were second-generation means that, whether consciously or unconsciously, they had to integrate two distinct assumptive worlds. The assumptive world posited by their parents (who for the most part were born and raised in Mexico) interacts with another assumptive world, that of North American society, which the women are exposed to through their American education. Thus culture, or in this case multiple cultures, and the degree of acculturation have an impact. This acculturation process is reflected in the American-influenced women's integration of previous generations' views of Our Lady of Guadalupe.

Yolanda: She may look quiet and calm and everything, but that takes a lot to do. That's why I believe in her the way I do, because I think she's very strong.
Carolina: She is a strong woman, in a quiet sense, in a "I don't have to tell the whole world that I'm strong, I know that I'm strong but

I'm doing it for my very special reasons that if I told you about it you wouldn't understand" kind of thing.

We find in these examples the interplay and the influence of their mothers' culture of origin and of U.S. culture. Despite these women's attempts to question and to integrate these two cultural sets of values in terms of what a woman should be, they are, in essence, creating or attempting to integrate a new understanding of what it means to be a woman. What we are witnessing is the struggle and emergence of a new understanding of themselves as Mexican-American women in U.S. society.

Another indication of the influence of acculturation is the differences in how they spoke of Our Lady of Guadalupe. Those women who were more in contact with their Mexican roots and who had active, daily interaction with other Mexican-American people tended to refer to Our Lady of Guadalupe in terms of "Our Mother" and spoke about her in a more familial, communal sense. In contrast, those women who were born in the United States and were acculturated to the point of perhaps not speaking Spanish well, or not really being affiliated with their culture of origin in terms of language and preference of customs, referred to Our Lady of Guadalupe as "the Mother of Jesus" or as "Mary."

This differentiating may thus be an indication of a certain amount of cultural distancing that these women have gone through or a cultural loss that has occurred in the acculturation process—and as such it is to be regretted.

It is both a cultural loss and a loss in general because Our Lady of Guadalupe functions in a restorative manner. She is a central religious and cultural symbolic memory and attachment for many Mexican-American women. For these women, she is a tool by which they make meaning of their assumptive world. Therefore, when acculturation and other means of distancing from the Mexican-American culture take place, these women lose their access to this primary source of cultural, religious, and symbolic meaning or attachment.

Perhaps the most significant factor in an individual's assumptive world is history. Whether these women are conscious or not of their legacy of colonization and oppression is not relevant; historical events have an effect whether we are conscious of them or not. The impact of systematic marginalization on Mexican-American women is that they find themselves in positions of no control over those institutions which influence them. We have no control over what family we are raised in, what race or sex we are, or what minority population we are born into. We have no control over the past. We have discussed the factors that have an impact on the assumptive world of the Mexican-American woman with regard to her position (traditional role) in the family and society. One such factor is history, a history of conquest, oppression, and social conditioning keeping these women in subordinate positions.

In light of the Mexican-American women's history, how can residues of hope, strength, and courage in their assumptive worlds be accounted for? Could the apparition and message of Our Lady of Guadalupe, a historical event that took place in the midst of devastation and conquest, be this carrier of hope, strength, and courage?

As noted in Chapter 3, Our Lady of Guadalupe instills hope, strength, and courage. She appeared at a time when the people had lost their will to live because everything they had known—their value system, their way of making meaning, their reason for being—had been destroyed. Our Lady of Guadalupe appeared and restored the indigenous peoples by coming to them within their cultural/symbolic system. She came as one of them (mestiza), speaking their language (Nahuatl), bearing their symbols (her image), and bringing a message of hope, presence, and love that restored and strengthened them, thus giving back to them their will to live. This dynamic repeats itself today when these women open themselves up to her.

When Our Lady of Guadalupe appeared to Juan Diego, she empowered him and all indigenous people. She offers hope and resurrection. This historical event continues to have an impact on the assumptive world of Mexican-American women today. As Julia comments, "To me, Our Lady of Guadalupe represents everything we as a people should strive to be: strong yet humble, warm and compassionate, yet courageous enough to stand up for what we believe in."

3. Who is Our Lady of Guadalupe?

Our Lady of Guadalupe has many identities. Historically, she is an "event." Sociologically and anthropologically, she forms and supports both cultural and religious identity. Theologically, she is the Mother of God and the Great Evangelizer. The question as to whether the apparition did in fact occur is inconsequential: for those who believe, no explanation is necessary; for those who do not believe, no explanation will satisfy. In reviewing the literature, though, and observing the impact that it has had on thousands and thousands of people, it is clear to me that something which happened in 1531 has evolved and grown and has become a very powerful influence on these people. My own pastoral experience with people in recent years of speaking on this subject matter has demonstrated to me that her influence over the last 450 years is still prevalent. I have seen crowds of people at workshops have transforming and conversion experiences after hearing my presentation of Our Lady of Guadalupe. I cannot explain it; I can only make an observation. People are deeply moved, they feel healed, they feel encouraged, and they do not feel alone. Somehow this image is able to transmit or communicate itself to people, individuals who will open themselves up to the experience.

A Source of Identification and an Enduring Presence

From a psychological position, Our Lady of Guadalupe is for these women someone with whom they identify. They confide in her, for she is consoler, mother, healer, intercessor, and woman. Our Lady of Guadalupe is the one who appeared to Juan Diego in 1531 and has never left the people or the Americas. This "felt presence" continues to be experienced even today and is key to understanding the impact of Our Lady of Guadalupe.

Spending time at the Basilica of Our Lady of Guadalupe in Mexico City, I spoke with indigenous women in order to elicit their own reflections about the importance of Our Lady of Guadalupe. It took some time to win their confidence and to encourage them to share with me. Gradually a rapport developed, and I asked one of the women:

"Well, what is the significance of Our Lady of Guadalupe? What makes her so different from the other Marys that have appeared around the world?" One indigenous woman in particular made a deep impression on me. I remember that she was the shortest and darkest of the women I was talking to and that she kept repeating that she had nothing to say because she wasn't educated. She rarely looked me straight in the eye; she kept her eyes downcast. When I asked this question, however, she looked at me, and her eyes twinkled. She responded, "Se quedó"— "She stayed."

What did she mean by this? Perhaps it means that with all the other Marian apparitions, Mary comes, makes some sort of request, and then leaves. Only Our Lady of Guadalupe comes, not to make a request, but to make an offering, and stays—in the image of herself that she left imprinted on the tilma of Juan Diego. And the people truly believe that she is alive and present for them.

> *Yolanda*: Her image has always been there in our house, in our home. She's always been there, just like whenever we saw her, there she is. Not in the sense of just the painting, whatever, but we all feel that we need to imitate her, and being a mother, how would she do, how would she handle it.
>
> *Irene*: I hope she never leaves me alone. When I really, really need her, I do feel her presence, when I'm really in trouble and I need help, I do feel it!

Sources of Strength

One of the major recurring themes that emerged in the sample interviews was that Our Lady of Guadalupe is a woman who has known suffering and who is strong. For these participants, Our Lady of Guadalupe was not only a strong woman but a source of strength. There seems to be a relationship between the strength that they receive from their relationship with Guadalupe and the comfort that it seems to bring them. Interestingly enough, when the women in the sample were asked how they knew that Guadalupe was a strong woman their response was that she had had to be strong to see her son suffer. Two manifestations of strength emerged, one being strength as the ability "to do," and the other as the ability to endure suffering.

> *Yolanda*: I think that I have always had her like a torch in my life, a torch that keeps burning, and there is nothing that can turn it off. [to endure]
>
> *Carolina*: She is a strong woman . . . in a quiet sense. [to endure]
>
> *Irene*: I mean, she'd have to be pretty strong to see her son nailed on the cross. [to endure]
>
> *Julia*: Our Lady of Guadalupe represents to me everything we as a people should strive to be: strong yet humble, warm and compassionate, yet courageous enough to stand up for what we believe in. [to do]
>
> *Catalina*: She must have been strong; I don't think any mother that is not strong could have handled all of that. All the punishment, the talk, just everything that happened to Jesus. And she had to. I'm sure she suffered for it also, because she is his mother. [to endure]

To understand the responses to "Who is Our Lady of Guadalupe?" the analysis must not isolate any one dimension of the psychosocial religious perspective. This inclusiveness is crucial for those in the helping professions if they are to help Mexican-American women who have Our Lady of Guadalupe as a prominent figure in their assumptive world. Once the full meaning of Our Lady of Guadalupe is captured, then we can help facilitate a deeper and more cognitive understanding of how this image can help nurture faith development.

Our Lady of Guadalupe can become both a religious and psychological resource for women, especially poor women, who have no other resource. That is, in her image they are able to reaffirm their identity and develop self-esteem. A Mexican-American woman—despite enduring the triple oppression of the dominant society's racism and sexism, as well as her own culture's sexism—can have a sense of belonging in a world where she may feel very isolated and alone. Guadalupe acts as a resource, a coping mechanism for those who have no other resources.

4. How is Our Lady of Guadalupe perceived by the Mexican-American women in this study?

By utilizing the Adjective Check List (ACL), I discovered that these women perceive Our Lady of Guadalupe as having personal worth for them. She is perceived as supportive, stable, accepting, relational, and nurturing, as one who engages in behavior that provides maternal or emotional benefits to others. The women did not see her as conforming, subordinate, critical, or skeptical. She is not seen as engaging in behavior that attacks or hurts others. In this same instrument, some contradictions of qualities did emerge. These women perceived Our Lady of Guadalupe as being both meek and strong-willed, independent and dependent, assertive and shy—all at the same time.

Those qualities of independence and assertion may at first glance appear to be in contrast to nurturance and relationality. The word "independence" lends itself to various shades of meaning: misunderstood, it tends to be thought of as the ability to stand alone, not need another, to be self-contained, rather than being autonomous but able to maintain meaningful relationships.

The contradictions are not necessarily oppositional. These women may be projecting onto Our Lady of Guadalupe the transitions (intrapsychic, spiritual, social-roles conflict, etc.) they themselves may be experiencing. These women, as believers, may use Our Lady of Guadalupe as a vehicle to make the transition from hardship to peace, from confusion to direction, or from despair to hope. It is difficult to make any kind of transition when met by criticism and aggression; most of us tend to respond by moving away or being immobilized and therefore preventing any movement, psychological or physical. Therefore, Our Lady of Guadalupe may be perceived as being open to these women. For example, someone who is longing for independence is made to feel that she has the ability to seek out and receive nurturance.

Acculturation

In Chapter 4, I discussed the tension of acculturation, the attempt by these women to integrate two distinct worldviews: one from their Mexican (Spanish-Indian) heritage and the other from North American society. Bringing these two worldviews together causes conflict. For example, an immigrant family may come to the United States to give the children better opportunities for quality of life, religious and political freedom, and education, while maintaining the parents' cultural ideals of caring for siblings, loyalty to the family, religio-cultural practices, and staying home. Mexican-American women are encouraged to be educated—but humble—in a society that values and encourages aggression, a combination which may evoke anxiety, conflicts, or mixed messages in the women. However, conflict may be seen as the first step in the process of a new creation of self.

Monica: I would love for my daughter to be growing up being herself, modest, strong, intelligent, beautiful. Some people think that Our Lady of Guadalupe is sort of passive and submissive and qualities that are, you know, that especially being a Latino and being in the United States, you don't want to be like that anymore. Well, I have my own ways. I'm kind of old-fashioned, so it's like nothing, they say, "Oh, well, you're old-fashioned," or you know, this and that, but I'm going to try hard to raise my daughter the way it should be, the right way, you know, not growing up around whatever is happening, you know . . .
Author: But what does that mean? What does it look like to be brought up right? What kind of attributes, what kind of traits, for a young girl?
Monica: Well, I know, like myself, I know her—she's, the way things are going now, people are going to look at her, "Oh, well, she's different." But that's going to be okay, in my eyes it will be okay.

Another way of expressing these differing and seemingly conflicting messages is that the bicultural person may be trained cognitively in one set of values and conditioned interpersonally with another set of values that do not dovetail with the former set. How does this conflict influence how these women view Our Lady of Guadalupe? Traditionally, they have been encouraged to emulate Our Lady of Guadalupe's qualities of humility, obedience, and ability to endure. If religious leaders stop at this limited view of Our Lady of Guadalupe, then the women will not have access to her other qualities: being faithful, tenacious, strong, a defender of the poor, and many more. If these latter values/ qualities were emphasized (as some women in this study begin to do: "Well, my grandmother thinks this is Our Lady of Guadalupe, but I think this"), then these women would have that much more to gain from this image of Our Lady of Guadalupe and she might remain a significant aspect of their worldview.

As a second instrument, I asked these women before the interview to write a paragraph about who Our Lady of Guadalupe is for them. She was most frequently perceived as a *mother-type* (fifty-five percent); as *someone to be prayed to* (thirty percent); as one who *brings comfort and peace* (twenty-five percent); and as someone who is *strong and/or gives strength* (twenty percent).

Responses that reflect Our Lady of Guadalupe as mother included the kind of mother ("perfect," "good"), "the mother of Jesus," "Mexican mother," "mother of the world," "Our Mother," and "Mother of God." In addition, Our Lady of Guadalupe elicited reflections on the respondents' own mothers ("She's strong like my mom"). This emphasis on the archetype of mother is not surprising given the significant religiocultural importance accorded to the ideal of motherhood.

These reflections also reveal a belief that Our Lady of Guadalupe will provide such things as peace, comfort, and strength. This belief is manifested by praying directly to Guadalupe for a variety of needs. Although this study was not designed to test Our Lady of Guadalupe as a coping mechanism, there does appear to be some evidence of her being utilized as such. Research will be needed to support this hypothesis.

A third instrument used was DeVos's (1973:19–23) categories (as discussed in Chapter 5) of the "basic motivational concerns in human relations." The structure of DeVos's categories was used as an interpretive tool. Our Lady of Guadalupe is viewed as having achieved something, as being competent, as in control, and as having power. To a larger extent, Our Lady of Guadalupe was most active in terms of expressive behavior—that is, she was perceived as harmonious and as a source of pleasure.

The women's comments suggest that Our Lady of Guadalupe is an image for and source of competence, power, and responsibility.

Twenty-five percent of the women perceive the relationship as both mutual and appreciative. This behavior may surface in popular practices where Our Lady of Guadalupe is asked for favors and, in turn, the women respond by lighting candles, bringing flowers, and praying to her.

The primary active agent under expressive behavior was the participant in regard to DeVos's category of Affiliation, which indicates that it is the woman who seeks to be in relation with Our Lady of Guadalupe. However, in the category of Nurturance, Our Lady of Guadalupe was found to be the active agent.

Our Lady of Guadalupe's instrumental behavior is seen as a force and symbol for the group in terms of potential power, achievement, and competence. The expressive aspects of behavior indicate a strong affective relationship between Our Lady of Guadalupe and this sample of Mexican-American women. The content of that relationship is that Our Lady of Guadalupe is a source of nurturance and pleasure, and the women respond with affiliation, appreciation, and harmony.

5. What is the nature and content of the relationship between Our Lady of Guadalupe and the sample?

This question is where some of the most powerful and affective material emerged. This relationship between Mexican-American women and Our Lady of Guadalupe gives these women a sense and a place of belonging. They are given a place in salvation history. The relationship gives them identity and direction as Mexican Americans, as women, and as mothers.

Many of the women expressed a connection between Our Lady of Guadalupe and their cultural roots, making reference either to their Mexican tradition or to the importance of their own history and customs, as imaged in the story or the iconography of Our Lady of Guadalupe: the color of her skin.

Ruth: I don't know too much, but I feel. You know, it's just some things you don't really know too much about. People make you think and watch the birth inside of you. She is a symbol, just that she's Mexican; it's my culture. I love her and she is part of my culture. . . . I feel proud that we have the Virgin of Guadalupe on our side. I think just having her the way she is, the color, and that she appeared to Juan Diego.

In identifying Our Lady of Guadalupe with their culture, there was an accompanying sense of their historical roots in terms of Our Lady of Guadalupe being a symbol for the indigenous and for the oppressed. There is also an understanding, appreciation, and identification with the role she plays, as woman, mestiza, mother.

Carolina: When I see the image I feel a lot of pain. She's got that expression on her face. There is a lot of pain and a lot of submissiveness. Maybe that's why Mexican mothers and families gather around to pray to her. Mothers always try to encourage their children to look towards her as a protector for the family. I guess they identify with her because she understands everything that they are going through, and it seems like they don't get enough credit for what they're doing, and only Our Lady of Guadalupe knows what they are going through and what their goals are: trying to raise a family and trying to accomplish something.

The world may not value these women; the world may not accept them or their ways. It may even consider their assumptive world superstitious. This religious language, belief, and behavior revolving around Our Lady of Guadalupe, however, is something that happens "among ourselves," within the Mexican-American community. The experiencing of Our Lady of Guadalupe is discussed among themselves, in their communities, where she is ever present—in murals on the "mom-and-pop" stores, worn around their necks on medallions, tattooed on the arms of the *cholos* (the Chicano youth subculture). Her image is seen in countless Mexican and Mexican-American restaurants and homes. She is present and visible in the community. Her image is a testimony that, although we may live in a world where we may not exercise control and are marginalized, the individual knows that he or she is called to a different way of relating, one in which we are sisters and brothers, and everyone is valued and has a place.

The way the women in this sample speak about Our Lady of Guadalupe is experiential, profound, affective, and reciprocal. This reciprocal exchange takes the form of the women coming to Our Lady of
Guadalupe with their concerns (marriage, children, health, problems,
comfort, etc.) and Our Lady of Guadalupe responding.

The Marian role as intercessor, as one who listens to and responds
to petitions, was very prominent in the responses from this sample.
Our Lady of Guadalupe is seen as having legitimate authority and
power, mastery and persuasion, so that she can intercede on the part
of the believer to God. She responds to the needs of the people and
acts on their behalf. These women believe that by asking Our Lady of
Guadalupe, by lighting a candle, by saying a prayer to her, she will, in
fact, deliver what they are asking for.

Rosío: I speak to the Virgin, you know, like as if she's my mother.
And I speak to her about things with me and I pray to her, and I
pray and I hope things are going to be okay, and if she can help
me, you know. And then I pray to God, you know, like she can
speak to him, you know. And maybe he can help her, you know,
and things can work out.

The area from which the content of the petitions comes usually involves marital problems, issues with children, pregnancy, family,
friends, or husband. The petitions are highly interpersonal, or relational, in nature. Other studies need to be done to measure the extent
to which these women answered the way they did because they were
mothers.

Yolanda: When we planned to have the baby, the first thing we
did is, before I actually got pregnant, my husband and I went to
church. We lit a candle at her picture, at her frame, and we asked
her please to help us, to guide us along with this, because she was
the one that we felt would help us through this. And that was the
intention there. I think we have always based our lives around her,
and now that I am a mom she's been more of a powerful image
to me.

Although this perceived exchange takes place in prayer, it is in many ways cathartic for these women. These women expose their vulnerability, their humanity to someone who is not judgmental, aggressive, or apathetic. Our Lady of Guadalupe will listen, will receive what they have to say, and will respond. This response brings healing, hope, courage, strength, and peace. Perhaps more importantly, it gives them the desire and the ability to go on with their lives.

The power, the lasting influence, and the effects that healing has on a person are worth noting. One subject's devotion to Our Lady of Guadalupe has been nurtured and sustained by her family's belief in the Virgin, not just in a popular devotional sense, but because of a concrete historical healing that took place in her life. One of this woman's most powerful childhood impressions is of her father, the symbol of traditional power, falling on his knees to thank the Virgin when told by the doctor that his daughter would be saved. In many ways, this act and the impression it left on the child reaffirmed for the daughter her own relationship with Our Lady of Guadalupe.

> *Yolanda:* Since I was small, I've always had her and I think I've come closer to her when I experienced and saw what my dad went through, thinking that he's going to lose me which I came to a point where if I would have stayed here it would have been one week and that's it—I wouldn't be here today. So I think that's strength for me . . . like because of my dad really believes in her, I think that made me say, "You are special."
> *Author:* Can you say more?
> *Yolanda:* I was six or seven and I got like a cyst or tumor on my face and here they gave me a really hard time about it and so my dad said, "Well, let's go to Mexico, the Virgin will help." So I remember him taking me there and the doctor said she's going to make it. I remember this very clear. I was just a little kid, I remember him falling on his knees saying "gracias" to the Lady of Guadalupe.

There is some evidence that this catharsis is made possible because Our Lady of Guadalupe is a woman, a mother, and one who knows what it means to suffer.

Ruth: I would like to do some things like her . . . to be a strong person, to believe in God and raise your kids the best you can; that's important to me, just to know that she is a mother.

Catalina: It brings inner warmth to talk to another woman. It brings an inner warmth. With God it's more like a satisfaction; with a woman it's more like just talking, being able to talk with someone that had a child, that had . . . and it's more like, I don't know, gee, it's hard to explain. . . .

Monica: All the agony, all the—just to see her own son, you know, die, that's why I say she must have been really strong. You know, like say now, I'm a mom, and I can see, I can put myself in a position, or something, you know. I know that before I would have had my little girl I couldn't understand, like my own mother, you know, couldn't understand the reason she would do things. But now I see. It really opens your eyes.

The role models Guadalupe manifests for these women are those of good woman and perfect mother. The adjectives, however, used to describe Our Lady of Guadalupe were sometimes contradictory, as discussed above. This reflects and affirms the results of the Adjective Check List.

For example, when these women looked at the image of Our Lady of Guadalupe and were asked what kind of woman they thought she was, they responded with such adjectives as kind, trusting, understanding, timid, humble, loving, courageous, strong, shy, sad, patient, gentle, and helpful. After describing those characteristics, they were asked if they wanted to imitate her or be like her. Many of them responded that they might like to, but they could not. This indicates some ambivalence, although it may also be a realistic appraisal of what is not attainable—being the perfect woman. They appreciated or valued these characteristics, but felt incapable of measuring up to them. Despite their inability to live up to the ideals they project onto Our Lady of Guadalupe, as Yolanda said, "I have her like a torch in my life. . . . It keeps me going. It keeps me active."

These women strive to be humble like Our Lady of Guadalupe; unfortunately, they do not appreciate the humility they do possess. When they realize their inability to match their prototype (Our Lady of Guadalupe), it is experienced as a deficiency. The male-dominated culture has presented a limited picture of who Our Lady of Guadalupe is, with too much emphasis on her humility and passivity. This limitation, a predominantly male projection of Our Lady of Guadalupe, is oppressive and only a small piece of who she is.

Our Lady of Guadalupe is not seen in terms of a feast day but as a person with whom the women relate on a daily basis, a person with whom these women can be intimate, honest, and frank about their lived situation. It is interesting to note that the feast of Our Lady of Guadalupe is only mentioned once in the interviews; this is surprising, given that Mary is very important in Hispanic religious life, as the study by the Northeast Catholic Pastoral Center for Hispanics showed (González and LaVelle 1985:103). Some possibilities for the omission in my study are (1) the wording of the question, using the word "holiday" instead of "feast" or "fiesta"; (2) their responses may be a reflection of acculturation into North American Catholic society; or (3) their responses may be the product of their religious education in the North American church.

Our Lady of Guadalupe does not play a prominent role in North American Anglo-Saxon culture, nor do the educational systems (both church and secular) encourage separate cultural symbols. As a result of their attempt to join the dominant culture, and with the pressure of socialization, it is feasible that Our Lady of Guadalupe would not emerge as an important church holiday for these women. The omission may also be an indication that the questions were coming out of the model of organized or institutionalized religion, rather than out of popular religiosity or the people's devotion.

When I first noticed that Our Lady of Guadalupe did not appear to be significant with respect to this question, I called the participants and asked if they had an image of Our Lady of Guadalupe in their homes. Eighty-five percent ($N = 17$) answered "Yes," suggesting that Our Lady of Guadalupe is not a part of organized religion, but rather a part of life, the realm of popular religiosity.

The responses to the questions in this chapter have given evidence of the way Our Lady of Guadalupe exists in the daily lives of these women. They speak to her in their hearts, not only in church. They touch her image, bring flowers, light candles, walk in processions, wear her image around their necks. These are all characteristics of the world of popular religiosity.

6. How does this faith experience of Our Lady of Guadalupe affect the women's overarching assumptive world?

This faith experience of Our Lady of Guadalupe stands in opposition to the scientific, objective, and rational assumptive world of the dominant culture. Therefore, this experience of Our Lady of Guadalupe is perhaps not the most effective medium by which to communicate with the dominant culture the possibilities of merging two different cultures and creating something new. But the story and experience of Our Lady of Guadalupe is a way these women can survive in that dominant culture and its assumptive world.

The story, belief, image, and cultural memory of Our Lady of Guadalupe help Mexican-Americans to envision a different world. In Christian terminology, it is an eschatological experience. In this experience, the marginalized have a special relationship with God, one which is especially meaningful for the people who have no other relationship with anything powerful in this world.

This relationship with Our Lady of Guadalupe—and thus, with God—is a means of empowerment. In this relationship women are not subordinate but rather are invited into a relationship of mutuality and reciprocity. These dynamics are described and supported by the cultural norm of faith (in which Our Lady of Guadalupe is a significant figure) and are visible and made manifest by a recurrent pattern of behavior (reciprocal affection/exchange, daily conversation, and cathartic prayer). The outcome is that the women change, perhaps only attitudinally and not behaviorally, but they feel comforted and this change allows them to make sense out of their world. With this empowering feeling comes the ability to theologize and be active.

Profile of Julia

I began this chapter by articulating the necessity of incorporating this psychosocial religious perspective with living, breathing people. What follows is a profile of one woman from the sample involved in this study, analyzed in light of Fowler's theory of faith development.

Julia is a 28-year-old, first-generation Mexican-American Catholic woman. She is married to a Catholic Latino who is of Costa Rican and Irish descent. They have two children: a son, age seven, and a daughter, three and a half. She completed one year of college and is a full-time homemaker. The data indicate that she has undergone a significant upward movement in her economic status. The family she grew up in had an income of $15–20,000. Her present income is over $30,000. She has participated in both religious and Mexican-American activities. As a teenager, she was involved in church activities, such as prayer groups and youth ministry. As a married woman, she has participated in Marriage Encounter. She is consistent in aligning what is important to her religiously and how she ranked holy days. Julia writes: "Our Lady of Guadalupe represents to me everything we as a people should strive to be: strong yet humble, warm and compassionate, yet courageous enough to stand up for what we believe in no matter how tense the pressure. Above all, obedient to God's will."

Julia demonstrates that she has engaged in some reflection (Individuative-Reflective Faith). She knows the story about Juan Diego and she knows that Our Lady of Guadalupe is Mary. She is capable of seeing beyond the symbol to connect with God. She comes out of her cultural history with an appreciation for the story and appears to have integrated Our Lady of Guadalupe into her psychic life. She is not dominated by the myth and gives evidence of thinking for herself and being who she wants to be: "I had to make up my own mind, my own choices." This is a woman who is educated and has some college education. She is free of economic concerns and has both the opportunity and leisure time to reflect on religious concerns in life, as indicated by her participation in Marriage Encounter (a Roman Catholic activity for marriage enrichment). Julia displays a certain self-confidence; she appears to feel good about herself and about her faith and to feel hopeful about the world. She gives no indication of being in a crisis situation.

Her experience of Our Lady of Guadalupe is that she is refined and yet strong. As Julia states, "She took care of business with Juan Diego." For her, Our Lady of Guadalupe serves as a model for both women and men. Our Lady of Guadalupe is there by her presence, a presence that influences. Julia goes so far as to suggest that Our Lady could influence God.

I would place this woman somewhere between Synthetic-Conventional and Individuative-Reflective Faith. Some of her comments might even indicate that she has glimpses of Stage 6—Universalizing Faith. She has had to face "contradictions": "when you talk to God, I guess there are times when . . . nothing happens. But then there's times when you know you're understood." She obviously has had the experience of God not responding and has dealt with this and incorporated it. Further, she demonstrates her critical reflection when she compares her mother with Our Lady of Guadalupe and concludes that they are not alike: "Maybe I see her through what I think . . . I see her the way I think that God sees her . . . you know she's like, well, I don't even think of my mother that way because my mother is not, well, my mother is very aggressive." Julia concludes that the presence of Guadalupe is a gentle presence: "I see her as being delicate."

She also goes beyond a purely personal understanding of Our Lady of Guadalupe and sees her as representing God—one who affirms "His hope for the world. . . . She has always been there for God, she has always represented Him. Some people don't like the idea or the image that portrays a woman representing a man, but that's the way it has always been. She has always been an activist representing Him."

There are some indications of her connectedness to Our Lady of Guadalupe because of her cultural history: "She is the one I turn to sometimes . . . I guess instinctively because I am Mexican. . . . I've never been attached to . . . the Blessed Mother . . . it's more Guadalupe."

Julia's experience demonstrates that the role of Our Lady of Guadalupe in the women's conscious life varies. That is, at different times, and at different psychological stages Our Lady of Guadalupe is called upon to satisfy different needs. This woman goes to Guadalupe for "marital problems" and "things that unconsciously I know a woman would understand better."

Julia also describes Our Lady of Guadalupe as being courageous, humble, peaceful: "courageous in the fact that she did God's will and she did what was right." When I asked her what feelings came to her when she reflected on Guadalupe, Julia answered, "I guess an understanding, I don't know if it's camaraderie, it just at times makes me feel peaceful. You know, you have, like I said, things for a lot of people aren't easy on earth. You have to look forward to something else . . . when you go to her and you have problems just like when you talk to God, I guess there are times when you talk . . . when you know you're understood."

Although Julia struggles to articulate what it means to have this presence in her life, she is very clear that Guadalupe is nurturing, encouraging, peaceful, and accepting. At the same time, Guadalupe is a symbol that says something to her about God and also about her own identity. When I asked Julia if she had any final statements she wanted to make about Our Lady of Guadalupe, the only thing she had to add was, "She is very beautiful."

This profile illustrates how the responses to the six questions can help us to work with and relate to these women. Julia is educated, knows the story of Our Lady of Guadalupe, and is not in crisis. Although she appreciates Our Lady of Guadalupe, there is no evidence of profound affectivity.

This psychosocial religious perspective helped me address the needs of these women by first directing me as educator and clinician to (1) access their psychosocial reality and (2) remind myself that in working with this population the psychosocial cannot be divorced from the religious and in fact increases the resources that can be accessed for further empowerment.

Conclusion

This analysis has revealed deeper insights into the Mexican-American women of this study's sample: (1) their worldview is one based in complex relationality; (2) there is evidence that most of the women have an affective relationship with Our Lady of Guadalupe; and (3) at different times and at different stages of psychosocial religious development, Our Lady of Guadalupe meets different needs for these women. Given this complex relationality, affectivity, and response to needs, what insights can be offered to those in theological praxis? This question is addressed in the next chapter.

SEVEN

Theological Significance

Within the Roman Catholic Church, devotion to Guadalupe's image and message has been used to discuss the significance and role of Mary (Mariology). While this is a very rich dimension in the faith life of Roman Catholics, I believe it is not the only or the best utilization of the story and image. There are three areas in which the understanding and application of the Guadalupe event may offer some theological insights to the larger church: (1) popular religiosity, (2) Guadalupe as symbol of God's unconditional love, and (3) the need for "feminine" metaphors for a more comprehensive understanding of the divine.

Guadalupe: "Of the People"

To appreciate the significance of Our Lady of Guadalupe it is crucial to understand the context in which she is recognized: popular religiosity. Popular religiosity—that is, how religion is lived and experienced by a majority of people (Schreiter 1985:122)—contributes to our understanding of Our Lady of Guadalupe. The adjective "popular" literally means "of the people." Although there is no comprehensive theory of popular religiosity, I offer a number of considerations that may assist in understanding this dynamic force.

One of the major elements of life among Hispanics in general and among Mexican-Americans in the United States is a system of folk customs and faith expressions termed popular religiosity or *religiosidad popular* (see Rodriguez 1990), which can be defined as the complexity of spontaneous expressions of faith which have been celebrated by the people over a considerable period of time (Elizondo, personal communication). They are spontaneous in that the people celebrate because they want to and not because they have been mandated by the official hierarchy, in this case the Roman Catholic tradition. When I speak of Catholicism in relationship to the Mexican-American culture, I am not referring to the institutionalized version of Catholicism, but to popular Catholicism, handed down through generations by the laity more than by the recognized and/or ordained clergy. There is a distinction between popular religiosity and what is called official religiosity (the institutional church). Although Hispanic popular religiosity has its historical roots in sixteenth-century Catholicism, it has evolved a life of its own that captures the identity and values and inspirations of the people in a way that I believe official religiosity has ignored. This way of being Catholic has always thought of itself as being the true faith of Christians, as being as "equally Catholic" as the clergy's version (Espín and García 1989:70–90).

From the point of view of the institutional church, popular religiosity has not been seen as equally Catholic, but as primitive and backward, perhaps even childlike. But popular religiosity is a hybrid with a life of its own: it continues to exist because for the poor and marginalized it is a source of power, dignity, and acceptance not found in the institutional church. Popular religiosity is not celebrated by a few, but by the majority of the people. It is an expression of faith which has survived over a considerable period with roots in the historical beginnings of Hispanic culture. Above all, popular religiosity is active, dynamic, lived, and has as its object to move its practitioners, the believers, to live their beliefs. That is, the people's own history, both personal and cultural, their own possibility for being saved in history, is expressed. Popular religiosity not only narrates a people's own history, but also acts it out and represents it. The life of the people is life as a human-divine drama in which the natural and supernatural claims are intimately intertwined. It is the humanization of God and the divinization of humanity. Humanity's cause (the poor) is the cause of God; God's actions for the cause of the poor are the actions that humanity must realize (Siller-Acuña 1981c).

In the example of the story and context of Our Lady of Guadalupe, she is God's action on the side of the poor, as is Juan Diego. In his encounter with the religious powers of the time, he is the protagonist, representing all who are marginalized. Similarly, Mexican-American women are the poor; Guadalupe comes and stands among them to reflect who they are—mother, woman, *morena*, mestiza—and gives them a place in a world that negates them.

Some of the documents of the church support this notion of popular religiosity. One of the fruits of the Latin American Church Conference at Medellín in 1968 was the serious discussion about popular religiosity. In *Pastoral Care of the Masses*, the Medellín Conference confirmed that in our evaluation of popular religion we may not take as our frame of reference the Westernized cultural interpretation (Second General Conference of Latin American Bishops 1973) and reaffirmed the vision of Vatican II that the Christian community should be so formed that it can provide its own necessities. (See Chapter 2, on the Nahuatl interpretation of the story and symbology.) This congregation of the faithful, endowed with the riches of its own culture, should be deeply rooted in the people. ("Decree on the Church's Missionary Activity, Vatican II," article 15, in Flannery 1975). The church attempts to discover and respect the presence of God in the concrete expressions of a particular culture. One such concrete expression has been revealed in the apparition of Our Lady of Guadalupe.

Popular religiosity is not only a vehicle for evangelization of many disparate Hispanic communities, but also functions as a form of resistance to assimilation. At the CTSA (Catholic Theological Society of America) Conference of 1989, Doctors Espín and García pointed out that popular religiosity is an important guardian of culture, history, and identity; without popular religiosity we (Hispanics in general and Mexican-Americans in particular) would not be the people we are. "Our identity as an integral part of the Catholic Church would not have survived the frequent clashes with the non-Hispanic—and often, anti-Hispanic—ways of the church in America" (Espín and García 1989:71).

When "we who are church" begin to theologize, we must be conscious that our theological methods are colored by who we are as individuals and which culture we are interpreting from. I express my ecclesiology with the expression "we who are church" to indicate ownership and identity as opposed to handing over of a church that is

something outside of ourselves and a nonevolving institution. Because
Our Lady of Guadalupe lives and breathes within this realm of popular
religiosity, our theologizing must come from within, in this case, Mexican Americans' popular religiosity. There are many living Gospel values
and metaphors of who and what God is that are expressed through
Mexican-American culture. Through popular religiosity, Our Lady of
Guadalupe's presence and message has been able to empower her
people as they interact with the society of the United States. The emphasis on family values, the notion of enduring suffering, the ability to
hope against all hope, a spontaneous feeling of connection and relationality, the unquestioned sense of God's providence as it is delivered
through Our Lady of Guadalupe, the warm conversational sense of the
presence of God, respect and love for all beings—all of these are found
in the image of Our Lady of Guadalupe, as expressed by the women of
the study in Chapter 6. Other popular faith expressions are pilgrimages, to the basilica for example; or sacred moments like Good Friday,
Las Posadas (a reenactment of Mary and Joseph seeking lodging), and
the making of *mandas* (promises). For Mexican Americans, the liturgical year begins with the Marian feast of Our Lady of Guadalupe.

These faith expressions of popular religiosity are readily accessible
to anyone without exception and no one is excluded from participating
in them. They provide a deep sense of unity and joy, while providing
a forum for shared suffering. They are participatory and everyone takes
an active role in them. The faith expressions, while serious, are not
overly organized. The challenge, I believe, is not to eliminate them or
simply to reduce them to a devotional celebration but to bring them
into constant dialogue with the Word of God as contained in Scripture,
tradition, and everyday revelation.

Some principal characteristics of popular religiosity (as set forth by
Schreiter 1985, Galilea 1981, and Marzal 1973) are the assertion that
God exists and everything is controlled by God; that God is rarely
approached directly—hence the importance of powerful mediators
such as Jesus and Mary (Schreiter 1985:158); and involvement and
participation of the whole community (Schreiter 1985:129). There is,
however, a private dimension to popular religiosity which we saw in
the interviews with the women of my study. This private dimension is
built upon the seeking of favors. The world is seen as interconnected

and controlled, which is to say that the concerns of the inhabitants are concrete and requests are directed as immediate needs. Prescriptions for religious activity of the official religion are usually not observed in popular religiosity. For example, attending mass is not considered as important as visiting the basilica (Schreiter 1985:130).

The work of José Luis González (1983) is helpful in expanding our understanding of popular religiosity. He asserts that it operates out of a principle of participation that integrates the world in such a way that everything is perceived as interdependent or relational. For example, I am who I am because I am somehow related to you. Members of community-oriented communities that live and breathe within the realm of popular religiosity refer to each other as *hermana o hermano* (sister or brother).

If God is immediately involved in all worldly affairs, then any event that happens, good or evil (that is, physical, natural evil as opposed to moral evil), can be attributed to God's decision. Even in daily conversation members of the Mexican-American community use the phrase *si Dios quiere* (if God wants).

Vital relationships with nature and nature's integration of positive and negative forces are part of the religious experience in popular religiosity. The world is seen as an interconnected and controlled place and this perception is confirmed by the forces of nature leaving little room for human maneuvering. For example, the earthquake in Mexico in 1985 was attributed to God's disfavor with the people.

Our Lady of Guadalupe's clear connection to nature is seen both in her image and in the fiestas that celebrate her. She is surrounded by the sun, the stars, the moon, and nature. In her fiestas all children carry roses to her image, indicating that a proper celebration of a divine event must contain beautiful elements of nature. In the celebration of Guadalupe, sacred space and time are particularly important. There is a specific day, December 12, designated to celebrate the feast and a specific time, dawn. The people rise at daybreak, the time of new beginnings and the rebirth of the sun, to sing *Las Mañanitas* (a dawn song) to her.

For those who participate in the realm of popular religiosity, religious experience permeates all space and time. There are spaces and times of special strength and power that are part of the religious experience. Some examples of these phenomena are home altars, shrines, processions, and grave sites. Our Lady of Guadalupe clearly represents a familial and relational component in Mexican-American life. She identifies herself as their mother and they are all brothers and sisters to each other. The notion of the sacred being immersed in history is seen as Our Lady of Guadalupe takes a central role regarding the vital necessities of life—food, shelter, safety, and concern for family. She is petitioned for everything from health to the protection of a family-owned business. Her image is found in many homes and businesses in the form of pictures, statues, and altars and is worn on people's bodies in the form of necklaces and even tattoos.

All of these examples are significant to the people and their religious life, but they are not institutionalized, that is, they are not formally structured with rigid rules and procedures.

It is crucial to understand that popular religiosity is rooted in marginality and oppression. Official religiosity usually rejects religious symbols that express the people's marginality, and in doing so also rejects the people. For example, a newly assigned pastor removed the Hispanic people's statue of Jesus, which graphically depicted his suffering. The people, who identified closely with the statue, were outraged and exclaimed, "If you do not want our Jesus then you do not want us either."

In the story of Our Lady of Guadalupe, as in the present, she is still not accepted by some officials of the church. Many parishes with large Hispanic populations still refuse to place an image of our Lady of Guadalupe in their churches. She is, however, recognized and welcome among the people, with whom she shares the experience of rejection.

In the realm of popular religiosity there is a longing to critique and alter our reality and understanding of the sacred. Values and beliefs expressed through liberation theology, such as the value of justice in which all people are co-creators of the reign of God, are part of this longing. I define liberation theology in the terms of Gustavo Gutiérrez (1973): it is a theology of the people whose focus is the struggle of the poor to overcome oppression. It is not a theology created by the intelligentsia, the affluent, or the powerful, but by the poor and oppressed. It is a theology that believes in a God of history, that believes that God is active and present in the world, and that it is not enough that the hearts and minds of women and men be converted, but that the very structures that perpetuate systems of injustice must enter a similar conversion process. This is of course to suggest a radical change in the current social and political situation and overturning the established order. In the same way that Exodus and the Gospels function as a source for theology of liberation, so too has Our Lady of Guadalupe been the driving force behind many struggles for justice among Mexicans and Mexican Americans. We need only look at the Mexican Revolution, the plight of the farm workers, and the emergence of the basic Christian community. When Father Hidalgo called out for the Mexican Revolution in 1821, he rallied the people under the banner of Our Lady of Guadalupe, as did César Chávez and Dolores Huerta in rallying the *campesinos* (farm workers) to fight for their rights as laborers. However, I caution against reducing Our Lady of Guadalupe to a political cause or ideology as the Christian God has been used. Liberation theology may also serve as a challenge to the popular religious notion of ethical and economic evil as being God's will.

Within popular religiosity social organization is predominantly horizontal, with temporal responsibilities which do not separate persons or give unequal weight to functions. In preparation for Las Posadas, Holy Week, Día de los Muertos, or All Souls' Day, everyone plays a role of equal importance, whether their task is to make the tortillas or proclaim the Word. In celebrating Our Lady of Guadalupe, social organization is present in a paramount way. No role is of higher status than any other. All are essential to the celebration, all are valued and affirmed. The presence of clergy, although desired, is not required and the fiesta could easily take place without them.

Guadalupe: Symbol of God's Unconditional Love

As seen in the practices of popular devotion, presence and immediate contact are vital in the world of symbols. The image of Our Lady of Guadalupe in the churches must be accessible and within reach, so that devotees may touch it or rub their hands across the frame or touch the candle before the picture. It is not enough to recognize a symbol; it must be held, experienced, and received. The symbols that emerge from the Guadalupe event are concrete: flowers, music, the sun. Not only does she come in her full presence adorned with cultural symbols that the people recognize, but she enters into their history. Through her affirmation and acceptance of her people, she gives them a reason to hope and to live.

The symbol of Our Lady of Guadalupe manifests the creating energy and creative power which is God. She is nothing less than God's self-giving, or grace. I understand grace in relational terms: not so much God as a person I love or God as a person who loves us, but God as love itself. God is love and the way of experiencing that love is within the dynamic of a relationship. Divine nature is relational and self-sacrificial: to share in the life of God, for God to give God's whole self to us, means that we live in some kind of relationship. How do we know we are living in that kind of relationship? We need to look at the relationships in our life to answer this question: Are they life-giving? Are they hopeful, affirming? Do they inspire growth? In Mexican-American women's relationship with her, Our Lady of Guadalupe comforts and renews their spirit.

God's grace is universally and unconditionally offered; it is God's self-giving. Our Lady of Guadalupe becomes a symbol and a manifestation of God's love, compassion, help, and defense of the poor. She restores her people's dignity and hope and gives them a place in the world and in salvific history. The first manifestation of God's creative energy and creative power is creation—to give life, to bring something forth. To this extent, I believe that Guadalupe may be a symbol of that grace of God. It is the dynamic giving of oneself to another, Guadalupe offering herself to the people in a life-giving and transforming way that is full of grace. One of the first things we say about the historical Mary is that she is filled with grace.

One of the stations of this grace, or God's self-giving, is experienced through the women's relationship with Our Lady of Guadalupe. Presence should be first among our pastoral tasks because of the high value Mexican-Americans place on relationality and interdependence. Within a pastoral context, then, presence is understood as visibility, accessibility, active listening, and sustained dialogue with Our Lady of Guadalupe. These factors are evident in the women's stories as they relate their relationship and their understanding of what and who Our Lady of Guadalupe is.

There is a danger of mistaking the *symbol* for the reality. Our Lady of Guadalupe is not God; she is a metaphor for God. All the qualities attributed to her (loving, comforting, present, maternal) are qualities of God. Her image is as a nurturing woman and mother, but God has what have been stereotypically designated as female as well as male qualities. Thus, the symbol of Our Lady of Guadalupe is a matrix of meaning: she tells us something about who we are (in the Mexican-American women's case, that they are female, mother, *morena*, marginalized), and she tells us something about who God is: God is the source of all life, maternal, compassionate, and present, and protects the poor and marginalized.

At the heart of any assumptive world for an individual or an overarching culture, there is always some ultimate symbol which ties everything together and which people can give themselves to. As anthropologists would say, an ultimate symbol should be capable of containing within itself the highest aspirations and desires of the people. In Julia's words, Our Lady of Guadalupe does this: "Our Lady of Guadalupe represents to me everything we as a people should strive to be: strong yet humble, warm and compassionate, yet courageous enough to stand up for what we believe in, no matter how tense the pressure. Above all, obedient to God's will." As a universal symbol Our Lady of Guadalupe bridges cultures: for Mexican-American women she affirms them because she looks like them and is a woman and a mother, and she affirms their Anglo-educated side, challenging sexism.

Although she may be more appealing to darker-skinned people than to light-skinned people, her message affirms the darker-skinned but also transcends ethnicity. She is grounded in Mexican history, but functions as a symbol of God's love, not only for Mexicans but for everyone.

Certain symbols may not be effective for an individual or for a group. For example, the symbol of God the Father may not work for the Mexican-American community, so the symbol of Our Lady of Guadalupe may speak more to them about the nature of God or about how God relates than do many of the classical symbols of God. Mexican-Americans may experience the Divine working through Our Lady of Guadalupe in symbols that are not the standard ones of official religiosity.

The understanding of *where* Guadalupe manifests herself is of utmost importance. Within the context of popular religiosity, that is, a context where the people are, a context and source of people's identity and values—this is where Our Lady of Guadalupe engages the people. The things for pastoral ministers and theologians to watch most closely are the ultimate questions her devotees ask, the places God is present in their lives, and how they celebrate and bring that to expression. These things I believe are revelatory.

Guadalupe: The Feminine Face of God

The significance of Our Lady of Guadalupe in popular religiosity must assume a dialectic posture with contemporary Catholic theology, and so we look at the insights that feminist theology has given us in terms of the maternal or feminine face of God.

Hispanic colonial evangelization taught that the Christian God was more powerful than the indigenous gods. The proof was that those who fought under the banner of the Christian God became successful conquerors. The Christian God was, more likely than not, imaged by those in power to reflect themselves. There is thus a metaphor and a constellation of images surrounding the God brought by the conquistadors.

Christianity preached forgiveness, mercy, compassion, and reconciliation. The symbol used by the dominant Spanish culture to communicate these values was the Virgin Mary. Representing Christianity to the newly conquered, the missionaries did not connect these fundamental Christian elements with God in their catechisms; they did connect them with Mary. These traits at the time were held to be maternal and also may have reflected the way the Spanish might have wanted the Indians to feel toward their oppressors. All of these "maternal" qualities were attributed to God by the missionaries, but in the conquered population's mind the association of God with the powerful and victorious was primary. Mary, however, was presented as loving, comforting, and accepting; she was clearly the faithful and solidarious one (Espín 1991:99).

Even in the early history of Hispanic Christianity, there is a dichotomy of attributes: those that are powerful but somewhat alienating were attributed to the male white European Christian God, and the more affective, maternal reconciling ones to the Virgin Mary. Dr. Espín (1991:98) asks, "How do Hispanics experience God as faithfully solidarious with them?" He suggests that perhaps we need to remove from the word "God" all the dominant, conquering demons it evokes.

If, instead of looking for the explicit use of the term "God" or other God-related activities, we look at instances when Mexican Americans seem to be relating explicitly or implicitly to a divinity closer to the Gospel's real God, we will discover a very clear presence of faithful solidarity in their operative definition of that God. The surprise is that this faithfully solidarious one is Mary, the Virgin, says Espín (1991:100). There is historical evidence that these stereotypical attributes of the feminine have been presented through Marian symbols and thus have traditionally been ascribed to Mary as Our Lady of Guadalupe. It is easy to perceive Our Lady of Guadalupe as the maternal or female face of God, because she evokes an unconditional love, solidarity, and a never-failing presence at the affective level. But in doing so, we inaccurately remove these attributes from where they rightly belong: to God.

I myself struggle with this concept, because naturally I am drawn to the caring and nurturing presence of Our Lady of Guadalupe, but I am committed to retrieving the basic meaning of her message and placing it within a new context. I am in a relationship with her; when a relationship is expressed, it reveals something about both the person and (in my case) that person's relationship with God through Our Lady of Guadalupe. What does the metaphor of Our Lady of Guadalupe tell us about who God is?

A tremendous amount of scholarly work has been done on Mariology, less on Our Lady of Guadalupe. Because Our Lady of Guadalupe is a Marian image, Mariology can contribute to an understanding of the image of Our Lady of Guadalupe and the truth about God which she expresses. In this section I rely heavily upon the insightful scholarship of Elizabeth Johnson.

The Marian phenomenon throughout history has been powerful precisely because it is a female representation of the divine, bearing attributes otherwise excluded from mainline Christian perceptions of God as Father, Son, and Spirit. In official religiosity, the feminine face of God has been suppressed and excluded, and female images of God have migrated to the figure of Mary. Now some Catholics feel what Johnson calls a theological necessity: to express the mystery of a Christian God adequately, God must be envisioned in ways inclusive of the reality of women and other marginalized groups. Those elements in the Marian symbol which properly belong to divine reality must be retrieved (Johnson 1989:500–501).

Toward a more gender-inclusive theology of God, the Marian tradition offers its powerful maternal and other female images of the Divine. Through this process of integration, the figure of Mary no longer has to bear the burden of keeping alive female imagery of the Divine, and the figure of God becomes our loving Mother to whom we entrust our needs. Again, for some, it may be difficult to image the male face of God as a loving provider, but the Marian image is not meant to replace but to enhance the personhood of God.

There are many incidents of the split of divine attributes traditional in Christianity. In an influential work, theologian Edward Schillebeeckx (1964:101–128) argued that God's love is both paternal and maternal but that the mother aspect of God cannot be expressed through the historical figure of Jesus as a male. God selected Mary so that the "tender, mild, simple, generous, gentle and sweet" aspects of divine love could be made manifest: "Mary is the translation and effective expression in maternal terms of God's mercy, grace and redeeming love which manifested itself to us in a visible and tangible form in the person of Christ, our Redeemer."

Feminist theologian Elisabeth Schussler Fiorenza (1979) explains the split by a long process of patriarchalization, as a result of which the divine image became more remote and judgmental, while Mary became the beloved "other face" of God. Intellectually a distinction was maintained between adoration of God and veneration of Mary, but on the affective, imaginative level people experienced the love of God and the saving mystery of divine reality in the figure of Mary (Johnson 1989:513; Schussler Fiorenza 1983:130–140).

What accounts for Hispanics' massive and persistent devotion to Mary? Latin American and U.S. Hispanic theologians view Marian images from a liberationist theology point of view: Mary's cult appeals strongly to the oppressed because she gives dignity to downtrodden people and thus renews their energy to resist assimilation into the dominant culture. Further, as Virgil Elizondo points out, the cult not only liberates downtrodden peoples but also liberates us from a restrictive idea of God (Johnson 1989:514; Elizondo 1977:25–33, 1983b).

Within the Roman Catholic tradition Our Lady of Guadalupe is a Marian image, and within the Hispanic culture she is a mestiza, a mixture of both Spanish and Indian blood. The event and figure of Our Lady of Guadalupe combined the Nahuatl female expression of God with the Spanish male expression of God which had been incomprehensible to the Indians' duality—their belief that everything perfect has a male and female component. Each understanding of God was expanded by the other, yielding a new mestizo expression which enriches the understanding of the selfhood of God (Johnson 1989:515). "The results of the new expressions of God and the Mother of God are an amazing enrichment to the very understanding of the self-hood of God. There is no longer the European expression of God-Nahuatl, but a new mestizo expression which is mutually interpreted and enriching" (Elizondo 1983b:61).

"Even for those who do not find Mary a personally viable religious symbol, she nonetheless does represent the psychologically ultimate validity of the feminine, insuring a religious valuation of bodiliness, sensitivity, relationality, and nurturing qualities. . . . The symbol of Mary as feminine principle balances the masculine principle in the deity, which expresses itself in rationality, assertiveness, and independence" (Johnson 1989:517).

Within the Roman Catholic tradition Marian devotion and the study of Mary are sources of understanding the divinity in female language and symbols. Johnson identifies five female images for God: mother, divine compassion, divine power and might, divine presence (immanence), and a source of recreative energy. I take the same five images and apply them to Our Lady of Guadalupe.

Our Lady of Guadalupe manifests God as mother: Our Lady of Guadalupe identifies herself as Our Loving Mother and people see her as a mother, a maternal presence, consoling, nurturing, offering unconditional love, comforting—qualities which tell us that mother is an appropriate metaphor for God. "Transferring this maternal language back to God enables us to see that God has a maternal countenance. All that is creative and generative of life, all that nourishes and nurtures, all that is benign, cherishes, and sustains, all that is solicitous and sympathetic originates in God/Her" (Johnson 1989:520).

Madonna Kolbenschlag's work *Lost in the Land of Oz* (1988:9) addresses the importance and necessity of the maternal. She identifies orphanhood metaphorically as "the deepest, most fundamental reality: experiences of attachment and abandonment, of expectation and deprivation, of loss and failure, and of loneliness." What message does Our Lady of Guadalupe offer to the spiritual orphans of the twentieth century through the metaphor of mother? That we are lovable and capable, that we belong, that we can grow and be transformed, and that there is a reason to live and a reason to hope.

Our Lady of Guadalupe manifests God's compassion: Our Lady of Guadalupe came to show forth her love, compassion, help, defense, and her presence among the people. "Returning this language to God, to whom it properly belongs, enables us to name the holy mystery as essentially and unfathomably merciful. God is the Mother of mercy who has compassionate womb-love for all God's children. We need not be afraid to approach. She is brimming over with gentleness, loving kindness, and forgiveness" (Johnson 1989:521). In the interviews with the women in my study, we have seen how they take their troubles to Our Lady of Guadalupe because they experience her as being compassionate and responsive to their needs, in a way which, if present, nevertheless has not been identified in their relationship to God. She will understand them better than the male face of God because she too is female and a mother.

Our Lady of Guadalupe manifests divine power and might: The word "power" comes from the Latin *posse*, meaning to be able, yet often when we think of power it is in terms of having power *over* someone or something, rather than having power *with*. Again and again, the women in my study found that in encountering and being in the presence of Our Lady of Guadalupe they regained their sense of self in an accepting and empowering relationship.

Our Lady of Guadalupe images power *with*, in a dynamism centered around mutuality, trust, participation, and regard. The power accessed by these women in their dialogue with Our Lady of Guadalupe is the power of memory, which she continues to stand for, justice, solidarity with the oppressed, belonging, unconditional love, the power of expressed feelings and sharing (women come to her and share their immediate needs and they feel heard). The power of commitment, the power to endure suffering, the power of caring, the power of risk ("As long as she is beside me, I'm going to keep trying"), the power of naming their fears, the power of knowing that the way things are is not the way things are meant to be, and with her help they are encouraged and given hope. She gives them not the will to suffer under injustice, but the will to continue *la lucha* (the struggle).

Our Lady of Guadalupe manifests, symbolizes, and activates the power of the people, in this case the power of the poor people. In the *Nican Mopohua*, it is the poor Indian Juan Diego who evangelizes the bishop, whose conversion enables him to work with the poor, the marginalized, and the indigenous. Siller emphasizes the Nahuatl image of *yollo* (the heart), which moves us to action; if a devotion to Our Lady of Guadalupe does not bring us closer to action and to solidarity with the cause of the poor, then the devotion is not authentically Guadalupana. This heart, love, relationship, and consciousness emerging from the poor call us to act on behalf of the poor.

Our Lady of Guadalupe manifests the presence of God: I have addressed this in the previous section about Our Lady of Guadalupe as a symbol of God's unconditional love.

Our Lady of Guadalupe manifests God as a source of recreating energy: "Attributing this imagery of plenty and new beginnings directly to God allows us to affirm that it is God's own self that is the source of transforming energy among all creatures. She initiates novelty, instigates change, transforms what is dead" (Johnson 1989:524). This is clearly seen in the timing of the apparition of Our Lady of Guadalupe. As argued in Chapter 2, she came at a time when the people were spiritually dead, abandoned by their gods, with no reason to live. Our Lady of Guadalupe's coming restored the people's reason to live and to hope. She identified herself using the familiar Nahuatl expressions of God, which showed the people that she came from the region of the gods.

In the Nahuatl culture the one supreme god, Ometeotl, was the god of duality, with both masculine and feminine principles. Because Ometeotl was invisible, there was no physical representation of this god, who was known by the titles of the Most True God, the God Who Gives Us Life, the Inventor and Creator of People, the Owner of What Is around Us and Very Close to Us, and the Owner and Lord of the Earth (Siller-Acuña 1989:48).

The Nahuatl names for God are not just dimensions but ultimate metaphors for who God is. And because they contain that which gave life to the people, those metaphors become a source of recreating energy.

EIGHT

Conclusions

Ultimately, this study is about faith and the impact of one particular religious symbol—Our Lady of Guadalupe—on the faith life of Mexican-American women. As a Latina woman, theologian, and clinician, I found that any one of the psychosocial or religious disciplines alone did not capture the complexity or dynamics of the relationship between Our Lady of Guadalupe and Mexican-American women. Therefore, I developed a more inclusive framework, the psychosocial religious perspective.

Our Lady of Guadalupe is a powerful cultural and religious symbol for people of Mexican descent, as evidenced in both historical accounts (Burrus 1981, 1983; Lafaye 1976; Watson 1964) and popular religiosity. Anthropological literature (Elizondo 1978, 1980b, 1983a, b; Siller-Acuña 1981a, b, c; Turner and Turner 1978) confirms that Our Lady of Guadalupe is a symbol of Mexican consciousness, combining elements of Spanish and indigenous roots. Theological literature views Our Lady of Guadalupe as, among other things, one of the unifying forces of the diversity of groups that make up the Mexican people (Lafaye 1976).

Although she is important to Mexicans and Mexican Americans, I believe that a significant personal or affective relationship exists between Our Lady of Guadalupe and Mexican-American women in particular. This relationship is expressed in feasts, devotions, pilgrimages, and the prevalence of the image of Our Lady of Guadalupe in all areas of their lives. Elizondo (1980b:112), a pastoral theologian, has written about the "good news of Our Lady of Guadalupe." He contends that the miracle of the apparition is that "it continues to penetrate the hearts of the Mexicans in such a way that they instinctively know that she is the mother of consolation and liberation."

As a theologian and a member of the Roman Catholic church, I am particularly interested in the influence that the image of our Lady of Guadalupe has on the self-image and religious identity of Mexican-American women. Although the authors cited above speak of the importance of Our Lady of Guadalupe, they lack data explaining the relationship between Our Lady of Guadalupe and Mexican-American women. Most of the literature presently available addresses the image of Our Lady of Guadalupe in general thematic terms rather than focusing on the experience of Mexican-American women. Lafaye (1976:1) states that the focus of his work on Guadalupe is "to shed light on the formation of Mexican national consciousness with the aid of its religious components." Elizondo (1980b:xiv) sees Guadalupe as "the key to a proper understanding and appreciation of the new Christianity of the new world and of the Mexican-American Christian consciousness today."

I would like to echo the importance and affirm the contributions that these authors have made. The position that I take is unique primarily because no one had ever asked Mexican-American women what they thought about the image of Our Lady of Guadalupe or how it influenced their lives. This is a voice that has not been heard, a voice that has been sought and articulated by one of their own.

This work focuses on understanding the religious life and perceptions of a group of Mexican-American women. It provides factual data that challenge the facile assumption that Mexicans are Catholics as if there was nothing more to say and challenges the perception that Guadalupe is the model of submissive, passive Mexican womanhood. Rather, she is a role model of strength, enduring presence, and new possibilities.

In looking at the sample in light of what the literature says about Mexican-American women in general, we find many differences. But the women's faith statements are representative of the larger population of Mexican-American women who continue to have devotion to Our

Lady of Guadalupe. This observation is further supported by my own pastoral experience and the experience of others.

The women in this study see Our Lady of Guadalupe as strong, competent, warm, humble, personal, patient, nurturing, maternal, and accepting. They relate to Our Lady of Guadalupe as a role model to whom they pray, a mother, one who intercedes, heals, affirms, gives them strength, and gives direction for a new world order based on love, compassion, help, and defense.

The psychosocial religious perspective and the questions that emerge are useful in addressing and identifying the relationship between Our Lady of Guadalupe and Mexican-American women. There is, in fact, a logic and system to the way these women view the world and the way they come to make meaning. And the core of how they make meaning, the core of the logic to their worldview, is relationship.

The Juan Diego paradigm of faith development that emerges from my research parallels the faith development of the women in this study. As the image of Our Lady of Guadalupe had a liberating effect in the life of Juan Diego in terms of his relationship to God and the world around him, this same image can have a liberating effect on these women if the message is lived out.

I discovered through the interviews (1) that the relationship of these women to Our Lady of Guadalupe parallels the initial perceptions and relationship of Juan Diego in that a strong affective bonding is achieved; (2) that these women have a limited knowledge of the one who appeared at Tepeyac; and (3) that, as happened with Juan Diego, encountering Our Lady of Guadalupe could lead to greater empowerment.

For the women in this study, their relationship to Our Lady of Guadalupe was expressed in terms of strength, hope, "I wait for her to answer me in my heart," "I really feel . . . she hears me and understands," peace of mind, gentle, caring, loving, comfort, "she brings me . . . happiness." The women in this study demonstrate that they do experience some connection with Our Lady of Guadalupe to varying degrees.

Most of the women in this study also recognize that Our Lady of Guadalupe is the Mary of the Roman Catholic tradition. They refer to her as "the mother of Jesus Christ and she is the one that stood by her son when they put him on the cross," "the mother of Jesus," "Mary the mother of God," and as "someone who can speak to God for me . . . the Queen of the Church."

To a certain extent, the women in this study reflect the same experience and the same relationship that Juan Diego had with Our Lady of Guadalupe. He trusts her; they trust her. He speaks to her in familiar, loving terms; the women see Guadalupe as someone they can talk to. He knows she is the Mother of God; the women are very aware of that fact. Yet this relationship is uncovered in the first and second apparitions of Our Lady to Juan Diego. What about the rest of the story? What about his being sent on a mission? What about his development as a person, as one who brought a message to "the establishment?" What about the support and encouragement that Our Lady of Guadalupe gave Juan Diego when he doubted his abilities, when he wanted to give up, when he was rejected by the bishop? These women do not experience themselves as being challenged by the message of Our Lady of Guadalupe, nor are they encouraged to be. The question arises, then, as to whether these women, and Mexican-American women in general, have been exposed to and understand the possibilities surrounding the Guadalupe event.

Juan Diego's relationship to Our Lady of Guadalupe undergoes progressive stages that move from the personal and affective to a challenge and call to mission. The Mexican-American women's relationship was found in this study to be involved in a similar process. They have had some encounter with "our Lady"; they experience joy, identification, peace, comfort, and understanding. They have demonstrated a bond with her and established trust in her, as a consequence of either a personal encounter or a family member's advice *pedir la virgen*, to ask the Virgin. Their relationship and understanding of Our Lady of Guadalupe must go beyond the relational mutuality, basic trust, and dependence on the literal observances of the Mexican-American and Catholic community to the liberating call of mission as experienced by Juan Diego. This call is to speak prophetically to both church and society about the "temple" as a place where the poor and marginalized can feel at home. These women are also called to a liberating faith that seeks a kingdom of peace and justice—a home for themselves and their families.

It appears that the relationship of these women to Our Lady of Guadalupe is the same as has been fostered in the Catholic church in regard to any Marian devotion. She is a "double-edged" symbol of human faith and discipleship and of the fact that God can be imaged with feminine and maternal characteristics (Johnson 1989:519). Perhaps missionaries in Mexico in the sixteenth century, steeped in the European Mariology of the time, "purified" the Guadalupe image by emphasizing those characteristics common to other Marian devotions. Given their confusion about the name and their association with the Virgin of Estremadura, Spain, it can be assumed that traditional teachings about Mary (motherhood, long-suffering, fidelity, purity, etc.) would be applied to appearances at Tepeyac. The result of this "tradition" appears to be that Guadalupe is not perceived as different from the apparitions at Lourdes, Fatima, Czestochova, and elsewhere, with the notable exception that she is Mexican, *morena.*

Although the women in this study were more educated than the general Hispanic population in the United States, they still did not know the story of the Guadalupan apparitions. They knew only of an "appearance" and a "miracle" having to do with flowers and an image. Lacking knowledge of the story and all the elements of symbolism within the narrative and the image, these women have been deprived of an important tool for their own development, a role model that goes beyond that of being a long-suffering mother, wrapped in blue, and set on a pedestal.

Unlike Juan Diego, the women in this study have never questioned or been challenged about their beliefs. In answer to questions in the interviews about the story and the passing-on of their beliefs, they gave the impression that they would pass on what had been passed on to them: the image of a mother who endured the sufferings of her son, who showed compassion and defense for the indigenous, someone who would "be there" in times of trouble. After the interview most of the women expressed surprise that someone would be interested in what they thought. They said that no one had ever asked them about Guadalupe, and they had never given any thought to who she was for them. Their questioning and reflection on meaning may be an indication of readiness for further faith development.

Once they have been challenged about their relationship to Guadalupe only as mother, as suffering, as perfect—that is, once they begin to rethink their image of who Guadalupe is and who, in turn, they themselves are—they will experience tension with their traditionally expected role within the home. In other words, once Mexican-American women begin to question the role model they are expected to follow, they will experience tension and conflict with the family's and the culture's expectations of them, which are also based on perceptions of Guadalupe. The two perceptions will conflict.

This tension will be aggravated as more and more Mexican-American women leave the home to enter the work force. Expected and taught to be gentle, quiet, and meek, these women will be faced with situations in which the personal skills demanded of them include being competitive, assertive, and articulate. Surprisingly enough, these needed skills are also demanded of Juan Diego. And it is Our Lady of Guadalupe who helps him to discover them.

Mexican-American women will also face this forced integration of traditional symbols and images with their new roles within U.S. society. Religious and cultural events will need to be celebrated with a mixture of traditional and newer symbols and meanings. The role of mothers as the principle caretakers of the children needs rethinking; perhaps husbands can take on some of those responsibilities. As acculturation becomes a fact of life, the exploration and rethinking of the image of Guadalupe can offer a powerful tool for Mexican-American women. Bringing the image and devotion of Our Lady of Guadalupe in line with the new situation of Mexican-American women in the United States is akin to what Guadalupe calls upon Juan Diego to do: take the traditional religious symbol of flowers into a new situation, give it new meaning, and thus transform it.

Likewise, upon reaching this stage, Mexican-American women will find themselves caught between their "new" vision of Our Lady of Guadalupe as one who empowers and the very real situation of a culture still in need of transformation. There is no doubt that there will be strong tension between women who embrace the whole story of a Guadalupe who empowers the "little one" and a culture and a society that much prefers the silent, suffering, perfect mother.

The women in this study were not involved in organizations of either a Mexican-American or a Catholic nature. Given the place that Our Lady of Guadalupe holds in the lives of these women, if they were to rethink their accepted image of who Guadalupe is, guided along the paths of development outlined above, I believe that they would be empowered to become involved, to demand a more active role in the church and in society. Supported by an inner strength and conviction nurtured by their relationship with this newfound Lady, Mexican-American women would soon find themselves, by sheer numbers alone, a powerful agent in the transformation of society. The institutional church can serve as a valuable support in this process of liberation. This, however, would demand a significant shift in attitude and practices with regard to women.

Mexican-American women must be made aware of the entire story of Our Lady of Guadalupe with all of its implications to gain a greater sense of pride in their cultural and personal identity. Building on the established relationship, Mexican-American women can be helped to see that, instead of accepting a limited cultural view of their roles as mothers, they are being called to relate and connect to the world outside the home. Just as Our Lady of Guadalupe affirmed Juan Diego in his moments of self-doubt and sense of unworthiness, Mexican-American women will find inner strength and conviction to make decisions outside of the domestic sphere. Mexican-American women have a unique opportunity to proclaim to the world the Guadalupan message of hope, love, and justice, a message of care and "connectedness" to the wider community. This universalization ultimately means that Our Lady of Guadalupe can be seen as a source of empowerment not only for Mexican-American women, but for all women. The story and iconography of Our Lady of Guadalupe is a starting point for further work in the areas of the personality sciences and religious studies. It is my hope that the larger church also experiences the healing presence and challenge of Our Lady of Guadalupe.

Appendix A-1:
Demographic Questionnaire

INTAKE QUESTIONNAIRE   NAME _____

                                        ADDRESS _____

                                        PHONE # _____

1. Sex: M   F
       1   2

2. Age: ____

3. Marital Status: (circle one) S M D W Sep Partnered
                                 1   2   3   4   5   6

4. Is your spouse:
(circle one) Mexican   Mexican-American   Chicano?

5. Is your spouse Catholic? Yes No

6. Do you have any children? Yes No

7. Have you had any children? Yes No

8. Please list their sex and age: _____

_____

_____

_____

_____

9. How much education have you had?
   Education (circle highest degree completed):
   1 2 3 4 5 6 7 8 9 10 11 12 College 13 14 15 16

   Advanced Degree _____ What _____

10. Occupation (title and description) _____

_____

_____

11. Your present income per year
    (check one, include spouse or partner)
    Under 5,000 _____(1)_____
    5–10,000 _____(2)_____
    10–15,000 _____(3)_____
    15–20,000 _____(4)_____
    20–30,000 _____(5)_____
    Over 30,000 _____(6)_____

12. The family I grew up in had an income of
    Under 5,000 _____(1)_____
    5–10,000 _____(2)_____
    10–15,000 _____(3)_____

15–20,000   _____(4)_____

20–30,000   _____(5)_____

Over 30,000   _____(6)_____

13. Your birthplace _____

14. Mother's ethnic/religious background _____

15. Father's ethnic/religious background _____

16. What generation Mexican American are you? _____

17. Length of Bay Area residence: _____

18. What other organizations or groups of a Catholic nature are you affiliated with?

   _____

   _____

   _____

19. What other organizations or groups of a Mexican-American nature are you affiliated with?

   _____

   _____

20. List the activities of a Catholic nature in which you are now involved:

   _____

   _____

21. List the activities of a Mexican-American nature in which you are now involved:

_____

_____

22. If you have children, please list the organizations or groups of a Catholic nature they belong to:

_____

_____

23. If you have children, please list the organizations or groups of a Mexican-American nature they belong to:

_____

_____

24. At what age did you get involved in church-related activities?

_____

_____

_____

25. What do you consider to be the most important and why?

   a. Church Holiday _____

   b. Symbol _____

   c. Belief _____

26. On a scale of 1–7 with 7 being the highest, rank the importance of the following:

Good Friday ___   Christmas ___

Easter ___   Feast of Our Lady of Guadalupe ___

Ash Wednesday ___   All Souls' Day ___

Ascension of Christ ___

27. On a scale of 1–7 with 7 being the highest, rank the following cultural holidays:

Cinco de Mayo ___   16th of September ___

Día de las Madres 5/10 ___   Día de los Muertos 11/2 ___

Día de la Raza 10/12 ___   Grito de Dolores 9/15 ___

Día del Trabajo 5/1 ___

Appendix A-2:
Level of Religious and Cultural Participation

1. **What other organizations or groups of a Catholic nature are you affiliated with?**
   - (1) Bible Study; Cursillos; Jóvenes.
   - (2) Youth Group.
   - (3) Marriage Encounter; Catechist.
   - (4) Victory Youth Outreach; Bible Study.
   - (5) Antes Bible Group.
   - (6–8) None.
   - (9) CCD Teacher.
   - (10) None.
   - (11) Lector; Parish Council Member; Eucharistic Minister; Choir; Cursillo.
   - (12) Encuentros.
   - (13–14) None.
   - (15) Marriage Encounter; Youth Group.
   - (16) None.
   - (17) Marriage Encounter; Choir.
   - (18) Marriage Encounter.
   - (19) Guadalupana; 200 Club.
   - (20) Encuentro Juvenil.

2. **What other organizations or groups of a Mexican-American nature are you affiliated with?**
   - (1–4) None.
   - (5) Mayo Club; Chicano H.S.

(6–10)   None.
(11)   High School Mexican-American club.
(12–14)   None.
(15)   Hispanic Marriage Encounter; League Latina; Soccer.
(16)   None.
(17)   MECHA—High School.
(18)   SSUC—Secretary.
(19)   High School Chicano club.
(20)   None.

3. **List the activities of a Catholic nature in which you are now involved:**
(1)   Bible Study; Catechist Training.
(2)   None.
(3)   Marriage Encounter; Catechist Training.
(4–8)   None.
(9)   Teaching children.
(10–14)   None.
(15)   Marriage Encounter.
(16–18)   None.
(19)   High School Chicano Club.
(20)   None.

4. **List the activities of a Mexican-American nature in which you are now involved:**
(1–20)   None.

5. **If you have children, please list the organizations or groups of a Catholic nature they belong to:**
(1–2)   None.
(3)   Catechism.
(4–8)   None.
(9)   CCD.
(10)   CCD.
(11)   None.
(12)   Catholic school.
(13–20)   None.

6. If you have children, please list the organizations or groups of a Mexican-American nature they belong to:

(1–20)   None.

7. At what age did you get involved in church-related activities?

    (1)   15—Encuentro Juvenil.
    (2)   17—Through friend with Youth Group.
    (3)   11–12—Assistant to catechist.
    (4)   24—Bible Study.
    (5)   16—Bible group.
    (6)   No involvement.
    (7)   13—Church choir.
    (8)   25—No involvement.
    (9)   25—CCD class.
  (10)   25—Bible Study.
  (11)   22—Cursillo.
  (12)   17—Encuentro.
  (13)   No involvement.
  (14)   No involvement.
  (15)   Always—Catholic schools; 17—Encuentro Juvenil.
  (16)   No involvement.
  (17)   Grammar school choir; 20—Marriage Encounter.
  (18)   17—Prayer group.
  (19)   No activities offered in church.
  (20)   16—Encuentro; Retreats.

Appendix A-3:
Most Important Church Holiday, Symbol, and Belief

1. **What do you consider to be the most important Church Holiday and why?**
   (1) Christmas—because it's the day Jesus Christ was born.
   (2) Christmas—because it brings the family close.
   (3) Feast of Our Lady of Guadalupe—because it's a celebration where I get together with my family.
   (4) Easter—because Jesus Christ rose from the dead; it means new life.
   (5) Christmas—because Jesus Christ was born.
   (6) Easter—God is risen.
   (7) Resurrection—because he died for our sins.
   (8) Christmas—because that's the day he [Jesus Christ] was born.
   (9) Christmas—because it's the birth of Christ.
   (10) Easter—because it's when God rose from the dead.
   (11) Holy Week—because you feel so bad; you think of the sacrifice and you're moved to be devout.
   (12) Christmas—because it's the birth of Christ.
   (13) Christmas—because Jesus Christ was born; he is the Savior; he opened up the gates of heaven.
   (14) Christmas—because it's the birth of Jesus Christ; when everything started.
   (15) Christmas—because Jesus was born to earth; it's hard to believe in a God who only stays in heaven; he came down as a human being; he lives, feels our emotions.

(16) Holy Week/Easter—because he [Jesus Christ] died and rose; everything was ugly before this.

(17) Christmas—because that's when Jesus Christ was born.

(18) Easter—because it means new hope.

(19) Christmas—because Jesus Christ was born; he is the Savior.

(20) Easter—because Jesus Christ died, suffered and rose; the whole process.

2. What do you consider to be the most important Symbol and why?

(1) Sign of the Cross—because it makes me conscious of God; I surrender to him; I have contact with him.

(2) Cross—because it's a symbol of God.

(3) Cross—because it represents resurrection and how we came to be through Jesus Christ.

(4) Water—because it's cleansing.

(5) Sign of the Cross—I don't know why.

(6) God—because he sent us Jesus Christ; he's a symbol of everything.

(7) Cross—No reason given.

(8) Baby Jesus—No reason given.

(9) Cross—because I associate the cross with his [Jesus Christ's] body.

(10) Christ Picture—because it's a symbol of truth and hope.

(11) Eucharist—because you can partake with other people; afterwards, there's a moment when everyone looks good/holy and we're a family.

(12) Crucifix—because it shows us that he [Jesus Christ] died for our sins.

(13) Cross—because it means God.

(14) Crucifix—because Jesus Christ is our savior.

(15) Cross—because it reminds me that God gave up his son for us out of love.

(16) Cross—because Jesus Christ is on it; because I believe in him.

(17) Cross—because we remember him [Jesus Christ]; he died for us.

(18) Presence—because it's more than a symbol.

(19) Cross—because it's a symbol of our savior who suffered for us.

(20) Crucifix—because it means Jesus Christ/God.

3. What do you consider to be the most important Belief and why?

(1) Communion—because I receive the body and blood of Jesus Christ; it makes me feel good and clean.

(2) Our Lady of Guadalupe—because of personal experience, i.e., because of her, I'm here; my father asked the Virgin to save me when I was six because of medical reasons.

(3) Through his body and blood we're saved and become part of his [Jesus Christ's] community and inherit his kingdom.

(4) Jesus Christ is alive.

(5) Jesus Christ.

(6) God.

(7) Jesus died for our sins.

(8) He [Jesus Christ] was born into the world.

(9) Prayers—because I'm always talking to God.

(10) That there is life after death.

(11) Holy Spirit—because it's ever-present.

(12) God is our savior and father creator.

(13) Jesus Christ died on the cross and rose—I don't know why.

(14) In God—because he saves; we return to him.

(15) God is willing to forgive.

(16) Mary and Jesus—because Mary gave birth to Jesus Christ (mother); Jesus Christ—nobody is empty.

(17) Mass—because we are united; worship God.

(18) That God loves us—because the world is so finite; there has to be something else.

(19) I believe that God is there.

(20) The Ten Commandments—because if you follow them you will have a good life.

Appendix A-4:
Most Important Religious and Cultural Holidays—Ranked

(1) **Religious**

7—Christmas
6—Easter
5—Ash Wednesday
4—Our Lady of Guadalupe
3—Ascension of Christ
2—Good Friday
1—All Souls' Day

Cultural

7—Día de las Madres—5/10
6—16th of September
5—Cinco de Mayo
4—Día del Trabajo—5/1
3—Día de la Raza—10/12
2—Día de los Muertos—11/2
1—Grito de Dolores—9/15

(2) **Religious**

7—Christmas
6—Our Lady of Guadalupe
5—Ascension of Christ
4—All Souls' Day
3—Good Friday
2—Easter
1—Ash Wednesday

Cultural

7—Día de las Madres
6—Día de los Muertos
5—Día del Trabajo
4—Día de la Raza
3—Cinco de Mayo
2—16th of September
1—Grito de Dolores

(3) **Religious**

7—Easter
6—Good Friday
5—Our Lady of Guadalupe
4—Christmas
3—Ascension of Christ

Cultural

7—Día de las Madres
6—16th of September
5—Cinco de Mayo
4—Día de la Raza
3—Día de los Muertos

2—Ash Wednesday
1—All Souls' Day

2—Día del Trabajo
1—Grito de Dolores

(4) **Religious**
7—Easter
6—All Souls' Day
5—Good Friday
4—Ascension of Christ
3—Ash Wednesday
2—Christmas
1—Our Lady of Guadalupe

Cultural
7—Día de las Madres
6—Día de los Muertos
5—Grito de Dolores
4—16th of September
3—Cinco de Mayo
2—Día de la Raza
1—Día del Trabajo

(5) **Religious**
7—Christmas
6—Easter
5—Good Friday
4—Our Lady of Guadalupe
3—Ascension of Christ
2—All Souls' Day
1—Ash Wednesday

Cultural
7—Cinco de Mayo
6—16th of September
5—Día de las Madres
4—Día de los Muertos
3—Grito de Dolores
2—Día del Trabajo
1—Día de la Raza

(6) **Religious**
7—Easter
6—Ascension of Christ
5—Ash Wednesday
4—Our Lady of Guadalupe
3—Christmas
2—All Souls' Day
1—Good Friday

Cultural
7—Cinco de Mayo
6—16th of September
5—Día de las Madres
4—Día de la Raza
3—Día del Trabajo
2—Grito de Dolores
1—Día de los Muertos

(7) **Religious**
7—Easter
6—Good Friday
5—Ash Wednesday
4—Ascension of Christ
3—Christmas

Cultural
7—Día de los Muertos
6—Día de las Madres
5—Cinco de Mayo
4—16th of September
3—Grito de Dolores

2—All Souls' Day
1—Our Lady of Guadalupe

2—Día de la Raza
1—Día del Trabajo

(8) **Religious**
7—Our Lady of Guadalupe
6—Ash Wednesday
5—Good Friday
4—Easter
3—Christmas
2—Ascension of Christ
1—All Souls' Day

Cultural
7—Grito de Dolores
6—Día del Trabajo
5—Día de los Muertos
4—16th of September
3—Día de la Raza
2—Cinco de Mayo
1—Día de las Madres

(9) **Religious**
7—Christmas
6—Easter
5—Ash Wednesday
4—Good Friday
3—Ascension of Christ
2—Our Lady of Guadalupe
1—All Souls' Day

Cultural
7—Día de las Madres
6—Día de los Muertos
5—Día de la Raza
4—Día del Trabajo
3—Cinco de Mayo
2—Grito de Dolores
1—16th of September

(10) **Religious**
7—Easter
6—Christmas
5—Good Friday
4—Ash Wednesday
3—Ascension of Christ
2—Our Lady of Guadalupe
1—All Souls' Day

Cultural
7—Cinco de Mayo
6—Día de las Madres
5—Día de la Raza
4—Día del Trabajo
3—Grito de Dolores
2—16th of September
1—Día de los Muertos

(11) **Religious**
7—Easter
6—Ash Wednesday
5—Good Friday
4—Christmas
3—Our Lady of Guadalupe

Cultural
7—Día de las Madres
6—Cinco de Mayo
5—16th of September
4—Día de los Muertos
3—Día de la Raza

2—Ascension of Christ

2—Día del Trabajo

1—All Souls' Day

1—Grito de Dolores

(12) **Religious**

Cultural

7—Christmas

7—16th of September

6—Good Friday

6—Cinco de Mayo

5—Easter

5—Día de las Madres

4—Our Lady of Guadalupe

4—Grito de Dolores

3—Ash Wednesday

3—Día de los Muertos

2—Ascension of Christ

2—Día de la Raza

1—All Souls' Day

1—Día del Trabajo

(13) **Religious**

Cultural

7—Good Friday

7—Día de las Madres

6—Easter

6—Cinco de Mayo

5—Christmas

5—16th of September

4—Ash Wednesday

4—Día de los Muertos

3—Ascension of Christ

3—Día de la Raza

2—Our Lady of Guadalupe

2—Grito de Dolores

1—All Souls' Day

1—Día del Trabajo

(14) **Religious**

Cultural

7—Christmas

7—Cinco de Mayo

6—Easter

6—Día de las Madres

5—Good Friday

5—Día de los Muertos

4—Ash Wednesday

4—Día del Trabajo

3—Our Lady of Guadalupe

3—Día de la Raza

2—Ascension of Christ

2—16th of September

1—All Souls' Day

1—Grito de Dolores

(15) **Religious**

Cultural

7—Christmas

7—Día de las Madres

6—Easter

6—Cinco de Mayo

5—Our Lady of Guadalupe

5—16th of September

4—Ash Wednesday

4—Día del Trabajo

3—Good Friday

3—Grito de Dolores

2—Ascension of Christ   2—Día de la Raza
1—All Souls' Day   1—Día de los Muertos

(16) **Religious**   **Cultural**
7—Easter   7—Día de las Madres
6—Christmas   6—Cinco de Mayo
5—Ash Wednesday   5—16th of September
4—Good Friday   4—Día de la Raza
3—Our Lady of Guadalupe   3—Día de los Muertos
2—Ascension of Christ   2—Grito de Dolores
1—All Souls' Day   1—Día del Trabajo

(17) **Religious**   **Cultural**
7—Good Friday   7—Día de los Muertos
6—Christmas   6—Día del Trabajo
5—Easter   5—Cinco de Mayo
4—All Souls' Day   4—Grito de Dolores
3—Our Lady of Guadalupe   3—16th of September
2—Ascension of Christ   2—Día de las Madres
1—Ash Wednesday   1—Día de la Raza

(18) **Religious**   **Cultural**
7—Good Friday   7—Cinco de Mayo
6—Easter   6—Día de las Madres
5—Christmas   5—Grito de Dolores
4—Ascension of Christ   4—16th of September
3—Our Lady of Guadalupe   3—Día de la Raza
2—All Souls' Day   2—Día de los Muertos
1—Ash Wednesday   1—Día del Trabajo

(19) **Religious**   **Cultural**
7—Christmas   7—Día de las Madres
6—Easter   6—Cinco de Mayo
5—Good Friday   5—16th of September
4—Ascension of Christ   4—Grito de Dolores
3—Ash Wednesday   3—Día del Trabajo

2—Our Lady of Guadalupe	2—Día de los Muertos
1—All Souls' Day	1—Día de la Raza

(20) **Religious**

7—Easter
6—Christmas
5—Ash Wednesday
4—Our Lady of Guadalupe
3—All Souls' Day
2—Good Friday
1—Ascension of Christ

Cultural

7—Cinco de Mayo
6—Día de las Madres
5—16th of September
4—Día de los Muertos
3—Grito de Dolores
2—Día de la Raza
1—Día del Trabajo

Appendix B-1:
The Adjective Check List (ACL)

Descriptions of Main Clusters of Study

Ideal Self Strong sense of personal worth; or harmony between what one is and what one wants to be.

Nurturing Parent Attitudes of support, stability, and acceptance associated with the concept of a "nurturing parent."

Nurturance To engage in behaviors that provide material or emotional benefits to others.

Affiliation To seek and maintain numerous personal friendships.

Self-Control The extent to which self-control is imposed and valued.

Adapted Child Attitudes of deference, conformity, and self-discipline associated with the concept of an "adapted" or very dutiful child.

Aggression To engage in behaviors that attack or hurt others.

Critical Parent Attitudes of evaluation, severity, and skepticism associated with the concept of a "critical parent."

Appendix B-2:
Sample Scores

ACL The Adjective Check List

NAME	ID	SEX	DATE SCORED

Sample size of group = 20

	Raw Score Mean	Raw Score Standard Deviation	Std. Score Mean	Std. Score Standard Deviation
Modus Operandi				
1. No. Ckd	68	28.16	41	8.20
2. Fav	42	14.52	57	6.24
3. Unfav	1	0.93	45	5.14
4. Com	11	3.83	44	8.54
Need Scales				
5. Ach	7	4.06	49	3.47
6. Dom	4	2.80	50	4.25
7. End	7	3.82	51	3.88
8. Ord	4	3.52	49	4.25
9. Int	12	5.00	53	6.72
10. Nur	16	4.53	57	5.65
11. Aff	18	5.88	56	4.96
12. Het	7	2.48	51	4.27
13. Exh	− 2	2.87	46	5.30
14. Aut	0	1.73	48	3.72
15. Agg	− 8	3.63	41	6.03

ACL The Adjective Check List (continued)

Sample size of group = 20

	Raw Score Mean	Raw Score Standard Deviation	Std. Score Mean	Std. S Stanc Devic
Need Scales				
16. Cha	2	2.16	46	5.(
17. Suc	−1	2.01	45	5.(
18. Aba	1	1.91	49	3.!
19. Def	4	3.39	53	6.<
Topical Scales				
20. Crs	0	2.85	43	8.<
21. S-Cn	3	2.68	55	6.(
22. S-Cfd	7	4.21	51	5.!
23. P-Adj	9	2.79	54	4.:
24. Iss	8	3.69	60	4.:
25. Cps	3	2.59	51	5.:
26. Mls	8	3.76	49	5.:
27. Mas	5	3.12	54	5.
28. Fem	10	3.86	48	7.:
Transactional Analysis				
29. Cp	−1	2.95	41	5.
30. NP	12	4.15	57	5.<
31. A	8	4.09	53	5.
32. FC	0	3.42	47	5.
33. AC	−9	3.98	43	5.
Origence-Intellectence				
34. A-1	5	2.57	57	6.
35. A-2	4	2.26	48	5.
36. A-3	8	3.02	55	6.
37. A-4	6	3.46	46	5.

Appendix B-3:
Categorization of Participants' Statements according to DeVos's Motivational Concerns

Instrumental Behavior (definitions from DeVos 1973: 22–23)

1. *Achievement:* "indicates behavior motivated by the desire to attain a goal, positively within a given set of standards or social codes, or negatively through what is socially defined as 'criminal behavior.'"

Participant	Statement	Active Agent
1	She plays an important role.	OLG P
2	No statement	N/A
3	I try to use her as a role model.	P OLG
4	No statement	N/A
5	She's the one that stood by when they put him on the cross.	OLG Jesus
6	No statement	N/A
7	She made many miracles, curing people; she's miraculous.	OLG O
8	She is miraculous.	OLG O
9	She's there for them . . . and maybe the background about her . . . what I've heard from my mom; I'd like for my kids to know more than I do; and them being able to pray to her.	OLG O N/A
10	No statement	N/A
11	No statement	N/A

12	I would pray to her to help me through it; I think she would give me some support.	OLG O
		N/A
13	No statement	N/A
14	No statement	N/A
15	No statement	N/A
16	No statement	N/A
17	No statement	N/A
18	No statement	N/A
19	She was a strong . . . woman . . . calm . . . she could take a lot . . . and she'd give a lot in return.	OLG O
20	To come to remind us of a love and spirit that does exist.	OLG O

2. *Competence*: "indicates behavior related positively to actualizing personal adequacy or capacity, or to a need to acquire competence negatively with a sense of failure and inadequacy."

Participant	Statement	Active Agent
1	To me for her to be the mother of God and to raise him and that God chose her; I think she is special. If He chose her, that means she had to have it all. . . .	God OLG
	to play a role like her you know, to be a good mother.	OLG O
	I don't know too much, but I could feel it.	N/A
		P OLG
	She gives me strength.	OLG P
2	Just touching the frame of where she's at, I feel that strength comes to me that keeps saying, ". . . you can do it, don't worry, I will always be here."	OLG P
3	She is strong . . . powerful.	OLG O
4	No statement	N/A

5	No statement	N/A
6	No statement	N/A
7	No statement	N/A
8	No statement	N/A
9	No statement	N/A
10	No statement	N/A
11	She put these signs and symbols into the world.	OLG O
12	I would pray to her to just help me. . . . It's kind of hard for me to really, I really, I'm not that knowledgeable about it myself.	OLG P N/A
13	I think that her strength and also when you believe in that, have faith, things do happen. She was . . . intelligent.	P OLG OLG O
14	When you pray to her you count on her; she's a strong woman to fulfill your needs all the time . . . gives you confidence that she will take care of you.	OLG O O OLG
15	I think of her as the perfect mother . . . she was a strong person . . . never fell apart.	P OLG OLG P
16	I pray and pray to her when somebody in my family is sick and she really helps me . . . she must have been a wonderful mother.	P OLG OLG P OLG Jesus
17	When somebody in my family is sick and she really helps me . . . she gets you out of worry and makes you happy.	OLG O
18	Courageous . . . she did what was right.	OLG O
19	No statement	N/A
20	No statement	N/A

3. *Responsibility:* "indicates behavior motivated by a sense of responsibility or obligation to internalized social directives, or the opposite:
avoidance of or flight from responsibility, or neglect of responsibility
due to profligacy, or irresponsible self-indulgence."

Participant	Statement	Active Agent
1	You know, to be a good mother.	OLG O
2	No statement	N/A
3	No statement	N/A
4	She signifies purity that was sent to be an example to us women.	OLG O
5	No statement	N/A
6	I want my boys to have some respect for me because I'm their mother. Well, they should have some respect for her because she is the mother of God.	P O OLG
7	No statement	N/A
8	Well, I will tell my daughters that she's "Our Lady" and to go to church . . . pray to bless themselves wherever they go . . . to pray whatever they need and for the "Lady Guadalupe" to hear their prayers.	P OLG
9	No statement	N/A
10	No statement	N/A
11	No statement	N/A
12	No statement	N/A
13	No statement	N/A
14	No statement	N/A
15	No statement	N/A
16	No statement	N/A
17	No statement	N/A
18	She had to be pretty courageous to avoid temptation.	OLG O

19	No statement	N/A
20	No statement	N/A

4. *Control/Power:* "indicates behavior directed toward the actualization of power, authority, or control in social relationships, negatively perceived, problems of dominance and submission."

Participant	Statement	Active Agent
1	I want my children to put their lives in the hands of the Virgin.	P OLG
2	If you believe in her nothing can go wrong. . . . I was six . . . got like a tumor . . . my dad said . . . "Let's go to Mexico, the Virgin will help" . . . the doctor said she's going to make it. I remember this very clear . . . I remember him falling on his knees saying "gracias" to the Lady of Guadalupe.	OLG O
3	She's powerful in a very loving way but yet she is still powerful.	OLG O
4	She is miraculous.	OLG O
5	No statement	N/A
6	No statement	N/A
7	I was pregnant and I was having problems . . . I was praying to her that maybe she'd save my baby.	OLG P
8	No statement	N/A
9	No statement	N/A
10	No statement	N/A
11	No statement	N/A
12	No statement	N/A
13	No statement	N/A
14	She gave me hope.	OLG P
15	She had a really strong character	OLG O

	and she knew what her limit would be.	
16	No statement	N/A
17	No statement	N/A
18	She took care of business with Juan Diego.	OLG O
19	She has more leverage [than I with God].	P OLG God
20	No statement	N/A

5. *Mutuality*: "indicates the phrasing of instrumental behavior in cooperative or competitive terms positively within social prescribed norms or negatively outside of them."

Participant	Statement	Active Agent
1	I love her and she is part of my culture; she is our *madre*. . . .	P OLG O
	I feel proud that we have the Virgin of Guadalupe on our side . . . having her the way she is . . . her color.	OLG O
2	I have her like a torch in my life. . . . It keeps me going. It keeps me active . . . I see that she's always been there for me. . . . I know that by . . . touching the frame of where she's at I feel that strength comes to me.	OLG P
3	No statement	N/A
4	No statement	N/A
5	No statement	N/A
6	No statement	N/A
7	No statement	N/A
8	When we pray to her she hears us.	P OLG
9	I feel warm as I pray to her.	P OLG

10	No statement	N/A
11	No statement	N/A
12	I have asked her for help many times . . . those times I would pray to her . . . she would give me some support.	P OLG
13	No statement	N/A
14	When you pray to her you count on her; she's a strong woman to fulfill your needs all the time . . . she gives you confidence that she will take care of you.	OLG O O OLG
15	No statement	N/A
16	I pray and pray to her when somebody in my family is sick and she really helps me. I can speak to her for comfort and help and feel relief and peace inside; some of my worries can kind of go away.	P OLG OLG P
17	No statement	N/A
18	I guess an understanding . . . camaraderie . . . peaceful . . . she brings a certain peace.	OLG P
19	No statement	N/A
20	No statement	N/A

Expressive Behavior (definitions from DeVos 1973: 22–23)

1. *Harmony:* "indicates positive behavior involving maintenance of peacefulness or harmony, or negatively concern with disharmony, discord, even violence and destructiveness in human relationships."

Participant	Statement	Active Agent
1	No statement	N/A
2	I feel that she's very peaceful and	P OLG

	tranquil and I try to perhaps imitate that tranquility.	
3	No statement	N/A
4	No statement	N/A
5	No statement	N/A
6	No statement	N/A
7	No statement	N/A
8	No statement	N/A
9	I feel warm as I pray to her.	P OLG
10	No statement	N/A
11	No statement	N/A
12	No statement	N/A
13	No statement	N/A
14	She gives you peace of mind.	OLG O
15	No statement	N/A
16	She really relaxes me . . . gives me a peaceful feeling inside.	OLG P
17	I talk to her and everything . . . I feel more like my heart opened.	P OLG
18	I guess an understanding . . . camaraderie . . . peaceful . . . she brings a certain peace.	OLG P
19	No statement	N/A
20	No statement	N/A

2. *Affiliation:* "indicates behavior related to feelings of interpersonal closeness and intimacy or their opposites, isolation, rejection, or interpersonal avoidance."

Participant	Statement	Active Agent
1	I love her and she is part of my culture; she is our *madre* . . . I feel proud that we have the Virgin of Guadalupe on our side . . . having her the way she is . . . her color.	P OLG O OLG O

2	She is here with me . . . she's always been.	OLG P
3	No statement	N/A
4	I can't really say.	N/A
5	I don't really know.	N/A
6	Not really.	N/A
7	I pray to her.	P OLG
8	When we pray to her she hears us . . . I trust in her a lot.	P OLG
9	When I'm troubled I pray and I talk to her.	P OLG
10	She was Mexican and I'm Mexican.	OLG P
11	I can't really relate as much.	N/A
12	[I] will always love her and trust in her.	P OLG
13	She's there whenever I need her . . . I don't think she ever turns anyone away.	OLG P OLG O
14	Not very much . . . (but respect).	P OLG
15	No statement	N/A
16	[Talks to her] about my day, my little girl, my husband . . . my family.	P OLG
17	No statement	N/A
18	I guess an understanding . . . I don't know if it's camaraderie . . . I guess instinctively because I am Mexican.	OLG P
19	I speak to the Virgin, you know, like as if she's my mother.	P OLG
20	I feel more love for her and I feel more comfortable and I feel more familiar with her than I do with . . . Mary.	P OLG

3. *Nurturance:* "indicates behavior involving care, succor, nurture, or, looked at from the standpoint of the recipient, behavior based on fulfillment of a dependent need or on its frustration."

Participant	Statement	Active Agent
1	She gives me strength.	OLG P
2	I have her like a torch in my life. It keeps me going. It keeps me active . . . I see that she's always been there for me . . . I know that by . . . touching the frame of where she's at I feel what strength comes to me.	OLG P
3	I have a tendency in my own to be vain . . . when I look at her she helps me.	P OLG
4	The Virgin de Guadalupe to me was like a guardian who watched over us.	OLG P
5	No statement	N/A
6	No statement	N/A
7	Very helpful.	OLG O
8	Very quiet.	N/A
	I will tell my daughters . . . to pray . . . whatever they need.	OLG O
9	When I'm troubled I pray . . . I talk to her.	P OLG
10	I think that she was a virgin that was very concerned about her people.	OLG O
11	She reaches the really oppressed.	OLG O
12	I have asked her for help many times . . . those times I would pray to her . . . she would give me some support.	P OLG
13	When I'm alone, when I need	P OLG

	someone to talk to, when I need help.	
14	She'd give me the strength to be strong.	OLG P
15	No statement	N/A
16	I can speak to her for comfort and help and feel relief and peace inside; some of my worries can kind of go away.	OLG P
17	She gets me out of worry.	OLG P
18	No statement	N/A
19	No statement	N/A
20	She brings me comfort . . . she knows what I mean; she'll know how I feel.	OLG P

4. *Appreciation:* "indicates a need for recognition or response from others—or its opposite, a concern with feeling ignored, unimportant, or disdained or depreciated by others."

Participant	Statement	Active Agent
1	I admire her for what she did.	P OLG
2	She's special because she's always been there in my life and I guess in my family's life too.	OLG P OLG O
3	I see the Mother of God as being extremely great, because my mother is extremely great to me.	P OLG
4	I just know she is the mother of Jesus Christ.	P OLG
5	No statement	N/A
6	Because she's the mother of Jesus.	P OLG
7	No statement	N/A
8	No statement	N/A
9	No statement	N/A
10	People feel a lot of respect for her.	O OLG

11	She is the mother of the world or a Mexican mother . . . waiting, caring, unselfish.	OLG O
12	No statement	N/A
13	No statement	N/A
14	No statement	N/A
15	Feelings of respect . . . it's tradition.	P OLG
16	I can go in there and just take a look at her . . . just being able to go in there . . . able to walk out feeling better . . . it's a gift.	OLG O
17	She's listening to you . . . she don't ignore you or nothing.	P OLG
18	No statement	N/A
19	No statement	N/A
20	And He [God] saw in her something very sacred and I would imagine that she could be a more mother-type if He chose her to conceive Jesus.	God OLG

5. *Pleasure:* "indicates behavior generally governed by a direct experience of satisfaction or pleasure or their opposites, of dissatisfaction or suffering within the self."

Participant	Statement	Active Agent
1	I feel proud that we have the Virgin of Guadalupe on our side.	P OLG O
2	She's beautiful; she's ours.	OLG O
3	No statement	N/A
4	No statement	N/A
5	No statement	N/A
6	No statement	N/A
7	No statement	N/A
8	She's a pretty woman; she's really perfect.	OLG P

9	No statement	N/A
10	No statement	N/A
11	No statement	N/A
12	No statement	N/A
13	No statement	N/A
14	No statement	N/A
15	No statement	N/A
16	I'd look up at her statue and think how beautiful and peaceful she looks.	OLG P
17	No statement	N/A
18	No statement	N/A
19	No statement	N/A
20	No statement	N/A

Appendix C:
Consent and Participation Agreement Form

I have been informed by the researcher, Jeanette Rodriguez, of the general nature of the questionnaire and interview. I understand that the researcher is a Ph.D. student at the Graduate Theological Union. I also understand that she is studying the relationship of Mexican-American women to Our Lady of Guadalupe. I understand that my name is not requested on the questionnaire and that identifying information will be coded/numbered so as to provide confidentiality. I understand that the completed questionnaire/interview may be kept for further research or publication use. I agree to participate in the research and to release any information acquired in the interview as long as my name is kept anonymous. Participation is voluntary and I understand that I do not have to answer any questions I feel may be personal.

Date _____ Signature _____

Bibliography

Acosta, Frank X. 1984. "Psychotherapy with Mexican Americans: Clinical and Empirical Gains." In *Chicano Psychology*, 2d ed., ed. Joe L. Martinez, Jr., 163–189. New York: Academic Press.

Acuña, Rodolfo. 1981. *Occupied America: A History of Chicanos*. 2d ed. New York: Harper and Row.

———. 1988. *Occupied America: The Chicano's Struggle toward Liberation*. (Rev. ed. of Acuña 1981.) New York: Harper and Row.

Alarcón, Norma. 1985. "What Kind of Lover Have You Made Me, Mother?" In *Women of Color: Perspectives on Feminism and Identity*, ed. Audrey T. McCluskey. Occasional Papers Series, vol. 1, no. 1. Bloomington: Women's Studies Program, Indiana University.

———. 1988. "Traduttora, Traditora: A Paradigmatic Figure of Chicana Feminism." In *Changing Our Power: An Introduction to Women Studies*, ed. Jo Whitehorse Cochran, Donna Langston, and Carolyn Woodward. Dubuque, Iowa: Kendall/Hunt Publishing Co.

Alegría, Juana Armanda. 1975. *Psicología de las Mexicanas*. 2d ed. Mexico City: Samo.

Almazol, Cynthia. 1971. "La Chicana and the Catholic Religion." Student paper, University of California, Berkeley.

Alvarez, Rodolfo. 1976. "The Psycho-Historical and Socioeconomic Development of the Chicana Community in the United States." In *Chicanos: Social and Psychological Perspectives*, 2d ed., ed. Carrol A. Hernández, Marsha J. Haug, and Nathaniel N. Wagner, 38–54. St. Louis: C. V. Mosby Co.

Anaya, Rudolfo A. 1972. *Bless Me Ultima*. Berkeley, Calif.: Tonatiuh International.

Andersen, Margaret L., and Patricia Hill Collins. 1992. *Race, Class, and Gender: An Anthology*. Belmont, Calif.: Wadsworth Publishing Co.

Anderson, Sherry Ruth, and Patricia Hopkins. 1991. *The Feminine Face of God.* New York: Bantam Books.

Andrade, Sally J. 1982. "Social Science Stereotypes of the Mexican American Woman: Policy Implications for Research." *Hispanic Journal of Behavioral Sciences* 4, no. 2 (June):233–244.

Anzaldúa, Gloria. 1987. *Borderlands: The New Mestiza.* San Francisco, Calif.: Aunt Lute Book Company.

————, ed. 1990. *Making Face, Making Soul: Haciendo Caras.* San Francisco, Calif.: Aunt Lute Foundation Books.

Arellano, Luz Beatriz. 1988. "Women's Experience of God in Emerging Spirituality." *With Passion and Compassion: The Third World Women Doing Theology,* ed. Virginia Fabella and Mercy A. Odvyoye, 135–150. Maryknoll, N.Y.: Orbis Books.

Arroyo, Antonio M. Stevens, C.P. 1980. *Prophets Denied Honor: An Anthology on the Hispanic Church in the U.S.* Maryknoll, N.Y.: Orbis Books.

Ascensio, Luis Medina, S.J. 1981. "Fuentes esenciales de la historia Guadalupana, Su valor histórico." In *Album conmemorativo del 450 aniversario de las apariciones de Nuestra Señora de Guadalupe,* ed. José Ignacio Echeagaray. Mexico City: Ediciones Buena Nueva.

Ascheman, Thomas J., S.J.D. 1983. "Guadalupan Spirituality for Cross-Cultural Missionaries." M.A. thesis, Catholic Theological Union at Chicago.

Atkinson, J. 1987. "Gender Roles in Marriage and the Family." *Journal of Family Issues* 8:5–41.

Ayer-Nachamkin, B., C. H. Cann, R. Reed, and A. Horne. 1982. "Sex and Ethnic Differences in the Use of Power." *Journal of Applied Psychology* 67, no. 4:464–471.

Baca Zinn, M. 1975. "Political Familism toward Sex Role Equality in Chicano Families." *Aztlán: International Journal of Chicano Studies* 6:13–27.

————. 1976. "Chicanos: Power and Control in the Domestic Sphere." *De Colores* 2:19–44.

————. 1979. "Chicano Family Research: Conceptual Distortions and Alternative Directions." *Journal of Ethnic Studies* 7:59–71.

————. 1980. "Employment and Education of Mexican American Women: The Interplay of Modernity and Ethnicity in Eight Families." *Harvard Educational Review* 50 (February):47–62.

————. 1982. "Chicano Men and Masculinity." *Journal of Ethnic Studies* 10: 29–44.

————. 1984. "Mexican Heritage Women: A Bibliographic Essay." *Sage Race Relations Abstracts* 9:1–12.

Bach-y-Rita, George. 1982. "The Mexican American: Religious and Cultural

Influences." In *Mental Health and Hispanic Americans: Clinical Perspectives*, ed. R. M. Becerra, M. Karno, and J. J. Escobar, 29–40. New York: Grune and Stratton.

Balderrama, Sandra. 1981. "A Comprehensive Bibliography on La Chicana." Unpublished manuscript. University of California, Berkeley.

Barber, Janet, I.H.M. 1992. "The Significance of the *Nican Mopohua*." Unpublished paper.

Basso, Sister Teresita. 1971a. "The Emerging 'Chicana' Sister." *Review for Religious* 30 (November):1019–1028.

———. 1971b. "The Emerging Chicana Women Religious." Student paper, California State University, San Jose, Seminar on the Social Psychology of the Chicano, July.

Benzo, Miguel. 1978. *Hombre profano—Hombre sagrado: Tratado de antropología teológica*. Madrid: Ediciones Cristiandad.

Bernal, G., and A. I. Alvarez. 1983. "Culture and Class in the Study of Families." In *Cultural Perspectives in Family Therapy*, ed. J. C. Hansen and C. J. Falicov, 33–50. Rockville, Md.: Aspen Publications.

Bierhorst, John. 1985. *A Nahuatl-English Dictionary and Concordance to the Cantares Mexicanos with an Analytical Transcription and Grammatical Notes*. Stanford, Calif.: Stanford University Press.

Blea, Irene I. 1988. *Toward a Chicano Social Science*. New York: Praeger.

———. 1992. *La Chicana and the Intersection of Race, Class, and Gender*. New York: Praeger.

Bock, W. Wilbur. 1965. "Symbols in Conflict: Official Versus Popular Religion." *Journal for the Scientific Study of Religion* 5 (October):204–212.

Boff, Leonardo. 1987. *The Maternal Face of God*. Trans. Robert R. Barr and John W. Diercksmeier. New York: Harper and Row.

———. 1990. *New Evangelization: Good News to the Poor*. Maryknoll, N.Y.: Orbis Books.

Bogardus, Emory S. 1929. "Second Generation Mexican." *Sociology and Social Research* 13 (January/February):276–283.

Brown, Lyle C., and William F. Cooper, eds. 1980. *Religion in Latin American Life and Literature*. Waco, Tex.: Markham Press Fund.

Burrus, Ernest J., S.J. 1981. *The Oldest Copy of the Nican Mopohua*. CARA Studies on Popular Devotion, vol. 4: Guadalupan Studies, no. 4. Washington, D.C.: Center for Applied Research in the Apostolate (CARA).

———. 1983. *The Basic Bibliography of the Guadalupan Apparitions (1531–1723)*. CARA Studies on Popular Devotion, vol. 4: Guadalupan Studies, no. 5. Washington, D.C.: Center for Applied Research in the Apostolate (CARA).

————. 1984. *Juan Diego and Other Native Benefactors in the Light of Boturini's Research.* CARA Studies on Popular Devotion, vol. 2: Guadalupan Studies, no. 7. Washington, D.C.: Center for Applied Research in the Apostolate (CARA).

Callahan, Philip Serna. 1981. *The Tilma: Under Infra-Red Radiation.* CARA Studies on Popular Devotion, vol. 2: Guadalupan Studies, no. 3. Washington, D.C.: Center for Applied Research in the Apostolate (CARA).

Campbell, Ena. 1982. "The Virgin of Guadalupe and the Female Self-Image: A Mexican Case History." In *Mother Worship*, ed. James J. Preston, 5–24. Chapel Hill: University of North Carolina Press.

Campos Ponce, Xavier. 1970. *La Virgen de Guadalupe y la diosa Tonantzín.* Mexico City: Ediciones JCP CED ISR.

Cárdenas de Dwyer, Carlota. 1980. "Mexican American Women: Images and Realities." In *Bridging Two Cultures: Multidisciplinary Readings in Bilingual Bicultural Education*, ed. Martha Cotera and Larry Hufford, 294–303. Austin, Tex.: National Educational Laboratory Publishers.

Cardozo-Freeman, I. 1975. "Games Mexican Girls Play." *Journal of American Folklore* 88 (January):12–24.

Carroll, Michael P. 1983. "Visions of the Virgin Mary: The Effect of Family Structures in Marian Apparitions." *Journal for the Scientific Study of Religion* 22:205–221.

————. 1986. *The Cult of the Virgin Mary: Psychological Origins.* Princeton: Princeton University Press.

Casas, J. Manuel, and Susan E. Keefe, eds. 1978. *Family and Mental Health in the Mexican American Community.* Spanish Speaking Mental Health Research Center, Monograph no. 7. Amado M. Padilla, Principal Investigator. Los Angeles: University of California.

Casavantes, Edward. 1976. "Pride and Prejudice: A Mexican American Dilemma." In *Chicanos: Social and Psychological Perspectives*, 2d ed., ed. Carrol A. Hernández, Marsha J. Haug, and Nathaniel N. Wagner, 9–14. St. Louis: C. V. Mosby Co.

Castillo-Speed, Lillian. 1980. "Chicano Studies, A Selected List of Material since 1980." *Frontiers* 11, no. 1:66–84.

Cawley, Martinus. 1983. *Guadalupe—From the Aztec Language.* CARA Studies in Popular Devotion, vol. 2: Guadalupan Studies, no. 6. Lafayette, Ore.: Guadalupe Abbey.

————. 1984. *Anthology of Early Guadalupan Literature.* CARA Studies in Popular Devotion, vol. 2: Guadalupan Studies, no. 8. Lafayette, Ore.: Guadalupe Abbey.

————. 1992. Personal conversation. November 25. Guadalupe Abbey, Oregon.

Centro de Estudios Guadalupanos, A.C. 1980. *Documentario Guadalupano 1531–1768*. Monumenta Historia Guadalupana, no. 3. Mexico City: Centro de Estudios Guadalupanos, A.C.

Chávez, Fray Angélico. 1954. *La Conquistadora: The Autobiography of an Ancient Statue*. Paterson, N.J.: St. Anthony Guild Press.

Clifford, James. 1988. *The Predicament of Culture: Twentieth-Century Ethnography, Literature and Art*. Cambridge, Mass.: Harvard University Press.

Clifford, James, and George E. Marcus, eds. 1986. *Writing Culture: The Poetics and Politics of Ethnography*. Berkeley: University of California Press.

Coltrin, Jeanne. 1971. "Influence of the Catholic Church on la Chicana." Student Paper, University of California, Berkeley.

Concha Malo, Miguel, O.P. 1981. "La Virgen de Guadalupe y la evangelización." *Servir* 17, nos. 95–96:377–394.

Cortés, Carlos, ed. 1974. *Church Views of the Mexican American*. New York: Arno Press.

Cotera, Martha. 1976a. *Diosa y hembra*. Austin, Tex.: Statehouse Printing.

———. 1976b. *Profile on the Mexican American Woman*. Austin, Tex.: National Educational Laboratory Publishers.

Cotera, Martha, and Larry Hufford, eds. 1980. *Bridging Two Cultures: Multidisciplinary Readings in Bilingual Bicultural Education*. Austin, Tex.: National Educational Laboratory Publishers.

Daly, Mary. 1973. *Beyond God the Father*. Boston: Beacon Press.

DeCock, Mary, B.V.M. 1985. "Our Lady of Guadalupe: Symbol of Liberation?" In *Mary according to Women*, ed. Carol Frances Jegen, B.V.M. 113–141. Kansas City, Mo.: Leaven Press.

Deiss, Lucien. 1972. *Mary—Daughter of Zion*. Collegeville, Minn.: Liturgical Press.

de la Torre Villar, Ernesto, and Ramiro Navarro de Anda. 1982. *Testimonios históricos Guadalupanos: Compilación, prólogo, notas bibliográficas e índices*. Mexico City: Fondo de Cultura Económica.

Del Castillo, Adelaida R. 1977. "Malintzin Tenépal: A Preliminary Look into a New Perspective." In *Essays on la Mujer*, ed. Rosaura Sánchez and Rosa Martinez Cruz, 124–149. Anthology no. 1. Los Angeles: University of California, Chicano Studies Center Publications.

Delgado, Sylvia. 1971. "Young Chicana Speaks Up on Problems Faced by Young Girls." *Regeneración* 1, no. 10:5–7.

DeVos, George. 1973. *Socialization for Achievement*. Berkeley: University of California Press.

DeVos, G., and Ross L. Romanucci. 1975. *Ethnic Identity: Continuity and Change*. Palo Alto: Mayfield Press.

Díaz, Vicente. 1985. "New Revelations from the Cloak of Juan Diego." *Colum-bia* 65, no. 12 (December):8–15.

Díaz-Guerrero, Rogelio. 1955. "Neurosis and the Mexican Family Structure." *American Journal of Psychiatry* 112 (December):411–417.

———. 1975. *Psychology of the Mexican: Culture and Personality.* Austin: University of Texas Press.

Dorney, Judith A. 1985. "Religious Education and the Development of Young Women." In *Women's Issues in Religious Education.* ed. Fern M. Giltner, 41–65. Birmingham, Ala.: R. E. Press.

Dri, Rubén R. 1981. "El mensaje liberador Guadalupano." *Servir* 17, nos. 95–96:355–376.

Eagleson, John, and Philip Sharper, eds. 1979. *Puebla and Beyond: Documentation and Commentary.* Trans. John Drury. Maryknoll, N.Y.: Orbis Books.

Echeagaray, José Ignacio, ed. 1981. *Album conmemorativo del 450 aniversario de las apariciones de Nuestra Señora de Guadalupe.* Mexico City: Ediciones Buena Nueva.

Eliade, M. 1957. *The Sacred and the Profane.* New York: Harcourt, Brace and World.

———. 1971. *Patterns in Comparative Religion.* New York and Cleveland: World Publishing Co.

Eliade, Mircea, and Joseph M. Kitagowa, eds. 1959. *The History of Religions: Essays in Methodology.* Chicago: University of Chicago Press.

Elizondo, Virgilio P. 1977. "Our Lady of Guadalupe as a Cultural Symbol: The Power of the Powerless." In *Liturgy and Cultural Religious Traditions,* ed. Herman Schmidt and David Power, 25–33. Concilium 102. New York: Seabury.

———. 1978. *Mestizaje: The Dialectic of Cultural Birth and the Gospel.* San Antonio, Tex.: Mexican American Cultural Center.

———. 1980a. "The Christian Identity and Mission of the Catholic Hispanic in the U.S." Paper presented to the National Conference of Catholic Bishops, Chicago, April 30.

———. 1980b. *La Morenita: Evangelizer of the Americas.* San Antonio, Tex.: Mexican American Cultural Center.

———. 1980c. *Our Hispanic Pilgrimage.* San Antonio, Tex.: Mexican American Cultural Center.

———. 1983a. *Galilean Journey: The Mexican-American Promise.* Maryknoll, N.Y.: Orbis Books.

———. 1983b. *Mary and the Poor: A Model of Evangelizing Ecumenism in Mary in the Churches.* Ed. Hans Kung and Jürgen Moltmann. New York: Seabury Press.

————. 1992. *The Future Is Mestizo*. New York: Crossroad Publishing Co.

Elizondo, Virgilio P., et al. 1980. *Los católicos hispanos en los Estados Unidos*. New York: Centro Católico de Pastoral para Hispanos del Nordeste.

Escalada, Xavier. 1965. *Santa María Tequatlasupe*. Mexico City: Imp. Murguía. 2d ed. 1968, 3d ed. 1978.

Espín, Dr. Orlando. 1991. "The Vanquished, Faithful Solidarity and the Marian Symbol: A Hispanic Perspective on Providence." In *On Keeping Providence*, ed. J. Coultas and B. Doherty, 84–101. Terre Haute: St. Mary of the Woods College Press.

Espín, Dr. Orlando, and Sixto García. 1989. "Lilies of the Field: A Hispanic Theology of Providence and Human Responsibility." In *The CTSA (Catholic Theological Society of America) Proceedings of the 44th Annual Convention* (St. Louis, June 7–10, 1989), 44:70–90. St. Louis: CTSA.

Espín, Olivia M. "Cultural and Historical Influences on Sexuality in Hispanic/ Latin Women: Implications for Psychotherapy." In *Race, Class and Gender: An Anthology*, ed. Margaret L. Anderson and Patricia Hill Collins, 141–146. Belmont, Calif.: Wadsworth Publishing Co.

Falicov, C. J., and B. M. Karrer. 1980. "Cultural Variations in the Family Life Cycle: The Mexican-American Family." In *The Family Life Cycle: A Framework for Family Therapy*, ed. E. A. Carter and M. McGoldrick, 383–425. New York: Gardner Press.

Flannery, Austin, ed. 1975. *Vatican Council II: The Conciliar and Post Conciliar Documents*. Boston: St. Paul Editions.

Flores, Rosalie. 1975. "The New Chicana and Machismo." *Regeneration Theology* 2, no. 4:56.

Flores-Ortiz, Yvette G. 1982. "The Impact of Acculturation on the Chicano Family: An Analysis of Selected Variables." Ph.D. diss. University of California, Berkeley.

Fowler, James W. 1981. *Stages of Faith: The Psychology of Human Development and the Quest for Meaning*. San Francisco: Harper and Row.

Frank, Jerome. 1961. *Persuasion and Healing: A Comparative Study of Psychotherapy*. New York: Schocken Books.

Freire, Paulo. 1970. *Pedagogy of the Oppressed*. New York: Herder and Herder.

Freud, Sigmund. 1964. *Future of an Illusion*. Trans. W. D. Robson-Scott. New York: Doubleday and Co.

Fuentes, Carlos. 1992. *The Buried Mirror: Reflections on Spain and the New World*. New York: Houghton Mifflin Co.

Galilea, Segundo. 1977. *Pastoral popular y urbana en América Latina*. Bogotá, Colombia: CLAR.

————. 1979. *Religiosidad popular y pastoral*. Madrid: Ediciones Cristiandad.

———. 1981. *Religiosidad popular y pastoral hispano-americano.* New York: Northeast Pastoral Institute.

Gallup, George, Jr., and Jim Castelli. 1987. *The American Catholic People: Their Beliefs, Practices, and Values.* Garden City, N.Y.: Doubleday.

Gandara, P. 1982. "Passing through the Eye of the Needle: High-Achieving Chicanas." *Hispanic Journal of Behavioral Sciences* 4, no. 2 (June):167–169.

García, John A., Theresa Córdova, and Juan R. García, eds. 1984. *The Chicano Struggle, Analyses of Past and Present Efforts.* Binghamton, N.Y.: Bilingual Press/Editorial Bilingüe.

García-Bahne, Betty. 1977. "La Chicana and the Chicano Family." In *Essays on la Mujer,* ed. Rosaura Sánchez and Rosa Martinez Cruz, 30–47. Los Angeles: University of California, Chicano Studies Center Publications.

Garibay, Angel. 1967. "Our Lady of Guadalupe." In *New Catholic Encyclopedia,* 6:821–822. 18 vols. New York: McGraw-Hill.

Geertz, C. 1973. *The Interpretation of Cultures.* New York: Basic Books.

Gelpi, Donald L. 1978. *Experiencing God: A Theology of Human Emergence.* New York: Paulist Press.

Gibson, Guadalupe. 1983. "Hispanic Women: Stress and Mental Health Issues." In *Women Changing Therapy,* ed. Joan H. Robbins and R. J. Siegel, 113–133. New York: Haworth Press.

Gilkey, Langdon. 1969. *Naming the Whirlwind: The Renewal of God Language.* Indianapolis and New York: Bobbs-Merrill.

Gilligan, Ann Louise. 1991. "Feminist Theology and Imagination: Exploring the Connections." *Womanspirit* 6, no. 1:5–8.

Gilligan, Carol. 1982. *In a Different Voice.* Cambridge, Mass.: Harvard University Press.

Gonzales, Sylvia. 1979. "La Chicana: Malinche or Virgin." *Nuestro* 3 (June/July):41–42, 45.

———. 1980. "La Chicana: Guadalupe or Malinche." In *Comparative Perspectives of Third World Women: The Impact of Race, Sex, and Class,* ed. Beverly Lindsay, 229–250. New York: Praeger Special Studies.

González, José Luis. 1983. "La religiosidad popular desde la práctica de la liberación." In *Iglesia y religión,* 16, 18–19, 26–27. Juárez, Mexico: Centro Antonio de Montesinos, A.C.

González, Roberto O., O.F.M., and Michael LaVelle. 1985. *The Hispanic Catholic in the United States: A Socio-cultural and Religious Profile.* Hispanic American Pastoral Investigations, no. 1. New York: Northeast Catholic Pastoral Center for Hispanics.

González Medina, Salvador, M.Sp.S. 1981. *El acontecimiento del Tepeyac: Mensaje de salvación.* Mexico City: San José del Atillo.

Gorsuch, Richard. 1968. "The Conceptualization of God as Seen in Adjective Ratings." *Journal of the Scientific Study of Religion* 7 (Spring):56–64.

Gough, Harrison, G., and Alfred B. Heilbrun, Jr. 1965. *The Adjective Check List Manual*. Palo Alto, Calif.: Consulting Psychologists Press.

———. 1992. *Guadalupe from the Aztec: Selections*. Lafayette, Ore.: Guadalupe Translations.

Grebler, L., J. Moore, and R. Guzmán. 1970. *The Mexican American People: The Nation's Second Largest Minority*. New York: Free Press.

Greeley, Andrew M., and Mary Greeley Durkin. 1984. *How to Save the Catholic Church*. New York: Viking, Elisabeth Sifton Books.

Grimes, Ronald L. 1976. *Symbol and Conquest*. Ithaca, N.Y.: Cornell University Press.

Griswold del Castillo, Richard. 1988. "The Chicano Movement and the Treaty of Guadalupe Hidalgo." In *Times of Challenge: Chicanos and Chicanas in American Society*, ed. Juan R. García, Julia Curry Rodríguez, and Clara Lomas, 32–38. Mexican American Studies Program, Monograph Series no. 6.

Guerrero, Andrés G. 1987. *A Chicano Theology*. Maryknoll, N.Y.: Orbis Books.

Gutiérrez, Gustavo. 1973. *A Theology of Liberation*. Maryknoll, N.Y.: Orbis Books.

Gutiérrez, Ramón A. 1991. *When Jesus Came, the Corn Mothers Went Away*. Stanford, Calif.: Stanford University Press.

Guzmán, Alicia P. 1984. "Promoción y dignidad de la mujer a la luz del Evento Guadalupano." In *Libro Anual—Conmemoración Guadalupana*. Mexico City: Instituto Superior de Estudios Eclesiástios.

Haight, Roger, S.J. 1979. "The Experience and Language of Grace." In *Rahner: Grace and History*, 119–139. New York: Paulist Press.

Hancock, Veliag. 1971. "La Chicana, Chicano Movement and Women's Liberation." *Chicano Studies Newsletter (UCB)* (February/March):106.

Handbook on Guadalupe, A. 1974. Kenosha, Wis.: Franciscan Marytown Press.

Hanke, Lewis. 1949. *The Spanish Struggle for Justice in the Conquest of America*. Philadelphia: University of Pennsylvania Press.

Harrington, Patricia. 1988. "Mother of Death, Mother of Rebirth: The Mexican Virgin of Guadalupe." *Journal of the American Academy of Religion* 55 (Spring):25–50.

Hellbom, Anna Britta. 1967. *Participación cultural de las mujeres indias y mestizas en el México precortesiano y postrevolucionario*. Stockholm: Ethnographical Museum.

Hernández, Carrol A., Marsha J. Haug, and Nathaniel N. Wagner. 1976. *Chicanos: Social and Psychological Perspectives*. St. Louis: C. V. Mosby Co.

Herrera, Marina. 1986. "Mary of Nazareth in Cross-Cultural Perspective." In *PACE* 16:236–238 (Winona, Minn.: St. Mary's Press).

Hishiki, Patricia C. 1969. "Self-Concepts of Sixth Grade Girls of Mexican-American Descent." *California Journal of Education Research* 20 (March): 56–62.

hooks, bell. 1984. *Feminist Theory: From Margin to Center*. Boston: South End Press.

Horowitz, R. 1981. "Passion, Submission and Motherhood: The Negotiation of Identity by Unmarried Innercity Chicanas." *Sociological Quarterly* 22 (Spring):241–252.

Hurty, Kathleen. 1983. "Power in a New Key: The Hidden Resources of Empowerment." Presentation at the World YWCA Council Meeting, National University of Singapore, November 1–14.

Isasi-Díaz, Ada María, and Yolanda Turango. 1988. *Hispanic Women: Prophetic Voice in the Church*. San Francisco: Harper and Row.

Jaco, E. G., ed. 1960. *The Sociological Epidemiology of Mental Disorder*. New York: Russell Sage.

James, William. 1958. *The Varieties of Religious Experience*. New York: New American Library of World Literature.

John Paul II, Pope. 1979. *Catechesi Tradendae: The Message Embodied in Cultures: Apostolic Exhortation on Catechesis*. Pamphlet 53. Washington, D.C.: National Conference of Catholic Bishops—United States Catholic Conference.

Johnson, Elizabeth A., C.S.J. 1984. "The Incomprehensibility of God and the Image of God Male and Female." *Theological Studies* 45, no. 3:441–480.

———. 1985. "The Marian Tradition and the Reality of Women." *Horizons: Journal of the College Theology Society* 12, no. 1:116–135.

———. 1989. "Mary and the Female Face of God." *Theological Studies* 50, no. 3: 501–526.

Kagan, Spencer. 1984. "Mexican American Children and Social Orientation." *Caminos* (November):24.

Kagan, S., and J. P. Knight. 1977. "Acculturation of Prosocial and Competitive Behaviors among Second and Third Generation Mexican-American Children." *Journal of Cross-Cultural Psychology* 8 (March): 273–284.

Keefe, S., and J. M. Casas. 1978. "Family and Mental Health among Mexican Americans: Some Considerations for Mental Health Services." In *Family and Mental Health in the Mexican-American Community*, ed. J. Manuel Casas and Susan E. Keefe, 1–24. Spanish Speaking Mental Health Research Center, Monograph no. 7. Los Angeles: University of California.

Keefe, S., and A. Padilla. 1987. *Chicano Ethnicity*. Albuquerque: University of New Mexico Press.

Keefe, S. E., A. M. Padilla, and M. L. Carlos. 1978. "The Mexican American Extended Family as an Emotional Support System." In *Family and Mental Health in the Mexican American Community*, ed. J. Manuel Casas and Susan E. Keefe, 49–67. Spanish Speaking Mental Health Research Center, Monograph no. 7. Los Angeles: University of California.

Kiev, Ari, ed. 1964. *Magic, Faith and Healing*. New York: Free Press.

Knaster, Meri. 1977. *Women in Spanish America: An Annotated Bibliography from Pre-Conquest to Contemporary Times*. Boston: G. K. Hall.

Knight, Margaret, ed. 1950. *William James: A Selection from His Writings on Psychology*. Middlesex, England: Penguin Books.

Kolbenschlag, Madonna. 1988. *Lost in the Land of Oz*. San Francisco, Calif.: Harper and Row.

Komarovsky, M. 1946. "Cultural Contradictions and Sex Roles." *American Journal of Sociology* 52:184–189.

Kung, Hans, and Jürgen Moltmann. 1983. *Concilium—Mary in the Churches*. New York: Seabury Press.

Kurtz, Donald V. 1982. "The Virgin of Guadalupe and the Politics of Becoming Human." *Journal of Anthropological Research* 38 (Summer):194–210.

Lafaye, Jacques. 1976. *Quetzalcóatl and Guadalupe*. Chicago, Ill.: University of Chicago Press.

Lang, Martin A. 1983. *Acquiring Our Image of God: Emotional Basis for Religious Education*. Mahwah, N.J.: Paulist Press.

"La Virgen de Guadalupe." 1980. *México Desconocido* (special ed.) 319 (June 13).

Lenz, Robert. 1987. "Juan Diego of Mexico." *Festivals* 5, no. 6 (December/January):25.

León-Portilla, Miguel. 1962. *The Broken Spears: The Aztec Account of the Conquest of Mexico*. Boston: Beacon Press.

———. 1963. *Aztec Thought and Culture*. Trans. Jack Emory Davis. Norman: University of Oklahoma Press.

———. 1969. *Pre-Columbian Literature of Mexico*. Trans. Grace Lobanov and Miguel León-Portilla. Norman: University of Oklahoma Press.

———, ed. 1980. *Native Mesoamerican Spirituality: Ancient Myths, Discourses, Stories, Doctrines, Hymns, Poems from the Aztec, Ycatec, Quiche-Maya and Other Sacred Traditions*. New York: Paulist Press.

Libro Anual: Año 1981–1982. 1984. Conmemoración Guadalupana Conmemoración Arquidiocesana 450 años. Mexico City: Publicaciones del Instituto Superior de Estudios Eclesiásticos.

Limón, José. 1990. "La Llorona." In *Between Borders: Essays on Mexican American/Chicana History*, ed. Adelaida R. Del Castillo, 399–432. Encino, Calif.: Flor y Canto Press.

López, Marta. 1979. "La Chicana: The Colonized Woman Emerges." *Equal Opportunity Forum* (September).

López Bucio, Baltasar. 1981. "Catolicismo Guadalupano." *Servir* 17, nos. 95–96:333–354.

Lucero, Robert, O.F.M. 1983. "Guadalupe and Immaculate Conception: Merging Streams of Hispanic and Anglo Spirituality." *St. Anthony's Messenger* (December):20–22.

McCluskey, Audrey T., ed. 1985. *Women of Color: Perspectives on Feminism and Identity*. Occasional Papers Series, vol. 1, no. 1. Bloomington: Women's Studies Program, Indiana University.

McDargh, John. 1985. "Life on the Road: The Development of Faith." *PACE* 16:112–116 (Winona, Minn.: Saint Mary's Press).

MacGregor, Jean, ed. 1992. *The Columbus Quincentennial: A Sourcebook*. Olympia: Washington Center, Evergreen State College.

McWilliams, C. 1968. *North from Mexico: The Spanish-speaking People of the U.S.* New York: Greenwood Press.

Madsen, William. 1964. "Value Conflict and Folk Psychology in South Texas." In *Magic, Faith, and Healing*, ed. Ari Kiev, 420–440. New York: Free Press.

———. 1967. "Religious Syncretism." In *Social Anthropology*, ed. Manning Nash, 369–391. Vol. 6. *Handbook of Middle American Indians*. Austin: University of Texas Press.

Major, Linda. 1974. "The Psyche-Changing Role Creates Latino's World of Conflict." *Agenda* (Spring):6.

Marina Arrom, Sylvia. 1985. *The Women of Mexico City 1790–1857*. Stanford, Calif.: Stanford University Press.

Marins, José, and Team. n.d. *Basic Ecclesial Community: Church from the Roots*. Quito, Ecuador: Imprenta del Colegio Técnico Don Bosco.

Markides, Kyriakos S., and Thomas Cole. 1985. "Change and Continuity in Mexican American Religious Behavior: A Three-Generation Study." In *The Mexican American Experience: An interdisciplinary Anthology*, ed. Rodolfo O. de la Garza et al., 402–409. Austin: University of Texas Press.

Martinez, Joe L., Jr., ed. 1977. *Chicano Psychology*. New York: Academic Press.

Marx, Karl. 1970. *Capital: A Critical Analysis of Capitalist Production*. Trans. from the third German edition by Samuel Moore and Edward Avelind. Ed. Frederick Engels. London: W. Glaisher.

Marzal, Manuel. 1973. "Investigación y hipótesis sobre la religiosidad popular." In *Pastoral y lenguaje*. Bogotá, Colombia: IPLA.

Medina Ascensio, Luis, S.J. 1979. *The Apparitions of Guadalupe as Historical Events*. CARA Studies on Popular Devotion, vol. 2: Guadalupan Studies. Washington, D.C.: Center for Applied Research in the Apostolate (CARA).

Melville, Margarita B. 1980. *Twice a Minority: Mexican-American Women*. St. Louis, Mo.: C. V. Mosby Co.

————, ed. 1988. *Mexicans at Work in the United States*. Houston: Mexican American Studies, University of Houston.

Mexican American Cultural Center. 1977. *Faith Expressions of Hispanics in the Southwest: Workshops on Hispanic Liturgy and Popular Piety*. Vol. 1. San Antonio: Mexican American Cultural Center.

Meyer, Michael C., and William L. Sherman. 1987. *The Course of Mexican History*. 3d ed. New York: Oxford University Press.

Miles, Margaret R. 1985. *Image as Insight: Visual Understanding in Western Christianity and Secular Culture*. Boston, Mass.: Beacon Press.

Miller, David Hunter, ed. 1937. *Treaties and Other International Acts of America*. Vol. 5. Washington, D.C.: U.S. Government Printing Office.

Miller, Harriet. 1985. "Human Development: Making Webs or Pyramids." In *Women's Issues in Religious Education*, ed. Fern M. Giltner, 149–172. Birmingham, Ala.: Religious Education Press.

Miranda, Francisco. 1968. "Presupestos históricos de la religiosidad popular en México." *Iglesia y Religiosidad Popular en América Latina*. CELAM Document no. 29. Bogotá, Colombia: Oficina de Prensa y Publicaciones del CELAM.

Mirandé, Alfred. 1977. "Chicano Family: A Re-Analysis of Conflicting Views." *Journal of Marriage and Family* 39 (November):747–756.

Mirandé, Alfred, and Evangelina Enríquez. 1979. *La Chicana: The Mexican-American Female*. Chicago: University of Chicago Press.

Misioneros del Espíritu Santo. 1981. *Estudios teológicos: Santa María de Guadalupe, Año Jubilar 1531–1981*. San José del Altillo, Mexico City: Misioneros del Espíritu Santo.

Montiel, M. 1970. "The Social Science Myth of the Mexican American Family." *El Grito: A Journal of Contemporary Mexican American Thought* 3:56–63.

Mora, Magdalena, and Adelaida R. Del Castillo. 1980. "Mexican Women in the United States: Struggles Past and Present." Occasional Paper no. 2. Los Angeles: University of California, Chicano Studies Research Center Publication.

Morales, Rosa. 1973. "The Chicana Women—Yesterday and Today." *El Renacimiento* 4 (September 10):1–2.

Moran, Gabriel. 1981. "Developmental Theories in Religious Education." *PACE* 12:1–4 (Winona, Minn.: Saint Mary's Press).

Mörner, Magnus. 1967. *Race Mixture in the History of Latin America.* Boston: Little, Brown, and Co.

Morton, Carlos. 1975. "La Virgen Goes through Changes." *Caracol* (July): 16–17.

Murillo, N. 1976. "The Mexican American Family." In *Chicanos: Social and Psychological Perspectives,* 2d ed., ed. Carrol A. Hernández, Marsha J. Haug, and Nathaniel N. Wagner, 15–25. St. Louis: C. V. Mosby Co.

National Conference of Catholic Bishops. 1983. *The Hispanic Presence: Challenge and Commitment: A Pastoral Letter on Hispanic Ministry.* Publication no. 891. Washington, D.C.: National Conference of Catholic Bishops—United States Catholic Conference.

National Council of La Raza. 1982. *Hispanic Statistics Summary: A Compendium of Data on Hispanic Americans.* Washington, D.C.: Office of Research Advocacy and Legislation, Emily G. McKay, Executive Vice President.

———. 1992. *State of Hispanic America 1991: An Overview.* Washington, D.C.: Office of Research Advocacy, Raúl Yzaguirre, President.

Navar, Isabelle. 1974. "La visión chicana." *La Gente de Aztlán* 4 (March):3 (University of California at Los Angeles).

Newton, Frank, Esteban L. Olmedo, and Amado M. Padilla. 1982. *Hispanic Mental Health Research: A Reference Guide.* Berkeley: University of California Press.

Nieto-Gómez, Ana. 1975. "Women in Colonial Mexico." *Regeneración* 2, no. 4:18–19.

Nieto Senour, María. 1977. "Psychology of the Chicana." In *Chicano Psychology,* 2d ed., ed. Joe L. Martinez, Jr., 329–342. New York: Academic Press.

O'Donovan, Leo J., ed. 1989. *A World of Grace: An Introduction to the Themes and Foundations of Karl Rahner's Theology.* New York: Crossroads.

Olivárez, Elizabeth. 1975. "Women's Rights and the Mexican American Women." *Regeneración* 2, no. 4:40–42.

Padilla, A. M. 1980. *Psychological Dimensions in the Acculturation Process: Theory, Models and Some New Findings.* Boulder, Colo.: Westview Press.

Parente-Martínez, Margarita Z. 1986. Interview, March, Mexico City.

Paul VI, Pope. 1975. *Evangelii Nuntiandi.* Document 62–63. Washington, D.C.: National Conference of Catholic Bishops—United States Catholic Conference.

Paz, Octavio. 1961. *Labyrinth of Solitude: Life and Thought in Mexico.* New York: Grove Press.

Perry, Mary Elizabeth, and Anne J. Cruz, eds. 1991. *Cultural Encounters: The Impact of the Inquisition in Spain and the New World.* Berkeley: University of California Press.

Pesquera, Beatriz M., and Denise A. Segura. In press. "With Quill and Torch: A Chicana Perspective on the American Women's Movement and Feminist Theories." In *Third Wave: Feminist Perspectives on Racism*, ed. N. J. Alarcón, L. Albrecht, and M. Segest. New York: Kitchen Table Press.

Powers, S., and V. V. Sánchez. 1982. "Correlates of Self-Esteem of Mexican American Adolescents." *Psychological Reports* 51, no. 3 (December): 771–774.

Prieto-Bayard, Mary. 1978. "Ethnic Identity and Stress." In *Family and Mental Health in the Mexican American Community*, ed. J. Manuel Casas and Susan E. Keefe, 109–123. Spanish Speaking Mental Health Research Center, Monograph no. 7. Los Angeles: University of California.

Primer Encuentro Nacional Guadalupano. 1978. Mexico City, September 7–8, 1976. Mexico City: Centro de Estudios Guadalupanos, A.C., Editorial Jus.

Puente de Guzmán, Alicia. 1981. "Promoción y dignidad de la mujer a la luz del Evento Guadalupano." In *Libro anual—Conmemoración Guadalupano*. Mexico City: Instituto Superior de Estudios Eclesiásticos.

Rahner, Karl, S.J. 1963. *Mary, the Mother of the Lord*. New York: Herder and Herder.

———. 1977. *Theological Investigations*. Vol. 8. Trans. David Bourke. 20 vols. New York: Seabury Press.

Ramírez Jasso, Alfredo. 1975. *La religiosidad popular en México*. Mexico City: Ediciones Paulines.

Religion in America. 1987. Princeton, N.J.: Princeton Religion Research Center.

Ribera-Ortega, Pedro. 1974. "La Conquistadora: San Fe's Ancient Queen and Patroness." *La Luz* 3 (May):10–11.

Ricard, Robert. 1966. *The Spiritual Conquest of Mexico*. Translated by Lesley Byrd Simpson. Berkeley: University of California Press.

Roberts, Robert E., and Catherine Ramsey Roberts. 1982. "Marriage, Work and Depressive Symptoms among Mexican Americans." *Hispanic Journal of Behavior Sciences* 4, no. 2 (June):199–221.

Rodriguez, Jeanette. 1990. "Hispanics and the Sacred." *Chicago Studies* 29, no. 2:137–152.

———. 1991. "The Impact of Our Lady of Guadalupe on the Psychosocial and Religious Development of Mexican-American Women." Ann Arbor, Mich.: University Microfilms International.

Rodriguez, R. 1982. *Hunger of Memory*. New York: Bantam Books.

Rojas, Mario, trans. 1978. *Nican Mopohua: Traducción del Náhuatl al Castellano*. Huejutla, Hidalgo, Mexico: By the author.

Rojas Sánchez, Mario, and Juan Homero Hernández Illescas. n.d. *La estre-*

llas del manto de la Virgen de Guadalupe. Mexico City: Francisco Méndez Oteo.

Roof, Wade Clark, and Jennifer L. Roof. 1984. "Review of the Polls: Images of God among Americans." *Journal for the Scientific Study of Religion* 23 (March):201–205.

Rosaldo, M. Z. 1974. "Woman, Culture, and Society: A Theoretical Overview." In *Woman, Culture, and Society*, ed. M. Z. Rosaldo and L. Lamphere, 17–42. Stanford: Stanford University Press.

Rosaldo, Michelle Zimbalest and L. Lamphere, eds. 1974. *Woman, Culture and Society*. Stanford Calif.: Stanford University Press.

Rosenfeld, Anne H. 1985. "Music: The Beautiful Disturber." *Psychology Today* (December):49–56.

Ruether, Rosemary Radford. 1977. *Mary and the Feminine Face of the Church*. Philadelphia: Westminster Press.

Ruiz, Vickie. 1987. *Cannery Women, Cannery Lives*. Albuquerque: University of New Mexico Press.

Sahagún, Bernardino de, O.F.M. 1829–1830. *Historia general de las cosas de Nueva España*. 3 vols. Mexico City: Ed. Carlos María de Bustamante.

Salas, Elizabeth. 1990. SOLDADERAS *in the Mexican Military: Myth and History*. Austin: University of Texas Press.

Sánchez, Rosaura, and Rosa Martinez Cruz. 1977. *Essays on la Mujer*. Anthology no. 1. Los Angeles: University of California, Chicano Studies Center Publications.

Sandoval, Moisés, ed. 1983. *Fronteras: The History of the Latin American Church in the USA Since 1513*. San Antonio, Tex.: Mexican American Cultural Center.

Schillebeeckx, Edward. 1964. *Mary, Mother of the Redemption*. New York: Sheed and Ward (orig. pub. 1954).

Schmidt, Herman, and David Power, eds. 1977. *Liturgy and Cultural Religious Traditions*. New York: Seabury Press.

Schneiders, Sandra M., I.H.M. 1989. "Spirituality in the Academy." *Theological Studies* 50, no. 4 (December):676–697.

Schreiter, Robert. 1985. *Constructing Local Theologies*. Maryknoll, N.Y.: Orbis Books.

Schulenburg Prado, Guillermo. 1983. *Congreso Mariológico 450 aniversario (1531–1981)*. Mexico City: Editorial Melo, S.A.

Schussler Fiorenza, Elizabeth. 1983. *In Memory of Her: A Feminist Theological Reconstruction of Christian Origins*. New York: Crossroads.

Schussler Fiorenza, Elisabeth, and Mary Collins. 1983. *Concilium—Women Invisible in Church*. Edinburgh: T and T Clark, Ltd.

Second General Conference of Latin American Bishops. 1973. *The Church in the Present-Day Transformation of Latin America in the Light of the Council*, vol. 2, *Conclusions*. 2d ed. Washington, D.C.: United States Catholic Conference.

Secretariat for Hispanic Affairs. 1978. *Proceedings of the II Encuentro Nacional Hispano de Pastoral*. Washington, D.C.: National Conference of Catholic Bishops—United States Catholic Conference.

————. 1986. *Prophetic Voices: The Document on the Process of the III Encuentro*. Washington, D.C.: National Conference of Catholic Bishops—United States Catholic Conference.

Segundo Encuentro Nacional Guadalupano: 2 y 3 diciembre de 1977. 1979. Mexico City: Centro de Estudios Guadalupanos, A.C., Editorial Jus.

Sepulveda, Betty R. 1972. "The Hispanic Women Responding to the Challenges that Affect Us All." *La Luz* 1, no. 7 (November):59–60.

Siller-Acuña, Clodomiro L. 1981a. "Anotaciones y comentarios al Nican Mopohua." *Estudios Indígenas* 8, no. 2 (March):217–274.

————. 1981b. "El método de la evangelización en el *Nican Mopohua*." *Servir* 17 (93–94):255–293.

————. 1981c. *Flor y canto del Tepeyac: Historia de las apariciones de Sta. Ma. de Guadalupe; Texto y comentario*. Xalapa, Veracruz, Mexico: Servir.

————. 1989. "Para comprender el mensaje de María de Guadalupe." Buenos Aires: Editorial Guadalupe.

Simoniello, K. 1981. "On Investigating the Attitudes toward Achievement and Success in Eight Professional U.S. Mexican Women." *Aztlán* 12, no. 1: 121–137.

Smith, Jody Brant. 1984. *The Image of Guadalupe, Myth or Miracle*. New York: Doubleday and Company, Image Books.

Solórzano, Lucy. 1974. "Love My Macho." Menlo Park, Calif.: Chicano Press at Stanford, Nowels Publications. *Images de la Chicana* (Spring):23.

Soustelle, Jacques. 1970. *Daily Life of the Aztecs on the Eve of the Spanish Conquest*. Trans. Patrick O'Brian. Stanford, Calif.: Stanford University Press.

Spanish Speaking Mental Health Research Center. 1978. *Report to the President's Commission on Mental Health from the Special Populations Sub-Task Panel on Mental Health of Hispanic Americans*. Los Angeles: UCLA.

Spencer, Anita. 1982. *Seasons: Women's Search for Self through Life's Stages*. New York: Paulist Press.

Sutherland, Elizabeth. 1970. "Colonized Women: The Chicana." In *Sisterhood is Powerful*, ed. Robin Morgan, 423–426. New York: Vintage Press.

Sweeney, Judith. 1977. "Chicana History: A Review of the Literature." In *Es-*

says on la Mujer, ed. Rosaura Sánchez and Rosa Martinez Cruz, 99–123. Los Angeles: University of California, Chicano Studies Center Publications.

Tabachnik, Sam. 1985. "Jewish Identity Developments in Young Adulthood." Dissertation, Wright Institute.

Tambasco, Anthony J. 1984. *What Are They Saying about Mary?*. Ramsey, N.J.: Paulist Press.

Third General Conference of Latin American Bishops. 1973. *The Church in the Present-Day Transformation of Latin America in the Light of the Council*. Washington, D.C.: National Conference of Catholic Bishops, Secretariat for Latin American Affairs.

————. 1979. *Puebla: Evangelization at Present and in the Future of Latin America*. Washington, D.C.: National Conference of Catholic Bishops, Secretariat for Latin American Affairs.

Todorov, Tzvetan. 1987. *The Conquest of America: The Question of the Other*. New York: Harper and Row.

Turner, Victor, and Edith Turner. 1978. *Image and Pilgrimage in Christian Culture: Anthropological Perspectives*. New York: Columbia University Press.

The Unchurched American . . . 10 Years Later. 1978. Princeton, N.J.: Gallup Organization.

Urrabazo, Rosendo. 1985. "Machismo: Mexican American Male Self-Concept." Ph.D. diss., Graduate Theological Union, Berkeley.

U.S. Department of Commerce, Bureau of the Census. 1985. *Population Characteristics*. Series P-20, no. 403 (December). Washington, D.C.: Government Printing Office.

————. 1988. "Estimates of the Population of the United States to November 1, 1987." In *Population Estimates and Projections*. Series P-25, no. 1015 (January). Washington, D.C.: Government Printing Office.

Valeriano, Antonio. 1978. *Nican Mopohua*. Trans. Mario Rojas. Huejutla, Hidalgo, Mexico: By the Translator.

Vásquez, Enriqueta Langauery. 1970. "The Mexican American Woman." In *Sisterhood Is Powerful*, ed. Robin Morgan, 426–433. New York: Vintage Press.

Vásquez, M.J.T. 1982. "Confronting Barriers to the Participation of Mexican American Women in Higher Education." *Hispanic Journal of Behavioral Sciences* 4, no. 2 (June):147–165.

Veyna, Angelina F. 1985. "Una vista dal pasado: La mujer en Nuevo México 1744–1767." *Trabajos Monográficos: Studies in Chicana/Latina Research* 1, no. 1:28–42.

————. 1986. "Women in Early New Mexico: A Preliminary View." In *Chicana Voices: Intersections of Class, Race, and Gender, ed. Theresa Córdova et al., Austin: University of Texas Press.

Vigil, James Diego. 1980. From Indians to Chicanos. Prospect Heights, Ill.: Waveland Press.

Wahlig, Charles. 1974. A Handbook on Guadalupe: For All Americans—A Pledge of Hope. Kenosha, Wis.: Franciscan Marytown Press.

Warner, Marina. 1967. Alone of All Her Sex. New York: Alfred Knopf.

Wasser, Lyneil Lansing. 1973. "The Virgen de Guadalupe and the Dialectic of Solitude." Presented at the Third Annual El Alma Chicana Symposium, San Jose, Calif., April 30–May 4.

Watson, Simone. 1964. The Cult of Our Lady of Guadalupe: A Historical Study. Collegeville, Minn.: Liturgical Press.

Williams, N. 1987. "Changes in Funeral Patterns and Gender Roles among Mexican Americans." In Women on the U.S. Mexico Border: Responses to Change, ed. V. L. Ruiz and S. Tiano, 197–217. Boston: Allen and Unwin.

————. 1988. "Role Making among Married Mexican American Women: Issues of Class and Ethnicity." Journal of Applied Behavioral Science 24: 203–217.

————. 1989. "Theoretical and Methodological Issues in the Study of Role Making." In Studies in Symbolic Interaction: A Research Annual, ed. N. Denzin, vol. 10. Greenwich, Conn.: JAI Press.

Williams, Norma. 1990. The Mexican American Family: Tradition and Change. Dix Hills, N.Y.: General Hall.

Wolf, Eric R. 1968. "The Virgin of Guadalupe: A Mexican National Symbol." In Reader in Comparative Religion: An Anthropological Approach, ed. William A. Lessa and Evon Z. Vogt, 226–230. New York: Harper and Row.

Ybarra, Lea. 1977. "Conjugal Role Relationships in the Chicano Family." Ph.D. dissertation, University of California, Berkeley.

————. 1982a. "Marital Decision-making and the Role of Machismo in the Chicano Family." De Colores 6, nos. 1–2:32–47.

————. 1982b. "When Wives Work: The Impact on the Chicano Family." Journal of Marriage and the Family (February):169–178.

Zappone, Katherine. 1991. The Hope for Wholeness. Mystic, Conn.: Twenty-third Publications.

Zavella, Patricia. 1987. Women's Work and Chicano Families. Ithaca, N.Y: Cornell University Press.

Zimbalest Rosaldo, Michelle, See Rosaldo, M. Z.

Index

religious, 58–60, 63, 124. *See also* assumptive worldview
written reflections, 89–91, 105–107

Ybarra, Lea, 71

Zimbalist Rosaldo, Michelle, 77
Zinn, M. Baca. *See* Baca Zinn, M.
Zumárraga, Bishop Juan de, 17–18, 27